At the Limits of Political Philosophy

At the Limits of Political Philosophy

From "Brilliant Errors" to Things of Uncommon Importance

James V. Schall

The Catholic University of America Press
Washington, D.C.

This is a paperback edition, with minor corrections, issued in 1998.

The paper used in this publication meets the minimum requirements of
American National Standards for Information Science—Permanence of
Paper for Printed Library materials, ANSI Z39.48–1984.
∞

Library of Congress Cataloging-in-Publication Data
Schall, James V.
    At the limits of political philosophy : from "brilliant
errors" to things of uncommon importance / by James V. Schall.
        p.   cm
    Includes bibliographical references and index.
    1. Political science—Philosophy.   2. Christianity and
politics.   I. Title.
JA71.J277   1996
320'.01—dc20
95-8019
ISBN 0-8132-0832-7
ISBN 0-8132-0922-6 (pbk.)

Dangdale pol in fever of contemplative life

"We must not follow those who advise us, being men, to think of human
things, and, being mortal, of mortal things, but must, so far as we can,
make ourselves immortal, and strain every nerve to live in accordance
with the best thing in us; for even if it be small in bulk, much more does
it in power and worth surpass everything."
     —ARISTOTLE, *Nicomachean Ethics* (1177b31–78a2),
          Book 10, Chap. 7

"To replace political philosophy by the history of political philosophy
means to replace a doctrine which claims to be true by a survey of more
or less brilliant errors."
     —LEO STRAUSS, *The City and Man*

"The inseparable imperfection annexed to all human governments consisted, he said, in not being able to create a sufficient fund of virtue and
principle to carry the laws into due and effectual execution. Wisdom
might plan, but virtue alone could execute. And where could such sufficient virtue be found? A variety of delegated, and often discretionary,
powers must be entrusted somewhere; which, if not governed by integrity
and conscience, would necessarily be abused, till at last the constable
would sell his for a shilling."
     —SAMUEL JOHNSON, 1770, as Recorded by Rev. Dr.
          Maxwell, of Falkland, in Ireland, in *Boswell's Life of Johnson*

"Every professor of philosophy who is worth his salt writes his own text, a
text which is his course, whether he publishes it or not. The text exists in
his notes or in his head. If he does not "write" this text down in one way
or another, he is not a professor because he has nothing personal to say
about his subject."
     —FREDERICK D. WILHELMSEN, "The Great Books:
          Enemies of Wisdom"

CONTENTS

ACKNOWLEDGMENTS

Earlier versions of Chapter 2 can be found in *Faith & Reason* 16 (Spring 1990): 52–62; Chapter 5, in *Divus Thomas*, Piacenza, 92, no. 3–4 (1991), 273–79, and in *The Politics of Heaven and Hell: Christian Themes from Classical, Medieval, and Modern Political Philosophy* (Lanham, Md.: University Press of America, 1984), 83–106; Chapter 6 in *Gregorianum* (Rome) 71, no. 1 (1990), 115–39; Chapter 10 in the *Bulletin, Institute for Theological Encounter with Science and Technology* (April 1987): 4–7; and Chapter 11, in vol. 8, *Annual, Catholic Commission on Intellectual and Cultural Affairs*, Notre Dame (1989): 59–74. The author wishes to thank these journals for permission to use them here.

Kind appreciation is also due to George Carey, Michael Jackson, Glenn Tinder, and Jerome Hanus, who read and remarked most helpfully on this text in the various stages of its progress.

In particular, I wish to thank David McGonagle, director of The Catholic University of America Press, and Susan Needham, staff editor, for their interest and perceptive help in bringing this work to completion.

At the Limits of Political Philosophy

Introduction

At the Limits of Political Philosophy begins, as does politics itself
for most of us, with those imperfect and dire conditions of human
existence unsettlingly familiar to all actual human beings: with
death, evil, suffering, injustices, even—dare we say it?—hell, as it
presents the problem of freely chosen wrongs and their punishment. We are intellectually provoked, however, not only by our
tragic experiences but also by what is most delightful and happy
about our lot. Our world includes both of these realities. Such
common experience of our kind, sometimes glorious, sometimes
sad, oftentimes evil, cannot but stimulate in us a deep intellectual
curiosity. Political philosophy, looking back on these sad or joyous
realities, seeks to order them in the light of higher purposes that
are also intrinsic to the discipline. By its own inner intellectual
dynamism, political philosophy presses its own limits. The discipline continually leads us from its own circumscribed subject matter, human life in the city and its meaning, to more astonishing
and intriguing things—to things of uncommon importance, as I
call them. Political philosophy enables us to formulate precise
questions arising within the confines of actual political living and,
at the same time, to prepare us to acknowledge real answers to
these questions when they appear from whatever source. Political
life is thus also a life of intelligence. The "political" animal is a
"reasoning" animal also in his very politics.

A coherent account of political philosophy will include the dignity of life in the polity, together with man's frequent and defin-
able deviations from reason occurring within civil life. Likewise,
it will include those horizons that Aristotle called the "divine" in
man, even in the context of political things (1178b31). Political
philosophy legitimately asks, as Plato did, about the meaning of

1

the human good and human evil, as well as about the meaning of
any destiny that results from human choices, be they good or bad.
The subtitle of this book reminds us that the intellectual expla-
nations of why human things are disordered often lead to certain
"brilliant errors" that have great historical standing. These "brilliant errors," however, though their consideration is now an intrinsic part of the historical record of political philosophy, do not
adequately explain the reasons for the human evils or the human
goods that occur in actual human cities. For this reason, great
danger to the city as well as to human life can arise from these
very errors. Aristotle advised us not only to state "the true view,
but also [to] explain the false view. . . . For when we have an apparently reasonable explanation of why a false view appears true,
that makes us more confident of the true view" (1154a23–25).

Evil, however, though it is a great dilemma and must be carefully treated, is not the greatest perplexity of political philosophy.
Paradoxically, virtue, friendship, joy, and happiness are greater
mysteries, realities more difficult to explain or cope with than evil.
This is why these topics are also found in the great books of the
discipline; it is why, I think, they deserve a fresh consideration
here, because we seldom seek to explain them all together in a
coherent relationship.

I shall argue that a noncontradictory unity exists among three
aspects of political philosophy—the problem of evil or coercion,
the problem of virtue, and the problem of contemplation of the
highest things. The case for this unity is not often made within
the discipline. Beginning with the fact of our "fallenness" (Scripture) or "wickedness" (Aristotle), we are led to the meaning of
human life itself, whether it achieves a good and whether this
good is completely comprehended or achieved by politics. Political
life does exhibit a myriad of evils and of the virtues contrary to
them. But neither the reality of evil nor the possibility of good
within the city is completely explained within political philosophy.
I do not think this incompleteness of political philosophy is a defect in the discipline but it does indicate its very limit, the nature
of its own understanding of what it is, of what it can do. The
"logic" of thought about political things leads to political philosophy. In its turn, by reflecting on these very political things, political philosophy is open to metaphysics and revelation, them-

selves grounded in events, in things. This "logic" is what is presented in this book.

Those who think about political things need sober reminders about their own souls. The Czech philosopher Nicholas Lobkowicz wrote, "Almost everything that has gone wrong in the recent history of our culture originated in the minds of people such as ourselves, people who are university graduates and intellectuals."[1] St. Paul himself was concerned with the destructive consequences of philosophers who chose not to acknowledge the truth (Romans 1:18–32). Political philosophy, as these remarks suggest, is not an indifferent enterprise. Upon its right understanding, nations and empires rise and fall, human beings live well or ill. The complexity of political philosophy includes its seriousness: that is, the risk that its "brilliant errors," if not attended to, will prove destructive to human life in actual cities.

Four brief citations are found at the beginning of this book. The first, a justly famous passage in Aristotle, seems to downgrade politics in favor of the contemplative life. He advises us not to listen to those who tell us to study only human things, that is, economics, politics, and such things connected with practical human life. We are not to lose ourselves in them as we can easily do. Aristotle's warning is not, however, that political things are not worthy in themselves. Rather he reminded us of things more noble. Aristotle thought that even if we spend very much time on them, all of our lives perhaps, but in the process learn little about the truth of the highest things, our effort was still well spent. To be a city, the city needs more than the official custodians of the city. Political philosophy as we know it, however, in the schools and in our culture has in both theory and practice largely neglected or denied the need for this contemplative experience that Aristotle thought so important.

The second citation is from Leo Strauss (1899–1973). Strauss did as much as anyone in recent decades to revive political philosophy. He emphasized that political philosophy, being itself, is a "claim" on truth. What Strauss called "the history of political philosophy" can be, and often is, merely a minutely accurate description of sundry erroneous notions about politics. Too seldom

---

1. Nicholas Lobkowicz, "Christianity and Culture," *Review of Politics* 53 (Spring 1991), 188.

does political philosophy seek the answers to questions about the best regime, about the right order of things in the light of which alone errors, even brilliant ones, can still be called "intelligent" errors. The understanding of error is an essential part of the philosophical endeavor. "Brilliant" errors are the ones most likely to lead us, when we reflect on them, back to obvious truths.

The third citation is a remarkable one from Samuel Johnson, in many ways one of the wisest men who ever lived among us, a man who will appear often in these pages.[2] Indeed, passages from Samuel Johnson begin almost every chapter of this book and provide much of the spirit in which it is written. I originally entitled this book *The Inseparable Imperfections of All Human Government*, a title obviously taken from this passage of Johnson. This proposed title, though striking, is too narrow for what needs to be to considered. That is, I am concerned not only with the "inevitable imperfections" but also with the goodness of human nature as such. However, Johnson's vivid passage does identify one of the major issues in political philosophy, the one from which most political thinking begins.

The fourth passage, from Frederick Wilhelmsen, I have taken to heart. Wilhelmsen wanted professors to teach what they actually held, a task no doubt to be undertaken with a high degree of humility and a forthright willingness to state the truth as coherently as possible. Professors were to explain, at least once in their lives, what they espoused, their own "text," as he called it. The great things, the things of uncommon importance, need to be stated directly. This "text," this "reading" at the limits of political philosophy, is the fulfillment of a debt to students, colleagues, friends, and readers who have also pondered these issues in their souls.

Taken together, these four passages indicate the subject matter, that is, political philosophy, the style of treating it, and the uniqueness of the approach to it. The systematic method of treating political philosophy is after the manner of a "text." The "text" is the

2. Samuel Johnson (1709–84) is one of the most insightful and erudite men in the history of English letters and thought. His biography written by James Boswell is an abiding source of stimulation, wisdom, humor, thought, and judgment about almost every topic of human interest. Johnson wrote a dictionary of the English language, as well as poems, plays, essays, novels, biographies, and literary criticism, all steeped in philosophy and wisdom.

discourse of a professor, an individual human being, who has himself wondered with his students and his friends about where political philosophy might lead if its highest duties to itself were realized.

The "text" is personal, that is, it is written by a person. It intends to confront objective issues. It is addressed to other minds in that respectful attentiveness that allows us, without apologizing, to direct our discourse to the highest things when the evidence warrants it. The reader will find here the varied topics and subjects that must be treated when the whole scope of political philosophy is broached. Political philosophy, in a way that other disciplines do not, leads us normally and logically to these considerations. The interested student of political philosophy wants at least once in his academic life—perhaps once again in his maturity and old age—to have such issues clearly presented to him.

The spirit of this presentation is friendly. I am polemical only to the extent that disagreement must be stated for the sake of truth or of good order. I am aware that the really important and central truths in political philosophy are obscured and rejected most often for fear of where they might lead, their import for our thinking and our living. Everyone is invited to follow the "text," my "text," as presented. No one is asked to agree unless persuaded. I write these reflections on political philosophy with the realization that I too may be in "error"—with, no doubt, enough vanity to hope that, if so, it is at least a "brilliant" error.

This account of political philosophy intends to present "a doctrine which claims to be true," not merely another opinion. Revelation—information from Scripture or other sources of presumably divine interventions—as well as philosophy, claims to be true. But this claim of revelation to be true is not an appeal to fideism, to ungrounded belief. Reasonable evidence must always be found for the plausibility of revelation. I am a follower of Aquinas on this point. I think such evidence does exist. No pertinent topic that is dealt with in revelation is, as I see it, to be excluded simply on the grounds that such revelation arises in faith. Valid reasons can exist for what we do not ourselves believe. Yet, certain philosophical positions do reject the possibility of revelation. When they do, intellectual analysis examines the validity of premises that would lead to such an exclusion. The examination of philosophical premises and methods, including our own, is itself part of the enterprise of political philosophy.

A philosopher can understand a good deal about the content of revelation. If revelation deals legitimately or interestingly or even plausibly with an issue that naturally arises in politics, we must contend with its implications. Revelation at its best does not deny the validity of reason. Indeed, it presupposes reason. Likewise, when revelation is most circumspect or negative about reason, it still seeks to justify itself through the use of reason. Reason at its worst can deny its own very existence. At its best, it is capable of coming to terms with revelation, but only if both are respectful of truth and the logic of its conformity with reality. Both learn from each other. The whole includes both in a proper order.

Much of the labor to present and critique important political philosophers has already been accomplished in the discipline. While discussion about the meaning of Aristotle or Plato or Machiavelli or Nietzsche may still be vigorous, we know for the most part what they held and why. I do not want to provide here another "textbook" on great political thinkers; I do not analyze given historical or actual regimes. This book begins where such efforts leave off. The most profound issues of human life, paradoxically, come to the fore precisely when practical issues are most adequately explained and studied. Students who have been given only descriptions of the ideas of the political philosophers or who study only the institutional or current political side of actual governments will, if they remain at this level, miss the heart and drama of political philosophy. We want to know what lies beyond the workings of the regimes, what lies beyond the "brilliant errors" of the great thinkers in the field. If they are "errors," we are, nevertheless, concerned with the truth that their originators were getting at in proposing them.

For many things in life, to be sure, it is sufficient to have the solution for a problem, without knowing either how the problem arose or how the solution responded to it. We need not all be plumbers to drink pure water from a tap, nor auto mechanics to be able to drive our cars. But for the highest things, practical and usable knowledge alone is not sufficient. The highest things are the property of everyone. Nonetheless, a human being must find problems in his own soul before he will fully realize that solutions for them are at least proposed for his examination. The realization that certain fundamental queries exist in his own heart and that great thinkers offer certain, often contradictory, solutions to them is the real context and enigma in which political philosophy lives and, yes, flourishes.

The study of political philosophy, as Aristotle described it in Book 2 of *The Politics,* thus includes both an account of the sayings of the political philosophers and a careful analysis of the constitutions and organization of actual regimes under which men have lived. The words of the political philosophers and the experiences of men in contingent political regimes are taken for granted. The attentive reading of the classical texts in political philosophy is the normal way in which political philosophy as such appears, particularly for the student, who as yet lacks experience and some means to formulate and criticize it.

When Aristotle observed that the young were not apt students of politics (1095a2–5), he meant that they lacked the experience in themselves and others of those passions, principles, goals, and, yes, disorders that constitute the very stuff of politics and human life. But what might not initially be encountered or noticed in reality may be confronted or indicated in books, in examples to be contemplated before the actual experiences arise. When experiences do finally occur, they will be recognized for what they are, in their moral distinctiveness, because of the help of the philosophers. The common-sense encounter with political things is the context of the classical authors. Their teachings are directed to those students, citizens, and politicians who are educable, who are willing to form their souls in the light of the right order of things.

Political philosophy is not based on a skepticism about the validity or worth of human knowledge, finite though that be. Nevertheless, political philosophy does not provide full answers to questions that arise within it through its own legitimate intellectual inquiries. The realization of this "incompleteness," itself a good thing, opens the mind to wonder about what is missing or about what is more complete. The remedial aspect of political philosophy, the issues of crime and punishment, are of obvious concern and are to be included in any philosophical discussion of the nature of political living. These realities in every human life, moreover, manifest the disorder in human nature. They signify something is wrong, something is not as it should be.

Efforts to remedy evil and disorder are not equivalent, however, to another sort of incompleteness that arises quite apart from these disorders. Indeed, in the revelational tradition, evil, sin, death, and punishment did not exist in the original plan for creation. The Book of Wisdom (1:12) reads, "Death was not God's doing; he takes no pleasure in the extinction of the living." The substitutes for revelation in modern philosophy, the systems we often call ideologies, also seek to remove these things—evil, suffering, even death—by economic, psychological, or political means. Yet, these surely curious similarities of purpose are not, as such, a sign that revelation is itself somehow "ideological." Nor does it indicate that the disorders of human life are alone what causes human wonderment. If I might put it this way, political philosophy would lead to a search for the highest things even had there been no Fall, no disorder in the human condition.

Revelation, I argue, leads to the completion and fulfillment of political philosophy, not in any necessary or artificial way, but as an intelligible response to valid questions posed in the discipline itself. Revelation is a gift; it does not arise from human sources. It is thus not something that could be demanded or commanded. It is a rational gift, directed to the human intelligence as such. It is something to wrestle with, to ponder. It is important to observe, for example, that Aristotle's questions admit of answers for us that he himself could not have weighed, since he had not the gift of revelation. Aquinas remains a key to the compatibility of reason and revelation. In the depths of our consciousness, finite intellect is "pulled," to use a Platonic word, toward ends that it knows were not established by itself.

This book is divided into four sections of three chapters each. The first section, "The Stages of Political Philosophy," is about this history of political philosophy, about the enduring questions, about the brilliant errors and the sober responses to them. Here we use the terms classical, medieval, and modern political philosophy not as merely temporal identifications but as intellectual distinctions. They indicate different ways that reason reflects on political things. Political philosophy includes the efforts to formulate and answer its own questions.

The second section, "The Grounds of Political Realism," presents in a more detailed fashion the topics of evil, hell, and death. "Political realism" holds that death, evil, and suffering are permanent realities in this world. They cannot be eliminated by human means, even though certain types of ideological political thinking have sought to do so. They are part of the calculus for estimating the rightness and possibility of any human political action. Each of these realities is found in the classical authors. In one way or another, they remain central issues in political philosophy and need to be presented frankly as part of its own subject matter.

The third section, "At the Limits of Political Philosophy," treats of the deaths of Socrates and Christ, then of happiness and virtue. This section discusses topics that are intrinsic to the human condition and would have been, in some sense, present in it even if there were no evil, sin, death, or hell to be pondered. The transition to this section is through a consideration of the deaths of Socrates and Christ. In these trials and deaths, we see how ultimate issues arise in particular political instances and how answers that are given—immortality and resurrection—hint at responses to questions that can arise in any existing city. What is argued more explicitly in this third section is that political philosophy brings us to certain important human issues, but that each issue also leads beyond itself. It does this aside from any logical human power to make it otherwise. But political philosophy cannot legitimately refuse the task of thinking about these realities. No questions serve more clearly to show this higher characteristic of human life than those of the meaning of happiness and of virtue.

The fourth section, "Political Philosophy and the Things of Uncommon Importance," addresses science, law, and friendship. Here are raised questions of truth, good, and love that are not adequately understood if viewed only in their political contexts. The uncommon importance of these ideas requires that no political philosophy that claims to deal with actual human beings can neglect these considerations, for they constitute the deepest meaning of human experience.

The perplexities of political philosophy as seen in these realities that arise within the city direct us beyond the limits of the discipline. To understand political philosophy as pointing beyond itself in its own nature may seem odd. We compartmentalize political things and we do not see the implications of the whole to which its parts are leading us. The wholeness or completion of political philosophy, however, is the result, not of philosophic necessity, but of a converging persuasion about certain questions within the discipline and possible answers to them. Reason can at least consider revelation as a possible answer to its own perplexities that are not solved on reason's own terms. Reason cannot exclude revelation as not pertinent if these convergences constantly recur. The responses of revelation to questions arising in the city may or may not be "believed." But we cannot maintain that certain responses of revelation are not at least possible answers to questions properly posed in political philosophy. More than anything, the pointing out of such convergences is what constitutes the uniqueness and purpose of these particular reflections.

Philosophy cannot by its own methods arrive at revelation, except that it can be curious about the existence of arguments from reason that also appear in revelation (i.e., Romans 1:19–23). We have not two entirely unrelated discussions, one of reason and one of revelation, but one discourse in which both reason and revelation are coherent elements. This interrelatedness does not mean that reason by its own powers can rise to faith. Nor does it mean that faith will make us good philosophers without any effort or brains on our part. But a coherent exposition of the whole in which both reason and revelation are actively present is possible. A plausible presentation of the practical and theoretic whole is what is most lacking in contemporary discourse of political philosophy. The "brilliant errors" must be discussed as realities in political philosophy. The abiding questions are likewise essential. The answers of revelation and metaphysics to these questions cannot intellectually or morally be ignored, particularly when they are directed to the questions that political philosophy itself formulates. These answers are essential parts of the whole of political philosophy and appear properly at its very limits.

A student of politics who studies only politics cannot be a good political philosopher. Furthermore, the lack of a spare, sustained account of the higher reaches of political philosophy has on the one hand left politics open to ideology and on the other caused it to fail to understand its own proper dignity. After years of teaching political philosophy and meditating on its relation to the rest of human thought and experience, I concluded that the discipline needed a more complete account of the questions that bring political philosophy, from within itself, to its own limits. This discourse is what I present here. The subject matter is intrinsically exciting and moving, once we begin to feel the perplexing incompleteness that surrounds political philosophy at its best.

The alert student, professor, or reader in political things needs to know where the discipline of political philosophy might go with its questions if it freely follows its own logic. No one would suggest that the solutions to the world's problems lie in political philosophy alone. But mistakes in political philosophy can and do cause enormous sufferings and disorders in actual human cities. We needn't deny the reality of chance to observe that good action usually flows from good thought, from right understanding and good willing consequent on it.

Political philosophy cannot be blind to metaphysics, theology, literature, or science if its own questions naturally and logically lead us to these disciplines. But we will see how this intellectual progress might happen only when we begin in politics and in political philosophy itself. The philosophers, moreover, teach serious students—whom I will call, in the Platonic tradition, "potential philosophers"—what to look for in civil life. Experience, in turn, once possessed can ground and modify what was initially learned from the books of the philosophers. The philosophers' books are intended to teach us to recognize *what is*. When the philosophers themselves, however, are confused, reality—*what is*, that which provokes the origins of our consciousness—can correct their errors, brilliant or not.

Politics does deal, and properly, with the things of this world, with what goes on during our lives on earth, with the life of "doing" and of "making," as Aristotle called it. That is why the politics of human beings in actual cities must be treated in a complete philosophy. Much of the dissatisfaction with political philosophy is due to its own methodological limitations. Reality is reduced to a function of the method used to discover it. But there are methods that are not narrowly "scientific." Politics deals with human choices. Its subject matter can never be modeled on the principles that govern physical sciences, principles that do not find their subject matter rooted in free choice. The problem of methods properly belongs to the sphere of political philosophy, since it must estimate whether a method excludes the essential reality on which politics and human life are based.

Realities perceived but not adequately confronted in intellectual discourse disturb the souls of the potential philosophers. In modern experience, the soul remains empty even after it has been provoked out of its youth or its slumber or its habits by the challenging, searing words of the philosophers or by the unavoidable enigmas or degradations arising from living in real cities. Real beginnings of intellectual life are neglected or denied because of pressures of life, especially of disordered life, or because of the limitations of methods used to deal with it. The confusions of the philosophers themselves can hinder this enterprise. Likewise, a polity can, by its coercive power, prohibit honest questions and legitimate answers because it seeks to protect itself from being critiqued by philosophy or revelation.

Granted that political philosophy is a true, if treacherous, path to the uncommonly important things, how is one to set forth on it? Two ways seem plausible. One way is to follow a basic "text" or discourse that directly names the issues and presents the arguments that support their inclusion in political philosophy. The other way is to take the student or reader through the intellectual experiences, particularly those described in the classical authors, on which such a disciplined treatment of the basic issues was initially grounded.

In this book, I will follow the first way. I will present my "text" or "reading" of those essential themes of political philosophy that lead to the highest things. A corresponding program through the classical literature is suggested in Chapter 2, on the history of political philosophy. The ways complement each other. The basic "text" of this book is a sustained discourse about the reaches of political philosophy. Students are often surprised to find out where certain seemingly ordinary or common things, such as friendship, actually lead. Political philosophy cannot be itself if it is restricted only to those things normally considered "political" by the methodologies of the discipline or by the theories of the professors.

This "text" is a "declaration of independence," as it were. It does not find it strange that either Aristotle's *Metaphysics* or the Epistle to the Romans, let alone Plutarch or Samuel Johnson, might have something pertinent to contribute to the subject matter of political philosophy. With that sense of liberty, we can begin. When we finally end, we shall possess a more complete understanding of the wholeness to which political philosophy directs us.

Political philosophy is presented here soberly within the intellectual discourse of our times as we have received it from our predecessors. But it is directed to understanding the truth. This more complete statement about political philosophy is not easy to find, or to comprehend when discovered. In the end, this discourse argues to the truth of things through political things. A concern about truth remains the main reason for presenting any discussion of intellectual things as they touch human beings. Political philosophy in its most serious reflections does require us to wonder about the truth of things, including political things, and about the truth to which political philosophy leads us—at its limits, beyond itself.

PART I

The Stages of Political Philosophy

ONE

The Intellectual Horizons
of Political Philosophy

> *"Johnson arraigned the modern politicks of this country, as entirely devoid of all principle of whatever kind. 'Politicks (said he,) are now nothing more than means of rising in the world. With this sole view do men engage in politicks and their whole conduct proceeds upon it.'"*
> —SAMUEL JOHNSON, April 18, 1775[1]

1. The Character of Political Philosophy

This book is addressed without apology to Plato's "potential philosophers": to contemporary students, of whatever age or level, who are awakening in their very souls to the call of higher things. By being perplexed over the *things that are*, by passionately desiring to know *how* things really exist, by searching for guidance to questions that are not often or fully broached in the university or in think-tanks or media or even in ordinary life, such students become alive to what they have not previously encountered or what they have been unable to explain. Perceptive students notice the lack of a philosophic account of the meaning of the experience of politics and how this experience relates to their particular lives, more especially to their understanding of *what is*.

The practice of political philosophy requires the experience of having read the classical authors to assist in examining the central problems of political living. Through political philosophy one can sort out relevant principles and criteria and can arrive at judg-

---

1. *Boswell's Life of Johnson* (London: Oxford, 1931), I, p. 598.

ments about meaning and truth in the issues that arise in and beyond political living. Good students in modern universities are often at first perplexed and astonished by teachings that "claim to be true." Even more fundamentally, they are astonished by the claim that truth might be possible and worth pursuing. But they soon become rather frightened and discouraged by those often dominant academic doctrines that maintain in principle that there is no truth is to be had.

Allan Bloom's description of the philosophical presuppositions of an average student in the best university seems mostly accurate: "There is one thing a professor can be absolutely certain of: almost every student entering the university believes, or says he believes, that truth is relative."[2] However, no life or discipline (paradoxically, even relativism) is worth pursuing if it does not have at least a claim to be true.

Truth in practical matters—in politics, in things to be done—is a conformity of what we actually do with what we ought to do. We are the beings who "ought to do" some things; for doing or omitting them we are praised or blamed. Our very lives require of us, elicit from us, activities that complete and define what we are. We are beings who are not complete without our own free effort. The kind of beings we are from nature also presupposes that we know our relative place in the universe, in the relation of things to each other. Some actions we do perform are better than others, which is why we are praised or blamed for them. Aristotle rightly maintained that only those actions that are worthy of praise or deserve blame (actions rooted in choices that could have been made otherwise) are the proper subject matter of human ethical and political philosophy (*Ethics* 1110b1).

A knowledge of what is proper to ourselves leads to a consideration of what is meant by philosophy or by a knowledge of the whole. We are the beings for whom a knowledge of the whole—of philosophy, in other words—constitutes the essential uniqueness of our being, even though we do not ourselves constitute this whole. We are receivers of what is highest in us, of the word that is not from us. We identify or name all that is not ourselves. This human condition implies a certain essential limitation in man-

2. Allan Bloom, *The Closing of the American Mind* (New York: Simon & Schuster, 1987), 25.

kind. The acceptance or rejection of this limitation constitutes our deepest moral orientation to the world, to ourselves, and to what lies beyond our kind. Behind every human action exists a reference to how that human being—who by his choice initiated the particular action—stands to the world in its essential givenness. We are parts of the whole who seek to know the whole, whose intellects are *capax omnium,* capable of knowing all things without ceasing to be finite, without ceasing to be ourselves.

2. *Political Philosophy and the Givenness of Man*

Many beings and activities in the cosmos exist that are not caused by human beings. Indeed, the cosmos itself, though not unrelated to the human mind, is not caused by it, does not exist because of it. Against the background of these nonhuman existences and activities, human beings put forth particular actions that come only from their own inner choice and causality. Human activities (those actions that could and would not exist without the existence of human beings as composites of body and soul) are the subject matter of political philosophy. This subject matter does not mean that there are no human activities that are more than political or ethical. Aristotle characterized our highest activity, rational contemplation, as "divine," but even our higher activities must pass through the ethical and political, through that wholeness which includes man's material and spiritual elements. Political philosophy strives to understand the relationship between the traditional categories, thought and action. The wholeness of the human being corresponds to the intricate wholeness of reality itself, to which man is open by his powers of action and thought.

Political philosophy does not begin without the experience of politics. Politics does not begin without the experience of human life in its classic stages, from conception to birth, to growing up, to maturity, old age, and death. "Man does not make man to be man," Aristotle remarked in a famous passage, "but taking him from nature as already man, makes him to be good man" (*Politics* 1258a21–23). From nature, from our existing in this world, we already are what it is to be human. No human being has ever caused either himself or the whole of mankind to be what it is to be a human being. Each human being is already a certain kind of being, different from other beings in the universe. To be a human being is a given, a fruitful mystery that is part of the reality of every human life lived on this planet.

Every human life that has actually come into being is included in the proper subject matter of political philosophy. The fate of the whole order of mankind is at least initially derived from a question that politics presents to political philosophy: whether there is a common good and goal that includes all the actual human beings—each of them—that have ever been specifically human with an existence, however brief, in this world. This consideration arose in political history from considerations deriving from revelation, of which St. Augustine's *City of God* is the most sophisticated early Christian source. Yet the question is rooted in Plato, in the last myth of the *Republic,* which asked about the possibility of our ever properly re-ordering our lives toward the good in some other life if we do not do so in this one. The drama of each human life is infinitely enhanced by the truth of this teaching of Plato—that we would not in fact redeem ourselves if we were given another chance to try again in some other life. The Myth of Er in the *Republic* and the story in the New Testament of Lazarus and Abraham and the rich man (in which the rich man asks that Lazarus be allowed to return from the dead to warn the rich man's brothers) both attest to the importance of the actual life we are given.

We can reject or attempt to overcome this human form or condition as it is given in nature, as something itself to be transcended, as an object hateful or unintelligible to our being. Certain modern philosophers and scientists have sought to alter the human form itself. Many others have sought to free it from any grounding in a will other than man's own. But we will attempt this transformation only if we suppose that no certain form or essence in man exists from nature or if we deliberately rebel against what we are. The fact that we have existed as already man, from a source that is not itself of human making, is in some theories considered not binding on us. Modern philosophic rebellion, in its most overt as well as in its most subtle forms, has as its theoretic background a resentment or rejection of the kind of being that man has been originally given in his own making, which is from outside himself (Chapter 3). Political philosophy cannot avoid dealing with the questions, is it alright to be a human being in the first place, and is it our duty and our dignity to remain human beings (even if we could, as we can, propose something else and attempt to make the proposal into a reality).

This theoretic background raises these questions: in itself, does man's givenness as man merely designate something feasible (because *what is*, is possible) but not normative (because *what is* has no purpose)? Or, more seriously, does this givenness of the very structure of man's being indicate a prior intelligence addressing man's own mind through the fact of his being what he is? Or is man merely some sort of cosmic accident or even joke? If *what man is* derives from some intelligence benevolent to him (we cannot deny the force of Descartes's worry about an alternate diabolic intelligence that might deceive us), then this givenness is intended as a guide for what must be called the fullness of human living. Political philosophy inquires into the relation of politics to this fullness that signals man's own highest being and end. This human fullness or completion, which is not apart from man's own choice, is not exclusively of his own making. Included in political philosophy is an understanding of alternatives—the "brilliant errors"—that begin the remaking of man by rebelling against his givenness.

3. *Political Science*

This book is a treatise of political philosophy, not of political science. In the order of time, the latter precedes the former, as the family precedes both. But in the order of dignity, political philosophy is the culmination of political science and the path to philosophy itself. Political science describes our lives in actual cities and guides actions and policies to achieve what men have chosen in common according to the ends of their actions. Political science seeks to understand and classify the regularities and norms of rule and citizenship that are found in existing but differing regimes. It assists us in achieving the ends of polities. Political science even describes the ends of disordered polities, as Aristotle explained in his own *Politics*.

Political philosophy, in contrast, arises because of the questions that occur in actual cities, just as philosophy arises out of questions that remain perplexing in political philosophy. Finally, revelation itself seems to be given when questions of philosophy receive no final or definitive solutions in politics or philosophy. The intellectual treatment of what exists in reality does not have strict boundaries, even though there are differing kinds of considerations, whose subject matters and definitions are not arbitrarily drawn. A scientific method can yield only the results the method allows. It cannot eliminate answers that are produced by other methods, or perhaps by reality itself, prior to all methods.

The accurate description of the worth of our civil society (political science), the description of its conception of good and bad in human action as embodied in law and custom, is one of the most dangerous and difficult of human enterprises. Most men, most of the time, are reluctant to hear what it is they are really like, what it is they stand for, what their city in practice, not just in speech, defines as its good. Polities are even less likely than individual human beings to listen to their own disorder accurately described. The danger of this accurate description is what lies behind the drama of the death of Socrates in Athens.

From this drama we learn that there must be a legitimate place where the precise description of polities and of individual lives within them can occur, where the meaning of the diversities of regimes can be argued without having the argument lead to the destruction either of the regime or of the philosopher. The place of resolution of these questions may not lie in the city itself. (If the competence of the city is limited, its worth and necessity are not thereby denied.)

The study of particular forms of regimes, their laws and processes of rule—political science, in other words—is a legitimate intellectual enterprise with a distinct subject matter. Minute investigations into actual regimes do not reach to those ultimate questions that, because human life itself extends beyond political life, every existing regime touches. All tyrannical regimes, however, want to conceive themselves as worthy and beneficial to their citizens, or at least they would argue, as Thrasymachus did in the *Republic*, that everyone would be a tyrant if he could. This claim to right or service is why almost all regimes in the modern world call themselves "democracies," almost the only word we have left

for a good regime. Political philosophy, thus, needs the organized
analysis of political science for the examination of its own subject
matter—that is, the location of the best regime.

The understanding of what it is to be a tyrant is an essential
exercise not only of political science but, more deeply, of political
philosophy. Political philosophy penetrates to the roots of human
freedom; it inquires into the nature of deviations from the good
that are possible to human beings living in cities. If the lives of a
good percentage of the human race in most eras are lived under
tyrannical or less than perfect regimes, as they are, the question
of the worth and meaning of these often (in human terms)
wretched lives cannot be avoided. If human dignity is not resolved
at some level that is not political, most of these lives have been
lived in vain, except perhaps for providing an example of what
not to do.

4. *The Open-Endedness of Political Philosophy*

Political life, by its very living and in particular by its failures,
leads to questions that are not answered by politics as such. The
"success" of the tyrant must imply a meaning other than the political for those lives subjected to his disorder of soul. Are the lives
of the citizens of a tyranny simply worthless if they are not lived
in a polity that can claim to possess at least some good? Certain
issues, such as the worthwhileness of human life in the worst regimes, lead to considerations that are no longer merely political.
They lead to issues that any perceptive person must confront if
he himself is to be whole. The status of the tyrant and that of his
victims was why the questions of the immortality of the soul and
of a final punishment for violations of justice both appeared first
in political philosophy and not in classical religion (Chapter 5).

Political philosophy begins by formulating perplexing questions that arise out of human experience. When they are once
articulated, it leads the student beyond political philosophy itself,
to philosophy and even to transcendence and revelation. Political
philosophy must be able to acknowledge that some responses to
its own questions are found in revelational sources. But political
philosophy does this analysis by being first and primarily itself,
political philosophy. If, when asked "What are you studying," a

student responds, "Political philosophy," there is implied a definite subject matter unique and proper to the term. But political philosophy is open-ended. It is not a defect in political philosophy that it must seek certain answers outside of itself. This incompleteness of political philosophy is the other side of the completeness of being, of the knowledge of *all that is.* In choosing a discipline to study, one does not cease to be a human being implicated in all disciplines.

Many avenues can be found to the highest things, the pursuit of which Aristotle, at the end of the *Ethics,* said should be our primary concern (1177b26–78a8). We can begin such pursuit with thought, with love, with evil, with pain, with beauty, with the order of the heavens, with death, with the complexity of plants, with almost any reality about which our minds can wonder. We can also begin, as we do here, with the experience of political living. All things lead to everything, but the paths are different, even when they intersect and reinforce each other. Political philosophy is not indifferent to beauty, or to truth, or to evil, or to the order of the heavens. For its own integrity and completion it has to account for them, or at least know that they are accounted for. Philosophy is of the whole, itself perhaps open to a further completion that does not jeopardize its own intrinsic legitimacy.

Political philosophy is a part of this whole of philosophy. It is the part that accounts for human activity as an important and separate reality in the universe, as something with its own being that needs to be understood if we are to grasp the whole. If the purpose of politics is to do, to act, to "live well," as Aristotle held, the purpose of political philosophy is to know, but to know after the manner in which political things can be known. The defense of doing and acting depends on the validity and truth of knowing the form and order of one's own actions, based in óne's own given being—a being like unto that in others, all other human beings who now are or ever have existed or ever will exist.

5. *Political Philosophy and the Politician*

Political philosophy acknowledges itself an integral part of philosophy, the knowledge of the whole. Political philosophy in modern times, however, has been that intellectual discipline most prone to substitute itself for philosophy as the claimant for the knower of the whole. Political philosophy has been the leading candidate to replace metaphysics or theology as the queen of the sciences. The reasons for this temptation are themselves integral to the understanding of political philosophy. Essentially, they derive from a denial of any alternate intelligible order in the universe (especially within the human being himself) to which the human mind is open and on which it depends for the truth of things.[3]

The result is a theory of knowledge that admits as valid only what the human mind or hand can make or, better, only what it wills to make. The polity comes to be seen as something so subject to human making that all things, including human deeds and sayings, fall under its scope and authority. It is an easy step to maintain that all being and knowledge can be assigned to politics alone. Politics becomes the only explanation of *all that is*, because apparently there is nothing beyond its scope. In one sense, this absorption of all into politics, the politicization of language, action, and deed, is the most "brilliant" of the errors with which political philosophy has to deal.

Political philosophy is not only a philosophical consideration of things political, though it is at least that. Rather it is an effort to render philosophy intelligible to the politicians who rule the city.[4] The purpose of political philosophy is to allow philosophy to exist in the city. Ironically, philosophy depends on the non-philosopher. We cannot have a city populated only by philosophers. How to render the non-philosopher who rules the actual city sympathetic to philosophy remains, as Plato knew, one of the main tasks of political philosophy. One solution, practiced over and over in human cities, is to banish the philosopher from the city. A second solution would be to neutralize philosophy, to render it innocuous, to deny that it has any serious purpose in human living. From Marsilius of Padua and Hobbes, this latter alternative has been the solution of modernity, which has systematically sought to deny any civil authority to what is not subject to human making. Even

---

3. See Josef Pieper, *Living the Truth: The Truth of All Things and Reality and the Good* (San Francisco: Ignatius Press, 1989).

4. See Leo Strauss, *What Is Political Philosophy?* (Glencoe, Ill.: Free Press, 1959), 5–95.

the state itself was artificially "made" by man's own powers. For Aristotle, on the other hand, the state was "natural," even though it had to be organized and configured by human prudence, action, and experience.

Plato's alternative—the philosopher-king who knew an objective good in which the good of all was contained—was possible only in the city he "built in speech," not in any actual city. Further, were not both the philosopher and the politician, not to mention the craftsman and the merchant, needed? And, to speak for the politicians, were not some philosophers rather dangerous, some even mad? Aristotle observed with no little irony that the greatest of crimes were perpetrated not by the politicians or the dissolute or the poor but by the philosophers (*Politics* 1267a9–17). The claim of the philosopher before the city could not be independent of the validity of the philosopher's claim on truth.

The reference to "brilliant errors" in the subtitle of this book recognizes not merely the dangers that arise from human imperfection but those that arise from the philosophers. Political philosophy, itself directed to human happiness and mankind's good, accounts not merely for what is wrong in human lives and institutions but for the limits of the good that politics at its best begins to recognize.

Samuel Johnson spoke of "the inseparable imperfection of all human governments," about "politicks entirely devoid of principle." We might have chosen a similar passage from the tenth book of Aristotle's *Ethics* or from St. Augustine's *City of God* (a book whose very title is based on Plato), or we might even have selected Machiavelli, to show that politics must deal not only with human virtue but with human vice. Sometimes it deceptively appears that politics arises exclusively from disorders and defects in the human condition. Political philosophy begins with a reminder of political realism, a reminder that all human governments, as all human individuals, will display some often quite serious imperfections. These varied imperfections are widely recognized, especially by politicians, to be obvious characteristics of actual human beings.

The expectation that human beings can and will bring about their own perfect order by their own efforts, however, presents us with one of the most perplexing issues in political philosophy:

namely, why can we not find a "perfect" form of rule? Ought not
the establishment of this perfect form be what we should be
about? Surely it is a legitimate question. The most serious question of political philosophy concerns the nature and location of
the best regime. For it is this question about the best regime, more
than any other, that either establishes the limits of politics or en-
courages politics to abandon all restrictions from nature or reason
to form what it will. Or to put it differently, if politics has no limits,
is politics not itself the explanation of the whole?

Political philosophy is necessary, then, for the defense of actual
political life. In this world, imperfection may be far less dangerous
than "perfection" if perfection is not properly something that politics can achieve by itself. This incapacity may not be a fault in
politics at all. Indeed, it is not, which why, beyond the "brilliant
errors," beyond the best that politics can do with the finite beings
we are, there remain things to be completed. Political philosophy
may not be fully capable of achieving such completion, but it can
at least point to the experiences and questions that make the further considerations seem necessary, even welcome.

6. *The Place of Political Philosophy in the City*

Samuel Johnson suggested that the reason for this inability to
remove imperfection from "all human governments" was the insufficiency of "virtue and principle." He observed that "wisdom
might plan, but virtue alone could execute." Virtue, wisdom, and
principle were to be located not merely in civil laws but in the soul
of even the lowest "constable," who would sell his duty for a shilling if he did not possess something inside of him to prevent it,
something that derived from virtue, wisdom, and principle. The
answer to the inevitable imperfection of all human governments
was to be found in those depths of the human spirit that were not
directly political. These depths needed examination by the political philosopher, himself knowledgeable about the nature of his
own subject matter, about the nature of his own soul. The resolution of the disorders in the city at a deeper level may not depend
on politics. Even if the city must fail, it does not follow that man
is necessarily a complete failure in the universe. The New Testament question, "What does it profit a man to gain the whole

world and lose his immortal soul?" (Luke 9:25), is a question with which political philosophy also must wrestle. It is Socrates' question at his Trial, about not being sure that death is the worst evil, while he knew that acting wrongly was.

Political philosophy first appeared in the dialogues of Plato as a form of discourse between the philosopher and the potential philosophers, the classical predecessors of all good students who aspire to know the truth. This discourse was, as it turned out, a deadly serious enterprise. It dealt with the question of whether human life had a highest meaning and, if so, what this meaning could be. It also inquired about who was responsible or qualified to achieve it? Was it available to those arriving at full adulthood and on what conditions? The hypothesis that political philosophy was itself implicated in the decision to be a philosopher meant that political philosophy was prior to philosophy. Laws and coercive powers could prevent the conditions of philosophy. Fear and terror could corrupt or mitigate the possibility of philosophy in any polity, at least for most people.

7. The Conflict between Truth and Polity

Socrates, in his *Apology*, chose to remain a private citizen, though his teaching caused the young potential philosophers to speak of him to their fathers, the politicians. The annoyance of the father-politicians at being prodded by their sons caused his teaching to become unexpectedly public. If Socrates could be induced or coerced to remain a private citizen or to be silent, the city would remain calm. A peaceful polity would be one that forbade philosophy, the very fact of which prohibition, however, would preclude a fully human city, since certain fundamental human things were excluded. Not every polity would allow the philosopher to exist. Even classic democracy, as described by Aristotle, in which no one could tell the difference between the philosopher and the fool because there was no valid principle to distinguish among lives in such a polity, allowed the philosopher to exist at the price of the theoretic insignificance of philosophy. A philosopher may even be incompatible with all polities. Whether this is so is the main burden of political philosophy.

Political philosophy sought a regime compatible with philosophy. Meanwhile, the actual cities realized that not all philosophers sought the truth. Even Socrates was dangerous to the existing order of Athens, whose own order was based not on truth but on freedom to do whatever one wished. The gods of Athens upheld its order. There was no acknowledged criterion of distinction of worthiness among human actions. The seriousness of the conflict between truth and polity is reflected in every era when a state has terminated the life of the philosopher, the saint, the mystic, or even an opposing politician. Political philosophy first appeared as an effort to make the polis and philosophy compatible.

The discourse of the philosopher was directed to the souls of the potential philosophers who were wondering about the best form of life open to a human being, the life that was just and good. Was the political life the highest life available to man? Was the highest thing a father politician could do for his offspring to hand on to him the political mantle? Was the choice of Socrates to be a philosopher the wise choice, the only real choice for a good man to make? Or were other forms of life equally legitimate? Were not philosophers few and were there not many other things to be done? Was not the life of the poet, or the politician, or the craftsman (the professions of the three accusers of Socrates) equally attractive to the young citizen seeking to be what he ought to be? Did the roles of the craftsman, poet, and lawyer in the condemnation of Socrates reveal defects in the souls of his accusers, defects that led to the essential imperfection of every polity? Philosophers seemed helpless. They were laughed at by Thracian maidens because they fell into holes in the road, as Plato pointed out. While the philosopher asked questions that searched for answers, the politician wanted only order and peace.

Political philosophy appeared in the *Ethics* and the *Politics* of Aristotle as a treatise or text designed to classify political things as they appeared in the actual lives of human beings. Plato had been concerned with the art of choosing what one is to be in his life. Aristotle, looking at these choices in retrospect, sought to classify their relative worth and meaning in themselves and for the city. Political philosophy is concerned with the character into which the young will allow their souls to develop and manifest themselves by their actions in their polity.

Political philosophy began with Plato's account of the death of

Socrates, the philosopher. Socrates was accused of making the stronger argument the weaker, of disbelief in the gods of the city of Athens, and of corrupting the youth, the sons of those who ruled the city. The youth themselves, the potential philosophers, were not above using philosophic method learned from Socrates as a "sport" to annoy their fathers. They were young and irresponsible, still in a state of themselves choosing what is "good" in the life that followed on their choices. For the "good" they chose, they were responsible against some objective standard of good that they did not themselves make. They were not simply innocent. Political philosophy thus began with potential philosophers and politicians before the philosophers.

Athens was the best of the cities of its time, but it was not perfect. The drama of the trial and death of Socrates that took place in the soul of the young Plato, the potential philosopher, led him to account over and over for this death. He unceasingly inquired whether Socrates had to have been killed by his own city, the best of the ancient cities. Except for the city built in speech, toward which he argued in the *Republic*, Plato did not think that philosophy was safe in any actual city, except perhaps for a time in Athens before it killed Socrates. The philosopher was not recognized in a democracy as anything extraordinary. Socrates, however, lived for seventy years in his own city before the danger of his teachings came before the public assembly in his city. Philosophy does appear in actual cities, but as a threat to their integrity.

8. *The Best Regime and the Existing Regime*

When philosophy fled the city at the death of Socrates, where did it go? It went to the academy, to the home of the philosopher. The philosopher either was indifferent to politics or saw that virtue and goodness, while not to be denigrated, were not to be found flourishing in actual cities. Truth demanded an escape from the city, even while the philosopher lived in it. The "inseparable imperfection of all human governments" required that philosophy seek a home beyond the city. But if this was the case, of what "use" was the philosopher? Philosophy was the knowledge of the whole. If this whole did not include political knowledge, it was imperfect in its very origin. What after all was the meaning of the philosophic vocation if not everyone could be a philosopher? If philosophy had little relation to actual politics, how did it relate to most citizens?

The impasse over the status of the best regime and its location compared to actual cities such as the Athens that killed Socrates involved another consideration. If political philosophy sought to know what was the best regime, and if the best regime had no actual location outside the argument that established its necessity (which was what the *Republic* was about), what was the meaning and status of all actual or existing regimes? Life in imperfect regimes is the "normal" condition of the actual human beings, perhaps some 90 billion of them, who have lived or are still living on this earth. The meaning of human life has to be found either in imperfect regimes or else outside of all existing regimes. To understand history as the effort to establish down the ages one actual, though fleeting, regime that is "the best," might be possible. But it is unlikely that this one actual best regime could justify the existence of all actual but imperfect regimes. This unlikelihood of the best regime implied that it was precarious to define actual human life solely in terms of the best regime.

Socrates' denial that it was possible or advisable to establish in fact the best regime, however, left all actual regimes in their disorders and imperfections. At this point classical Stoicism argued that whatever was, was right. But this solution emptied specifically ethical and political actions of their basic meaning.[5] The philosopher attempted to show his own superiority to the actual world by his "apathy," by his passionlessness and indifference to all that actually happened in the world. Against this strongly argued and tempting position, political philosophers had both to defend the real worth of human action and, at the same time, to order it to philosophy, to a wisdom that does not solve the human problem by denying the freedom of human actions. Philosophy or something beyond it must remain to answer the questions, why human choice is possible and what it is about, all the while identifying

---

5. See James V. Schall, S.J., "Post-Aristotelian Philosophy and Political Theory," *Cithara* 3 (November 1963): 56–79; "Post-Aristotelian Political Philosophy and Modernity," *Aufstieg und Niedergang der Römischen Welt*, ed. Wolfgang Haase and Hildegard Temporini (Berlin: Walter de Gruyter, 1994), part 2, vol. 36.7, pp. 4902–36.

things to be blamed and praised both in human actions and in human polities. Human choice, however, will inevitably result in imperfect actions and their consequences. As these actions appear in the city, they are ordered through laws, customs, and constitutions, but they remain actions of individuals, who chose to put them into reality.

This book will treat in detail the issues in political philosophy that naturally lead to perplexities that not even philosophy can completely answer: the issues of virtue, friendship, happiness, law, evil, punishment, and death. Each of these topics brings us to a question, now properly formulated, for which an answer must be sought or discovered. The properly formulated questions, based on a lived, intelligible experience, are the value of political philosophy in itself. By being itself, political philosophy incites the human mind to consider whether responses exist to questions posed.

Let us first survey in more detail the field of political philosophy, highlighting the essential questions that arose in political philosophy and the answers that were given to these questions in the classical, medieval, and modern eras. In our survey let us not minutely analyze each response but rather gain insight into the character of the responses and their relation to the whole of political philosophy. In subsequent chapters we will turn to those particular issues in political philosophy that lead to considerations of the highest import.

TWO

The Sequence of
Political Philosophy

> *"But the Being, said Nekayah, whom I fear to name, the Being which made the soul, can destroy it."*
>
> *"He surely can destroy it, answered Imlac, since, however unperishable, it receives from a superiour nature its power of duration. That it will not perish by any inherent cause of decay, or principle of corruption, may be shown by philosophy; but philosophy can tell no more. That it will not be annihilated by him that made it, we must humbly learn from higher authority."*
>
> *The whole assembly stood a while silent and collected. "Let us return, said Rasselas, from this scene of mortality. How gloomy would be these mansions of the dead to him who did not know that he shall never die; that what now acts shall continue its agency, and what now thinks shall think on for ever. . . ."*
>
> —SAMUEL JOHNSON, *Rasselas*, Chapter 48[1]

1. *The Questions of Political Philosophy*

Political philosophy must explain itself, its concerns. The political realm must let what is not political exist in its own right if what is not political is to flourish. The understanding that non-political things exist is the prerequisite for understanding the things that are political. Otherwise, what is not political will not be allowed presence within the realm of the polity. The common

---

1. Samuel Johnson, *Rasselas, Poems, and Selected Prose*, ed. Bertrand H. Bronson (New York: Holt, Rinehart, and Winston, 1958), 610–11.

good of the polity allows private and transcendent goods to exist. The polity recognizes that these goods are also its own good, though not its own competence.

The basic questions of political philosophy are these:

a. What is the best city and where is it located? Since there are many existing cities, their differences and likenesses require us to ask: which of these existing regimes is better and why? The answer to the question of what is the "best" regime may or may not be the same as the question of where this best regime exists. The best regime according to the classics existed in speech, in argument, not in fact. This response was brilliant and at the same time unsatisfactory.

b. What is the nature of human happiness? Political "science" asks about the nature of human happiness in general and, separately, about human happiness insofar as man is a mortal during his time on earth. These questions are not identical. But the happiness of man in his mortal condition consists in the activation of potentialities that man receives from his given nature. Happiness, as Aristotle put it, consists in the activities of the virtues (see Chapters 8 and 9). Man must choose his happiness according to the right order of his given nature, but he does not himself determine the "what" that will make him happy, the "what it is" that results in his happiness. He discovers this happiness already existing for him as a given, even as a gift.

c. What is the relation of politics to happiness? Man is by nature a political being. Man does not make himself to be man. The sphere of politics is that of making him "good man" in Aristotle's terms, wherein "good" refers to the proper activities of all the potentialities given to man by nature. These capacities are to be activated according to man's highest faculties of intellect and will; that is, he is to decide whether and how to activate them. He is rightly to be praised or blamed for his own self-rule. What is at issue is the happiness of a particular man, not man "in general." Except in the mind, man "in general" does not exist; only Socrates, Peter, and Mary exist.

Politics is the location of the moral virtues insofar as these virtues touch others. But the moral or practical virtues, however worthy in themselves, naturally lead to the contemplative virtues, which are the proper activities of man's highest faculties. These speculative virtues transcend politics but do not deny their naturalness nor their orderedness to the practical virtues. Political philosophy also asks about the unity of these virtues and about the corresponding relations between the objects on which they are based.

2. *Classical Political Philosophy*

What is classical political philosophy? The search for the limits of politics, for "moderation," is the effort to define what things are political and what things are not. Classical political philosophy recognized that the most immediate and difficult issue it had to face was convincing the politician to claim competence in nothing more than politics. Man is a social and political animal in all his activities. Man transcends the city, as Leo Strauss said, only by what is best in him, that is, by his speculative powers.[2] In seeing what is required of the best city, we see the limits of politics. Moderation characterizes classical theory because classical theory recognizes truths beyond politics. To claim more of politics was "immoderate"; it was to claim to create reality, not to learn about it from *what is*. The philosophic books devoted to metaphysics are legitimate books. They deal with objects that are not simply political. At his trial before the politicians who ruled his city, Socrates responded to his "voice." The "voice" was not from Athens.

All actual cities, for the classical writers such as Plato and Aristotle, are less than the best. The best regime existed in speech, in the argument that established its necessity, the argument which all potential philosophers must re-create in their own souls through study and discipline. The conclusion of this re-creation is the vivid, intelligible realization that the best city must exist only in speech as far as limited human powers are concerned. The attempt to impose the best regime, when it is not left in the mind, destroys any actual city, which is composed of individual human beings with finite capacities in finite relations.

Rarely, indeed never, is any polity composed of unqualifiedly good human beings. No polity can be composed exclusively of

2. Leo Strauss, *The City and Man* (Chicago: University of Chicago Press, 1964), 49.

philosophers. Philosophers likewise display the failings of other human beings. The thought about the best man or best regime, however, is a necessary consequence of thought about the variety of actual cities. Men who do not see how the problem of the best man or regime arises from actual living in the polity will not inquire about the theoretical best and its location. Hence, they will leave themselves open in modern times to ideology. Ideology is a manmade substitute for the best regime. In classical times, men left themselves open to a religion that was itself untested by philosophy. Socrates still held for the existence of spirits, even though the gods of Athens did not meet the philosophic test.

Statecraft is reflective of the order of the soul within the individual citizens. The polity is not something totally apart from the virtuous or vicious life of its members. Rather, it is composed of human beings acting toward themselves or others virtuously or viciously. The various types of regimes reflect the differing ways that human beings can relate their souls to the highest things. Polities fall into the category of relation, not substance. They are not beings, autonomous or artificial, but ways of interrelatedness and action. The effort to classify a particular regime is at the same time an effort to judge the regime in its moral status, in its goodness or in its evilness. This intellectual endeavor explains why political philosophy, when honest, is a dangerous profession, since few regimes are willing to know what they actually are.

3. *Post-Aristotelian Political Philosophy*

The late Greek and Roman writers did not agree with Plato and Aristotle on the nature of man and his relation to the polity. For the post-Aristotelians (the Stoics, Epicureans, and Cynics), the city is not necessary for man's perfection. The passing of the classic city-state into the Alexandrine or Roman empires left man with no intermediary between himself and the All. The wise man should withdraw from actual cities toward the whole. The individual is to make himself incapable of being influenced by the emotions or actions that go on in the world. These were the very aspects of man that, for the classical Greeks, made man political.

In post-Aristotelian systems, man shows his superiority to nature and the polity by not allowing either to affect him. Perfection is a-political and independent of anything but the inner human will. We are to show our superiority by being "a-pathetic," that is, by not allowing anything to affect us, even our passions. Aristotle maintained that passions existed, should be ruled, and were in themselves good and indicative of virtue's subject and possibility.

Moral virtues in this new system after Aristotle were held to surpass theoretic or speculative virtues. This order was exactly the opposite of that found in the Greek classics, where the moral virtues were ordained to the theoretic virtues, whose purpose was to discover *what is*. The order of the city decided the order of the gods for the post-Aristotelians, not the other way around. Civil theology, not natural or revealed theology, ruled the city, whose good took priority over the gods and over philosophy. In effect, art became superior to prudence. The city in which man lived must be subject to nothing but man himself. The roots of modernity are already present in the post-Aristotelians. The city, the world, and the individual are identified. Man is superior to all that is not his own will. Nothing is capable of affecting him.

4. *Scripture and Political Philosophy*

The revealed religions initially existed independently of Greek philosophy. But eventually, the philosophers realized that religion was dealing with subjects familiar to it, while the religious leaders saw in philosophy either a threat to religion's legitimacy or a support to its teachings. What is the contribution of Scripture to political philosophy? In the Old Testament, Yahweh transcends the world and its orders, including the polity. Politics is limited by the divine will. Israel is subordinate to God and His commandments. Right civil order is right order with God.

The law is revealed. To live is to live the precepts of Yahweh, precepts that include love of God and love of neighbor. The best polity is the polity of Yahweh. Other polities were of little worth unless they imitated the laws of Yahweh. In Deuteronomy (4:5–6), Moses said: "I have taught you statutes and laws, as the Lord my God commanded me; these you must fully keep when you enter into the land and occupy it. You must observe them carefully, and thereby you will display your wisdom and understanding to your people." Revealed law appealed to understanding.

No specifically political content is found in the New Testament, except (but this was most important) to distinguish the things of Caesar from the things of God (Matthew 22:22) and to locate the origin of all authority, including civil authority (Romans 13:1–7). The things of Caesar and the things of God are both legitimate. To find out what belongs to Caesar, to the polity, we must turn primarily to philosophy, not revelation. To find out what God is like, we turn to revelation. Caesar is ultimately the recipient of his authority from God, as Christ at His trial told Pilate, the governor. This reception need not be understood as a direct "donation" of authority but as another way of saying that man's political nature requires established political authority, itself bound to *what man is* and what is his nature and destiny. New Testament revelation implies philosophy and proposes its completion.

The authority of Caesar is not fully autonomous. Hence Christ said to Pilate, "You would have no authority at all over me if it were not given by Yahweh" (John 19:11). Peter and John said in the Acts of the Apostles that "we should obey God rather than men" (4:19). Taken together, these statements about political authority meant that the obedience of God required, when reasonable, obedience to men. Men in authority were themselves subject to the order of Yahweh, not merely to themselves. They were limited.

The very fact that authority arose in human society and was necessary in reason meant that the origin of human nature in God confirmed the classical Greek notion that man was by nature "political." Man was to live in a political order in which some authority was necessary for man's own good and completion. The legal and constitutional working out of these two differing legitimate areas of competence allows for wide variety of relationships between religion and state. What is does not allow is the absorption of one by the other.

5. *The Relationship of Faith and Reason*

What is the connection between revelation and politics? Let us propose several ways we might formulate this relationship:

a. Thesis 1: Politics determines civil religion (Cicero and the Romans).

b. Thesis 2: Revelation determines the political order (theocracy).

c. Thesis 3: Both revelation and politics have their proper spheres, neither is complete by itself as an explanation of all things,

i. some of these latter theories hold that reason and revelation can be contradictory to each other and still live side by side with each other (two truths);

ii. others hold that both are harmoniously related to the same persons, to the same body of action and discourse. One does not contradict the other. Each aids men in the clarification of the other (Aquinas).

The theory of "two truths" (Thesis 3i), which is attributed to the Arab philosopher Averroes, maintained that the differences between faith and reason could not be reconciled. One truth comes from reason and one from revelation. Both of these truths were said to be "true," but philosophically they could be contradictory to each other. This contradiction meant that the same person could go about affirming two truths, with the necessity to act on them, but which were contradictory to each other.

Scholasticism (Thesis 3ii), the word generally given to Christian medieval thinkers, held that this two-truth situation must be shown to be impossible, both humanly and theoretically. Neither reason nor faith can be saved this way. The relevant but diverse data of reason and revelation can be organized and related. The classifications of what is political, what is philosophical, what is revelational are established in the resolution of apparent contradictions between reason and revelation. The "two truths" are stimuli to discover the consistency of one truth that may be known from different sources. Neither truth can contradict the other.[3]

6. *St. Augustine*

Many of the most important contributions to medieval political philosophy came from St. Augustine (d. A.D. 430), who was a

3. See Josef Pieper, *Scholasticism: Personalities and Problems of Medieval Philosophy*, trans. Richard and Clara Winston (New York: McGraw-Hill, 1964), 100–109. See also Thomas Pangle, "The Theological-Political Problem," in Leo Strauss, *Studies in Platonic Political Philosophy*, ed. Thomas Pangle (Chicago: University of Chicago Press, 1983), 18–23.

citizen of the still-existing Roman Empire and not strictly speaking a "medieval" man. Everyone reckoned with him, not least St. Thomas. St. Augustine remains not only one of the most stimulating but one of the best-known men of ancient or any times. He practically invented, in his *Confessions,* the art of informing us what went on in our souls. Everyone must still reckon with him.[4]

In political philosophy, St. Augustine was a follower of Plato, in the sense that he recognized that Plato had asked the right question, namely, "What is the best regime?" The question had to be asked if we were to have any philosophical integrity. St. Augustine realized that, with the evidence at his disposal, Plato had given the right answer: The best regime must be located only in speech, only in philosophic arguments. But that the best regime was located only "in speech" was not accepted by St. Augustine.

Politics, for St. Augustine, is the result of the Fall. Agreeing implicitly with Aristotle at the end of *The Ethics,* Augustine held that coercive government ought not in principle to exist but did exist because of the fallen condition of man. This disordered condition was not rooted in human nature or in the polity but in the human will. Evil (or good) is operative regardless of the sort of actual city in which man lives. By any objective criterion, most men are sometimes good, often quite bad. Augustine continued one line of political thought from the classics: political thought must account for the evil actions of men as a fact of the public order. This fact often requires the use of force to control evil actions. The authorities in the state itself are not exempt from evil workings within themselves.

St. Augustine acknowledged that members of any state, even the Roman Empire, could be members of the City of God. Membership in the City of God—St. Augustine's phrase for all those who do choose God over themselves—depended not upon civil citizenship but upon grace and discipline. Yet, as St. Augustine also argued, these same believers ought, because of their belief, be better citizens, soldiers, businessmen, and craftsmen. St. Au-

---

4. See *St. Augustine,* ed. M. C. D'Arcy (New York: Meridian, 1957); Herbert Deane, *The Political and Social Ideas of St. Augustine* (New York: Columbia University Press, 1956); *Augustine Today,* ed. Richard John Neuhaus (Grand Rapids, Mich.: Eerdmans, 1993); Charles Norris Cochrane, *Christianity and Classical Culture* (London: Oxford, 1977), 359–516.

gustine did not see that the City of God, however much it answered the question of the location of the city in speech, had no
effect on the world, itself doomed to pass away. The Roman Empire was ruled by a long succession of dying men, St. Augustine
once said.

The search for the highest things and the accurate knowledge
of the worst things—the City of God and the City of Man, in St.
Augustine's terms—was legitimate. But neither city could be fully
realized in this world. St. Augustine was a direct heir of Plato, for
whom, at the end of the *Republic,* rewards and punishments for
personal and political virtues and vices were given in immortality,
not in this life. The central notion of political philosophy—the
search for the best regime—was, for Augustine, itself legitimate.
This conclusion was presented to political philosophy through
revelation. Man was not in essence a futile or contradictory being
who had been given unfulfillable desires or goals, however much
it seemed that way from philosophy alone.

St. Augustine insisted that the achievement of these higher
goals was not in man's own power, nor were they achieved in this
life. Grace, with the Kingdom of God, was primarily a gift, not a
direct product of political prudence or art or action. In this view,
all actual cities were defective and would remain so in practice
and in theory. The foundation of the political realism, which describes actual cities, is associated with St. Augustine (Chapter 4).
However important politics might be, the real drama and action
in the world has to do with the City of God and the City of Man,
neither of which could be located in an existing polity but passed
through the hearts and choices of each person.

7. *Feudalism*

Before examining how medieval philosophy met these questions about the City of God that arose out of classical and Old
Testament thought, let us touch on the structure of the medieval
world, which is described as "feudalism." Feudalism resulted after
the sixth century from the breakdown of the central Roman authority over finance, army, bureaucracy, and politics. Life became
localized in the various centers of Europe that had to fend for
themselves against invasions of new peoples and armies. Initially

feudalism represented the loss of the Roman articulation about the differing orders of social being. Much of the memory of Rome about universal rule and brotherhood remained, both in practice and in symbol, particularly in the Church.

The new people from the North and East sought both to imitate the Roman civility and to take on some form of Christian belief. The feudal order contains within its very operative structure both civic tradition and revelation. This presence of these two sources is what makes western feudalism different from any other kind of feudalism existing in the world. Feudalism already had within itself generations of men who had read St. Augustine's *City of God*. Those same men had to finance and defend their own lands without the aid of any central power.

The subsequent intermingling of civil, economic, political, and ecclesiastical questions and institutions (the pope had temporal jurisdiction; the emperor and kings had spiritual influence) resulted in a vast confusion (investiture controversy) of the various issues. Revelation caused the great intellectual efforts to understand, both in theology and in law, what this revelation specifically demanded and how it was to be understood. Revelation replaced neither the philosopher nor the politician. The temporal power of a priest or bishop arose from a temporal source, not a revelational one. Medieval intellectual thought demanded that all the orders of natural being and activity be accurately understood.

All of this confusion, however, took place within a people now Christianized and to some extent Romanized. Revelational questions and principles were part of any effort to sort out proper realms of politics, Church, economy, family.[5] The equality of man, the dignity of the person, the necessity of service to all, the irreversible nature of history became part of the normal way of resolving the conflicting orders and problems. Right order meant that Roman law was gradually established within the Church through the formation of canon law. This legal structure clarified the various feudal and civil legal traditions, so that they had an orderly relation with one another.

5. See Harold J. Berman, *Law and Revolution: The Formation of the Western Legal Tradition* (Cambridge: Harvard, 1983).

8. *Aquinas*

The thinker who is rightly credited with organizing these varying traditions and principles into the unique medieval synthesis was St. Thomas Aquinas (d. 1274). What was his contribution to political philosophy? Christian, Jewish, Islamic, and feudal traditions were all affected by the rediscovery of Aristotle. St. Thomas wrote a detailed Commentary on Aristotle's *Ethics* and began one on his *Politics*. He paid careful attention to what Aristotle had to say. Under the guidance of Aristotle, the political was seen not as a result of evil, but as itself good and necessary. Yet, Aquinas agreed with St. Augustine that actual disorder had to be accounted for and that it was to be located in the will. Aquinas sought to resolve these differing approaches in one unified order.

St. Thomas took up all the questions in Aristotle—those of friendship, justice, law, and virtue. He related them to the virtues and ends of human life as presented in both the philosophical and revelational traditions. Further, Aquinas sensed that resolvable order exists between philosophy properly understood and revelation. Feasible, noncontradictory responses to unanswered philosophic questions could be found in revelation. The initial questions were those found in Plato and Aristotle arising from wonder about friendship with God, about the union of mind and spirit, about the reward of the good and the punishment of evil, and about the meaning of the immortality of the soul. Some answers to these questions were also present in political philosophy in an inadequate form. St. Thomas knew the questions and the proposed answers both from reason and from revelation.

St. Thomas did not replace revelation with reason. Nor did he understand revelation as a kind of detailed law. Rather he demonstrated that what revelation presented in its own terms and its own manner did respond to questions that were legitimately asked by the philosophers. The vocation of the philosopher and the excitement of this vocation remained for St. Thomas. For him, there were not two truths, but there was an order with different sources for the same truth. Since revelation was a gift, it was not the result of philosophy. But issues treated in revelation also oc-

curred in philosophy. In fact, the particular question of the existence of God led Aquinas to argue that the same source was
responsible for both faith and reason. Human intelligence could
and must embrace both realms, without changing the nature of
either. The result would be an increase in philosophic accuracy
and depth together with an understanding of just why revelation
might be given, why it might not be simply irrational.

9. Beginnings of Modernity

The nominalist theories, especially those attributed to William
of Occam (d. 1349) and Marsilius of Padua (d. 1342) in the century after St. Thomas, are about the nature of the primacy of the
will and the consequent lack of order in nature, except on the
basis of will. Thomism held, following Genesis, that nature did
not need to exist. But given that it did exist, existing secondary
causes (what was not God, in other words—say, a tree or a man)
acted according to what they were, by their own powers. In late
medieval theology, such "limitations" from nature, from *what is*,
were rejected.

The arbitrary political state of early modern theory was first
prefigured by the arbitrary God of nominalism. God was seen as
simply will. God's sovereignty was said to be limited if He were
not free to make anything whatsoever, even contradictory actions.
Such a theory maintained that it was exalting God by refusing to
limit Him by His own being. It argued that the distinction between good and evil depended only on God's will. Ironically this
theory made it possible, when religion was subject to the Leviathan, to replace God by the polity. A polity modeled on an
arbitrary God, or one which subsumed His powers, would be unlimited.

Marsilius of Padua was the first of the moderns in political philosophy and the last of the medievals. He was a commentator on
Aristotle. He held that Aristotle did not account for one key dis-
ruptive force in a polity, namely, the priest. He solved the conflict
between reason and revelation by reducing the priest to purely
spiritual affairs. No relation between spirit and matter could be
found, a view just opposite Aristotle's. The king exercised purely
material force for the good of the community. The spiritual was

privatized. It could not affect the public order. The single order, in which politics dominated all other spheres, came to prevail. The dual order of the medieval period, in which both revelation and reason had legitimate functions, came to an end. No longer one society and two swords, but a single polity, a single sword, and a single head. The spiritual was reduced to the inner conscience. It either did not matter or did not have any order except that of political will.

10. *Essence of Modern Theory*

Without the medieval reality, modern political philosophy would not have many of its most basic characteristics and institutions. Limited rule, parliaments, representation, civil constitutions, higher law—these are all medieval ideas and forms. Modern political philosophy, however, can be looked upon in two ways. The first, begun by Marsilius but perfected by Machiavelli and Hobbes, looks on man as autonomous. It proceeds to construct the polity from premises that are not derived from the order of being found in man as given by nature. Civil society is "constructed." The forms of constructed politics are found solely in the human will.

The second way of looking at the origin of modern political institutions began before St. Thomas with roots in St. Augustine and Aristotle. Here was retained the idea that no perfect kingdom could exist in this world. But it held that actual human betterment was possible. This approach, as recorded by writers like Christopher Dawson and Ellis Sandoz,[6] freed politics from utopian or Machiavellian claims, without denying that good and bad actual polities were possible. A better worldly order depended on the proper, nonpolitical understanding of the nature and location of the highest things. There existed in the world forces of kindness and charity, which could not be anticipated by the classic polity. If spiritual motives or sources existed, they could be accepted but not fully accounted for by philosophy. If men and women were better because of spiritual forces (even by philosophical stan-

6. See Christopher Dawson, *Religion and the Rise of Modern Culture* (Garden City, N.Y.: Doubleday Image, 1991); Ellis Sandoz, *A Government of Laws* (Baton Rouge: Louisiana State University Press, 1990).

dards, though not for philosophical reasons), the polity would be better, no matter what its form. The sources of human virtue and action were not limited to this world or to its sciences. They had, nevertheless, actual effects on human lives. The privatization of the spiritual life as proposed by early modernity in Marsilius and Hobbes was a denial of the full personhood of the actual people who lived with grace and reason.

Machiavelli rejected classical or Christian political philosophy at its very root. He held that we were not to look to what men ought to do, but to what they did do. He differed from the classics and the medievals, who likewise knew as clearly as he did the evil that men did "do." Machiavelli did not retain any primacy of "oughtness," by which we could distinguish good and evil within politics. What was good was simply what was successful to secure political peace. What was evil was what failed.

Socrates, to recall, had maintained that to do evil was the worst thing, that death was preferable to doing wrong. Machiavelli lowered the sights from the good and from the transcendent to the actual. This lowering eliminated any moral distinction of good and evil, the key subject matter of ethics and politics according to the classics. The soul of man was not open to the transcendent city. We were to begin with the analysis of power and success and not ask about their ultimate justification or implications. Classical and Christian thought had attributed a meaning to man other than that of life in the city conceived in terms of success or failure, but with Machiavelli, modern theory loses that higher meaning.

Hobbes held that the *summum bonum* in the classical or Christian sense was not a factor in man, but that man's deepest motivating force was fear of violent death. In stark contrast, this fear of death was precisely what Socrates had maintained should not prevent us from acting on the highest things. With Hobbes, all philosophical or religious issues could be settled by a polity willing to use this fear of death for its own ends of peace and order. Order was not a principled agreement, brought about by virtue and argument, but a struggle rooted in fear of force, designed to counter what Hobbes felt was religious and philosophic fanaticism. The order of the Leviathan was an order rooted not in reason but in will or force. It was constructed solely out of the mind of man, not conformed to any transcendent order either of man or of what was beyond him.

The second instance of modern thought, deriving from St. Thomas, tried to save certain clear advances that were not necessarily linked with the complete autonomy of the human will. In this view, the modern world represents the completion of a given nature open to the incentives of revelation. The human work of improving the world could be accomplished only if the final questions of man's meaning were decided and lived out in practice on the basis of principle. The proper use of politics was not as an explanation of all things; specifically, if metaphysics and theology addressed the first questions, politics and economics could be left to be themselves to work for the relative betterment of the life of man qua mortal. This confusion is what happened when politics and economics claimed competency beyond their own realms.

Modernity is a struggle between "the modern project" inaugurated particularly by Machiavelli and Hobbes against classical and Christian theory. The modern project proposes that man, in order to be man, must replace or even destroy all that is given to him in nature about what he is and ought to be. Marx, for example, wanted to create a world in which he could see only autonomous man everywhere he looked. By contrast, the classical tradition names as the man of responsible openness to being the one who seeks the highest things beyond politics. Yet he sees it is possible to retain a reflection of these highest things in his own life and in his own city because of the sort of being it is who is called to the highest things. These highest things are now presented to the philosopher by revelation.

Modernity in its autonomous sense sought to eliminate the question of God by solving the question of politics. Medieval political philosophy at its best sought to solve the question of God; it thereby found a solution to the question of politics. "Seek ye first the Kingdom of God and all these things shall be added to you." Medieval political philosophy is nothing less than the articulation of this proposition among the heathen. It is at this theoretical point that we can begin to see the need to return both to the classics and to medieval philosophy to meet problems caused by the trials and failures of modern political philosophy as well as of modern practice. Modern theory at its later stages—sometimes called post-modern theory—in this sense is not something different from modern political philosophy but a drawing of its own logical conclusion when the return both to revelation and to reason is rejected on grounds that can only be traced to will.

The sequence of political philosophy, as I have described it, provides the general context within which we can eventually proceed to the classical questions and the import of the responses of medieval theory to those abiding questions. First, however, we must say something further about the nature and importance of modernity as a philosophic concept that stands for human autonomy. The responses of classical and medieval theory can be understood as living and viable alternatives to the modern proposals that were designed to replace them but which, in the empirical order, have proved their dangers and startling inadequacies.

The "brilliant errors" of modern political philosophy demonstrate the sober sanity of classical and medieval argument. They demonstrate as well the genius of the human mind to formulate answers to its abiding questions when it refuses those answers found in the intellectual tradition of reason and revelation. Although I do not propose a "return to the middle ages," yet I agree with Samuel Johnson: these alternate solutions of genius arising out of political philosophy, when given their due, remain "gloomy," not merely to him who holds, with the tradition of Socrates and revelation, that "what now thinks shall think on for ever," but to the formulators of modernity itself.

THREE

Modernity

> *"Every man in the journey of life takes the same advantage of the ig-*
> *norance of his fellow travellers, disguises himself in counterfeited merit,*
> *and hears those praises with complacency which his conscience re-*
> *proaches him for accepting. Every man deceives himself while he thinks*
> *he is deceiving others; and forgets that the time is at hand when every*
> *illusion shall cease; when fictitious excellence shall be torn away; and*
> *All must be shown to All in their real state."*
>
> —SAMUEL JOHNSON, *The Adventurer,* August 25, 1753[1]

1. The Word "Modernity"

No one likes to be called "anti-modern" or out-of-date, even if
he is. To be up-to-date, however, is often to be out-of-date, and
what is called "modern" is more and more a product of past ages.
This is why we hear talk of the "post-modern" and even the "post-
post modern world," even though the premises that ground these
later theories are themselves firmly rooted in modernity itself.
The nineteenth-century theory of progress was largely crippled
by the reality of World War I. That is, things were evidently not
getting better and better. Political philosophy should discuss at
least with itself its own terminology and its meaning.

As an antidote to the ills of more recent thought—and this is
by no means an "antiquarian" position—I will suggest some return to classical and medieval thought in its essential outlines. It
is important, in this light, to continue the discussion from the last

---

1. Samuel Johnson, *Rasselas, Poems, and Selected Prose* (New York: Holt, Rinehart, and Winston, 1958), 166.

chapter on the importance and understanding of modernity. This chapter is intended, not to reject the whole modern world, but to clarify and finally to reject certain foundations of modern thought. It is not that much of this "modern" thought has not been understood or analyzed by classical or medieval thinkers at least in its abiding principles. In a basic sense, most ideas and theories, even modern ones, do have intriguing classical foundations in one form or another. But there is also something different that can be articulated in terms intelligible to classical and medieval philosophical reflection.

The word "modern" is a fluid term that means simply the "now," with the immediate future and the recent past, both latter usually understood to be some indeterminate yet recognizably limited distance from the now. Every time was at some moment modern. Likewise, every modern time will become past or ancient time. Even a "post-modern" now will become a past now. Modernity, as the term is used in this book, stretches roughly from the late fifteenth century at least into the twenty-first century, with appropriate gradations of emphasis sometimes captured by the terms "early modern," "late modern," or "post-modern."

If, then, the twenty-fourth century should call itself something other than modern, "modernity," as a description of the period from the Discovery of America until the Third Millennium, will no doubt seem as remote to the twenty-fourth century as Columbus or even the invention of the automobile does to us. Historians with some irony will call our era the "Age of Modernity." Our age will be a past age. Historians and philosophers will be curious to see what we were about. Even theories that are classified as "the end of history" or post-modern are themselves products of modernity, of the idea that man could accomplish what he set out to do. The trouble is that, in the end, he may find what he does by himself boring, or uninteresting, or even unintelligible.

Samuel Johnson, who does not seem to have used the term "middle ages," was, however, annoyed to hear the ancients praised before the praises of modern times, which for him, meant the eighteenth century. "Men in ancient times dared to stand forth with a degree of ignorance with which nobody would dare now to stand forth," Johnson wrote.

I am always angry when I hear ancient times praised at the expense of modern times. There is now a great deal more learning in the world than there was formerly; for it is universally diffused. You have, perhaps, no man who knows as much Greek and Latin as Bentley; no man who knows as much mathematics as Newton: but you have many more men who know Greek and Latin, and who know mathematics.[2]

One was more likely in Johnson's time than now to hear the ancients praised at the expense of the moderns. Though still possible and even necessary, as Eric Voegelin and Leo Strauss have argued, it has been more rare for at least a century. To imply that things were better in past or ancient times suggests that the present is a kind of rejection of or retrogression from something once thought to be better. Early theories of history, symbolized by the accounts of a Golden Age and the Garden of Eden, held that things were better in the beginning. History, far from being an advance, was a falling away from what was perfect in the past. What was "modern" was what was corrupt and disordered. Advancement meant going back.

Yet, particularly with the theory of Progress in the nineteenth century (a theory that held that things were both better and more true because they were more recent), it became popular, even supposedly "scientific," to hold that because something is modern it is therefore superior. Obviously some things were improvements, but whether men were "better" remained a question. The classical philosophers, no doubt, would have held that whether a time or era is better or worse depends not on its relative position in some temporal sequence but on how it compares with a fixed standard. This standard, though it may appear or even disappear in time, is not dependent for its validity on time itself but on its truth. Though men could change their minds, ideas as such did not change. As Aristotle put it, Socrates could stand or sit, but what it was for Socrates to sit down was an unchangeable idea.

Many classical authors, most notably the Greek historian Thucydides, held a cyclical view of history. This theory affirmed that good and bad came around in a predictable sequence, and that therefore nothing new ever really happens, but only eternal rep-

2. *Boswell's Life of Samuel Johnson* (London: Oxford, 1931), II, 494.

etition of what has already occurred. (Nietzsche, at the end of modernity, is famous for suggesting a return to this very theory.) According to cyclic theory, when we understand the cycle of necessarily recurring events we understand what will happen in the future.

These classical theories maintained that what was good or evil was still identifiable by what each, good or evil, was in itself. Both good and evil were stable over time, not relative to some place in the recurrent cycle of the ages. Murder, for example, though it might and did often occur, did not become right with time even in cyclical theories but remained wrong in any time in which it might occur. The stability of the meaning of good and evil over time was what gave meaning and coherence to human history. The Roman historian Tacitus remarked that some German tribes thought that stealing was permissible. Historicism and cultural relativism took this to mean that, simply on the basis of custom, what was good (or evil) in one place or time was not necessarily good (or evil) in another; in other words, that good and evil were grounded only in culture and custom, not in nature. St. Thomas, by contrast, held that it is possible for individuals or peoples to fail to see the validity of some principle, but that does not make the principle wrong (I–II, 95, 6). Time does not change principle.

2. Exhaustion of Ideologies

We have recently come to use the term "post-modern" to indicate a body of thought or experience that is beyond the "modern." This usage implies that modernity, or "the modern project," is now itself out-of-date or overcome by thought and events. Whether this change of intellectual content is true or not, or whether it is rather merely a further carrying out of principles already implicit in modernity, is a problem that modernity presents to political philosophy. A widespread feeling no doubt exists that some great historical period is now ending. "The end of history," "the end of socialism," "the beginning of a new world order" have become common themes.

Other thinkers hold that modernity's intellectual crisis has given new legitimacy to the classical philosophy and religion against which it first arose. Still others would like to see the modern project carried to the extremes of its initial premises, to the complete elimination, that is, of any sign of a transcendent presence or natural order in human life. Finally, we have those who would see in the failure of modernity an occasion for some completely new religion or philosophy that rejects modern materialism. Fundamentalism is both praised and excoriated on these grounds. A return to pure classical philosophy (without the additional input of revelation) is considered by still others to be the best way to overcome the errors both of modernity and of the religious wars incident in modern history.

Theories of progress more recently have been challenged by theories of apocalypse. The world is not getting better and better; rather, it will soon end with a crash. Initially nuclear weapons, and now scenarios of environmental and medical disaster, have fueled ideas of doomsday. Such theories are in fact quite popular. Doomsday theories (whether of an anti-war, or an anti-technological, or a pro-ecological nature) are themselves rooted modernity, which claims total human control over nature or, often, the control of man through control over nature.

No doubt the sense that the "modern" is itself to be overcome seems particularly valid in the light of the crisis in the marxist world. In much philosophical analysis, the crisis is regarded, as the conclusion of at least one major aspect of modernity that began in the sixteenth century. Whether the core issue that modernity raises—the complete autonomy of man—has ended or merely changed emphases is one of the most serious issues with which contemporary political philosophy has to deal. This concern (that, in fact, the premises of modernity continue but in different, though intellectually related, form) constitutes the content of any discussion of "post-modernity."

Modernity after Rousseau presumed a theoretical "malleability" of human nature—that is, there is no such thing as a stable human nature. Mankind is open to transformation by human will and power, usually by the instrumentality of the state, because it is limited by no norms other than itself. Positions in political philosophy that include the classical and religious traditions of original sin, human imperfection, and the limitation of the state, however, remain philosophically defensible but anti-modern in intellectual spirit and substance.

Ironically, the anti-dogmatism and relativism on which modernity is based leave mankind open to ideologies that claim no truth but rely only on the human will to achieve whatever it wants. No abiding human nature remains to criticize their concepts of human form. The reason for this ideological result is this: a world in which there is supposedly no natural order based on some mind or intelligence beyond man has no theoretic means to resist any claim that arises from human intelligence, particularly academic or collective intelligence.

The philosopher Eric Voegelin observed that there would be no new "ideologies" in the twentieth century, but rather a working out of the ones already formulated in the nineteenth century and before.[3] A certain line of thought in modern philosophy had reached its end or completion; nothing further could be added to it because of its inner consistency. Socialism, anarchism, and liberalism exhausted the possibilities open to them on their own premises. What has happened in the twentieth century, in Voegelin's view, has been the incarnation of these initially abstract ideologies, their projection onto space and time through political movements, that is, through a will that imposed them and tried to make them work. The failures of these efforts, notably socialism, have become part of the philosophic evidence with which we must deal in our understanding of modernity.

The origin of modern totalitarian states, including those democratic in form, lies in the insistence that, for the good of all, it was permissible to put ideological arrangements into operation in the world, even by force. The subsequent testing of these ideologies by experience has been the history of the twentieth century. In religious terms, modernity is the effort of man to save himself by presenting and putting into being an alternate project to the very being of man and cosmos. This alternate conception of man's good is dependent only on his own intelligence, not that found in nature and in the God who created nature.

Modern ideologies embrace the goals and assumptions of a society based on human will in its autonomy. The relation of classic revelation to ideology is clear on the level of doctrine: revelation is opposed to ideology, for classical theology holds that the human

3. *Conversations with Eric Voegelin,* ed. R. Eric O'Connor (Montreal: Thomas More Institute, 1980), 16.

will is free but also dependent on an intellect that can discover the intelligibility in being, including its own being. To the degree that religion itself has taken over essential features of the modern project, however (and this is often considerable), it appears not as religion but as ideology. When the thinking of religion and of modernity have converged, the transcendent has been left unattended or taken over by movements that do not bear the delicate balance of classical revelation.

Eric Voegelin wrote:

We observe, for the last two hundred years, that every possible locale where one could misplace the ground [of being] has been exhausted. This expresses itself in the fact that we have, since the great ideologies of the mid- and late nineteenth century, since Comte, Marx, John Stuart Mill, Bakunin (and so on), no new ideologist. All ideologies belong, in their origin, before that period; there are no new ideologies in the twentieth century. Even if one could find a new wrinkle in them, it wouldn't be interesting because the matter has been more or less exhausted emotionally. We have had it.[4]

The exhaustion of the ideologies, which is the meaning of the end of modernity, makes again clear the force of the classical and medieval philosophical positions from which modernity thought to dissociate itself. The understanding of modernity includes understanding the classical and medieval positions. Philosophy reflects on its own aberrations as legitimate evidence of its own validity, indeed of its own morality. The study of modernity unavoidably re-proposes the question of the truth of classical philosophy and revelation against which modernity was constructed. Since it cannot establish its own relativist premises, modernity is intrinsically precarious and is unable to explain satisfactorily its own observations.

3. *Progress and Limitation*

Nietzsche spoke of replacing the "modern" man with a superman, someone who took seriously the "truth" that God was dead, as modern men in practice believed to be the case. Whether "modernity" as an intellectual and political concept has come to an

4. Ibid.

end becomes intelligible in the context of the nature of modernity as it has been understood in political philosophy. Modernity has, philosophically, exalted politics as the ultimate science, whose function it is to solve all of mankind's material and spiritual disorders. Politics replaced theology as a way to benefit man.

Classical ethical thought admitted that, while it was wrong to do so, men were free to destroy themselves. Paradoxically human life depends on its own will. A philosophy based on will alone appeals only to itself and not to the world or God for the justification of what man thinks or does. Classical philosophy and revelation held that man could and often did choose to reject the given world. A life of disorder was possible for every individual or society. The careful classification of these rejections of order manifested in personal vices and corrupt regimes was in part what ethical and political science was about.[5]

"All must be shown to All in their real state," Samuel Johnson observed of our proneness to deceive even ourselves. The problem that modernity has presented is whether the ideas or forms that have served to define the modern world are valid. But this validity is not a question of the time in which ideas appear. Rather it is an examination of ideas and concepts against a standard or norm that does not change with time. At its most extreme forms, rather than to admit the possibility of a theoretically justified standard, the very instrument of reason itself is denied. What results is a completely unfettered will.

Voegelin's idea that the ideologies are exhausted was not a kind of pessimism with regard to human innovation. Rather it was an account of the human mind that desperately sought to replace the real being of *what is* with something completely of its own construction. Real being, *what is,* was the concern of classical and medieval thinkers; it bore within itself inexhaustible freshness. The concern of modern political philosophy was a product completely of man's mental construction. Pitted against the reason found in things, reason whose origin is transcendent, the human mind could never "imagine," never construct, a reality quite as wondrous as the one that was given.

---

5. See Paul Johnson, *The Intellectuals* (New York: Harper & Row, 1988); E. Michael Jones, *Degenerate Moderns* (San Francisco: Ignatius Press, 1993).

In opposition to given reality, the ideological construction of what humans thought "ought" to exist could be either materialist or spiritual. A willed intellectual construction in the name of liberty depended on nothing but will itself. This construction was to be placed into existing reality, into *what is*. From the modern viewpoint, reality had no source of meaning in reason, but another arbitrary will, itself equally independent of any grounding in what is. Between such divergent wills no resolution could endure, only conflict.

This conflict could be resolved in but two ways: (1) A Hobbesian Leviathan, who had all power in himself and therefore could use fear of death, could be appointed by citizens to guarantee their peace. That is, absolute state power could limit the conflicting ideas. Or (2) all ideas and ideologies could be reduced to insignificance through a concern only for what was conceived to be common, that is, prosperity and material well-being. Men could strive to make ideas irrelevant to their "real" concerns or they could establish a force, called law, based on will alone. The law decided what form the public order should take. The "law" in this sense would be conceived to be a common will, not a common reason, as Aquinas already anticipated (I-II, 90, 1, ad 3).

Any consideration of modernity begins in Machiavelli, in Descartes, and in Bacon, whose principles are, respectively: (1) the rejection of any moral authority of the classical philosophers through the denial of any distinction between what men ought to do and what they in fact do; (2) the radical separation of thing, sense, and mind; (3) the proclamation of modern science as itself capable of meeting the "needs" of mankind in a way the ancients never could have thought.[6]

The ancient Greeks failed to produce the marvels of modern science, not because they did not know how or were incapable of learning how to produce them, but because they saw where experimental science, freed from the contemplative order, would lead. Science, they thought, would end by undermining human nature as such, by attempting to reconstruct it on grounds at odds with its initial givenness. The foundation of this givenness is the

6. See Leo Strauss, "The Three Waves of Modernity," in *Political Philosophy: Six Essays*, ed. Hilel Gilden (Indianapolis: Bobbs-Merrill, 1975), 81–98.

effort of classical and medieval political philosophy to relate itself to what metaphysics is about, to *what is*.[7]

The Greeks rejected science on moral and philosophical grounds, not on grounds of ignorance. In recent years, increased attention is being given to this side of the classical authors that was dubious about the autonomy of science. The progress of science is no longer so easily accepted as a good in itself, particularly when man himself becomes the "object" of science. When the purpose of science is to overcome what is thought to be "mal-constructed" in man's nature (primarily his evident incapacity to produce a perfectly good life or polity in this world), the progress of science demands a freedom from the limitations presumably caused by human nature.

4. *Human Nature and Progress*

Leo Strauss put the problem this way:

The change in the character of social science is not unconnected with the change in the status of the modern project [modernity]. The modern project was originated as required by nature (natural right), i.e. it was originated by philosophers; the project was meant to satisfy in the most perfect manner the most powerful natural needs of men; nature was to be conquered for the sake of man who himself was supposed to possess a nature, an unchangeable nature; the originators of the project took it for granted that philosophy and science were identical. After some time it appeared that the conquest of nature requires the conquest of human nature and hence in the first place the questioning of the unchangeability of human nature: an unchangeable human nature might set absolute limits to progress. Accordingly, the natural needs of men could no longer direct the conquest of nature; the direction had to come from reason as distinguished from nature.[8]

In these words we find an exact description of the nature and character of modernity. The original "needs" of men—food, clothing, shelter—were understood, especially by writers like Ba-

7. See Charles N. R. McCoy, *The Structure of Political Thought* (New York: McGraw-Hill, 1963).

8. Leo Strauss, *The City and Man* (Chicago: University of Chicago Press, 1964), 7.

con, not to have been met by ancient or medieval philosophy, science, or religion. Since the way to meet these needs could not be discovered in nature or in the human intellect's own functions, human nature apparently had to be reformulated by reason.

Directed primarily at man's higher needs, the following were the impractical questions asked by classical and medieval philosophy, at the expense, it was maintained, of the practical: What was truth? Who was God? How ought human life to be lived? What is the good? Because of the time and energy it took, the all-absorbing effort to answer these questions was said to be the "cause" of any failure to meet the needs of mankind, needs that arose not from man but from nature. The religious answers, summed up by giving a cup of water or providing a cloak, had, it was claimed, failed. Modern reason, not religion, was obliged to meet these requirements of nature. It would turn to more efficient ways for meeting the basic material needs. This not ignoble purpose was what modernity set out to accomplish.

But what initially motivated this pursuit to meet men's natural rights or needs was itself something from nature. Nature was given. It was open to human understanding to comprehend its exigencies in terms of the basic needs of man himself. Men had an obligation to provide for these natural needs. What science was supposed to have been able to do—hence the "newness" of modernity—was to provide for these needs for all without violation of anyone's "rights." In its modern philosophical usage, "rights" has come to mean "what we will for ourselves." This fulfillment of needs was proof of modernity's "spiritual" side. Classical political bodies were said to have limited their production and distribution of goods to only a few, and even this required slavery. Modernity would democratize these aristocratic riches. As Aristotle himself foresaw, slavery would be made obsolete by technology, not by politics.

If science was truly universal and had no limitations on what it could investigate, what reason could be given for not studying human nature itself? Human nature was said to limit science because it was unchangeable. In medieval philosophy, human nature was unchangeable because it existed as a result of an act of creation on the part of God, the intelligibility of which act was to be found in human nature reflecting on itself. Man was not the cause of himself. Medieval thought understood man to be better made by nature than by man himself, because of his origin in God. No alternative to *what man is* could be found to be superior to the classical and revelational articulation of what man ought to be.

However, in a line of thought that extends from Scotus and Occam to Descartes, Bacon, and Hume, it is argued that human nature does not depend on God's reason. Human nature itself was put into question. Since it could no longer provide a limit to a science that did not recognize anything but material causes, the human mind was free to provide the models based on its own analysis of itself about what it could want. The modern project or modernity was developed in this context. This eventuality is what Strauss meant by finding a direction from "reason" and not "nature" as the source of what man was. As Strauss understood, this sort of reason independent of nature was the worst possible threat to human nature.

5. *Metaphysics and Modernity*

Two approaches in modernity have come to be proposed for solving man's higher needs to society and to his own ends. The first, the individualist or liberal approach, left the higher questions to the private order of soul. Whatever anyone might choose for his highest good was valid so long as it did not interfere with or even have anything to do with the corresponding choice of others. No common end or good existed, only a sufficiency of material goods. No possibility of rational adjudication of theoretical differences was possible, since in principle in modern philosophy values were subjective and located in an autonomous will, a will limited by no nature. This is the ultimate origin of the "fact" and "value" controversy in modern social philosophy.

The second solution, the collectivist solution, proposed that the greatest good for everyone could not be achieved except through a society with one will and one energy, a proposition we owe primarily to Rousseau, though Hobbes formulated its main lines. For its own good, the individual will had to be placed in subjection to a higher will. In modernity, the collectivist solution laid claim to a certain nobility and selflessness. Rightness consisted not in truth but in conformity to this will, itself located in the chosen collective power of the polity.

In either case, the individualist or the collectivist, human nature presented no limits on the individual or the collective will, which was capable of producing a man no longer restricted by the older limits of nature. Since in modernity man was himself theoretically malleable in all aspects of his corpus and his mind, the limits of bodily requirements or moral virtues were, it was maintained, overcome in principle. Whatever man chose himself to be was right, because what was right was what conformed to his will, presupposed to no duty or obligation prior to his personal or collective will. Freedom was the highest virtue. "Right" was rooted in freedom, not nature. Reason followed on freedom, a reversal of the order found in classical and medieval theory.

The individualist position holds toleration—not interfering with willed decisions or understandings of another's good—to be the newest and most necessary virtue. Indeed, it meant aiding them, fostering them. This fostering became the essential purpose of government. Freedom could bear no limit except itself, not even of truth or nature. Any criticism of this result coming from the classical understanding of nature or revelation was rejected on the grounds that it was "unscientific." Science came to mean the rational ordering of nature according to the free mind itself. It did not refer to any norms or rules found in nature, present there from a superior mind and discoverable as intelligence.

In a lecture given at Indiana University in the 1939–40 academic year, Etienne Gilson addressed the nature of science and political ideologies. He wrote in terms rather similar to those cited above from Leo Strauss:

Mankind is doomed to live more and more under the spell of a new scientific, social, and political mythology, unless we resolutely exorcise these befuddled notions whose influence on modern life is becoming appalling. Millions of men are starving and bleeding to death because two or three of these pseudo-scientific or pseudo-social deified abstractions are now at war. For when gods fight among themselves, men have to die. . . . The trouble with so many of our contemporaries is not that they are agnostics but rather that they are misguided theologians. Real agnostics are exceedingly rare, and they harm nobody but themselves. . . . Much more common, unfortunately, are those pseudo-agnostics who, because they combine scientific knowledge and social generosity with a complete lack of philosophical culture, substitute dangerous mythologies for the natural theology which they do not even understand.[9]

Gilson connected the rise of modernity, of political ideology, with the decline of metaphysics and the faith compatible with it.[10] Also, he implied the close connection between the philosophical question of the existence and nature of God with secular theologies designed to replace Him.

The essence of modernity was the imposition of humanly formed and willed abstractions on a reality that bears unacknowledged signs of intelligence. No one would want to substitute a manmade abstraction for reality unless something in reality seemed to need rejection (see below, Part II). Modernity refused to accept the fact that there were things men "ought" to do, or things they could not do if they only did what they ought. In doing these things they ought not to do, they, in the view of classical and medieval thought, violated their freedom and nature. That is, they sinned or broke the law given to them in their being. Certain norms or laws of our being oblige us by nature and God to obey, but obey after the manner of men, that is, freely. To escape from such a position, modernity held that we must first eliminate from reality any sign or standard not put there by man himself.

If reality is a chaos, a bewildering confusion, or simply unknowable because of the incapacity of the human intellect to know anything outside of itself, this same reality, this *what is*, cannot guide a rational creature. The alternative to order of reason found in nature (with a rational proof for the origin of this reason in God) is autonomous reason in man. Autonomous reason is not dependent on *what is*. Reason is independent of everything but itself. The epistemological controversies of modernity from Descartes to Hobbes, Locke, Hume, and Hegel are important for political philosophy because they leave, supposedly, the mind free of any dependence on anything but itself.

Modernity does not see itself constrained by a mind open to

9. Etienne Gilson. *God and Philosophy* (New Haven: Yale University Press, 1941), 136–37.
10. See Etienne Gilson, *The Unity of Philosophical Experience* (New York: Scribner's, 1937); *Being and Some Philosophers* (Toronto: Pontifical Institute of Mediaeval Studies, 1949).

reality for its proper workings or sources, a reality that itself reveals an order not originating in any human mind, yet intelligible to it. Modernity is left free to project onto reality, particularly human reality, whatever it can freely conjure up by its own reasonings. Indeed, this projection becomes something of a human right or even duty, because a world with no sign of any intelligence at all is barren and despairing.

Opposed to a modernity rooted in will is a metaphysics rooted in being, in *what is*. The study of this reality is the study that frees man from himself, from the belief that what is first encountered is his own self. Aristotle's theoretical sciences stand as a guarantee that *what man is* will be seen as grounded in something other than himself. In a sense, this means that the *what is* of man is better than he could make himself to be—this without denying that he can and ought to choose to be what he already is.

6. *Freedom in Modernity*

The apparently exhilarating sense of "freedom" characteristic of modernity is rooted in this phenomenon of a world that presumably reveals and can reveal no intrinsic order but that which the mind proposes to itself, even if that proposal is only one of power and self-interest. This feeling is reminiscent of, even rooted philosophically in, the Stoic notion that man made himself independent of any feeling or effect on him from the world. Different minds cannot agree on a common truth that exists independently of these same minds because there is no such independent truth, even of man. All that is possible is nonintellectual obedience, forced or voluntary, to a single will or to a compact that leaves all ideas privately in the hidden mind with agreement possible only on the material "needs" of human nature. This nature is no longer seen to have any norms or demands other than what men legislate for themselves. "Rights" are legislated by a will and defined by it. This autonomous status of rights constitutes their essential danger in modernity.

The content of modernity can be epitomized by the phrase in Genesis, now applied to man and not God, that man has claimed the power himself to formulate the difference between good and evil. If this autonomy were the only element of modernity, however, every age would be a "modern" age, since this claim lies behind every disorder in every age. Nonetheless, one explicit element in modernity is the claim that any distinction between good and evil is due, not to God or to nature, but solely to man's own autonomous freedom. He decides the moral content of his actions and puts this theory into practice. This content is expressed in "rights."

What distinguishes modernity from classical or medieval thought is not that there are necessarily more people who do evil things in the modern world, but that what is considered to be evil depends exclusively on a human decision subject to nothing other than itself. If that decision is expressed politically, it is a "law," that is, something willed to be true with no other criterion but itself (see Chapter 11). Only by virtue of norms that do not change could we be aware of moral evil in the world.

If modernity depends on autonomous will, what does that will choose? In medieval thought about the will, it was said to have two aspects: (1) the ability to act or not to act, and (2) the ability to act in this way or that. If men chose to follow in their actions the criteria described by Aristotle in the *Ethics* or in the similar Ten Commandments, that would imply that human freedom was subject to something other than itself. It is, of course, possible to "obey" the commandments on the assumption that their content is human and worthy yet unconnected with anything but the free human will. The commandments, in this latter sense, would be seen merely as products of a rational will with no other justification but that will. Kant's duty ethic is of this character.

Indeed, one might even expect that the commandments could well be the norms most attractive to man in any case. This sort of ethic, however, would still be a form of pride or autonomy, unless it is also seen to be rooted in an intelligence other than human intelligence. To the extent that even a natural law ethic is based in a refusal to acknowledge the real nature of things, it would be an act of pride. At bottom, this theoretic independence is the problem of "modern natural law," as it is called.[11]

11. See A. Passerin D'Entreves, *Natural Law: An Historical Survey* (New York: Harper Torchbooks, 1954); Henry Veatch, *Human Rights: Fact or Fancy?* (Baton Rouge: Louisiana State University Press, 1985); John Finnis, *Natural Law and Natural Right* (New York: Oxford, 1980); Russell Hittinger, *A Critique of the New Nat-*

The most obvious and most graphic claim to autonomy is to maintain that what were considered evils in the tradition of ethics and revelation are now classified as good deeds to be lived out and embodied politically as good. To establish human autonomy is to proclaim the traditional vices to be not evil but good, or at least available to man as part of his perfection and available to him as tools of action and rule. Again, this position is not entirely new. The position against which Socrates argued was that the happiest man was the one who was free to do exactly what he chose to do, including calling evil good. The worst state of the soul, according to Socrates, was to do what is evil and be praised for it as if it were good.

The content of modernity as it has worked itself out from its own premises is to be taken from traditional ethics and morality. Murder or adultery or stealing or dishonorable speech was said to be forbidden because of a law to which men ought to conform and conform according to their being. They were to observe it because they were capable of knowing and choosing it in its persuasive force. The autonomous man, however, freed from this law, would be liberated to use any action for his own purposes, to establish his freedom from any claim that natural law might have on him. If he did not use evil means, it was because he willed not to use them. There would be times and circumstances in which their use was perfectly logical and good.

Tradition held that children should be begotten and raised in a family, consisting of a husband and a wife and at times other relatives, and that this order is the natural order of things. The defiance of such a position would be anything from simple divorce to the scientific begetting of children outside of marriage, even outside of the womb, or the raising of children outside of homes in state-controlled institutions. Again, the validity of the traditional position was considered by Plato and by Aristotle. Socrates seems to have thought that this scientific dealing with human life

---

ural Law Theory (Notre Dame: University of Notre Dame Press, 1987); Heinrich Rommen, *The Natural Law* (St. Louis: Herder, 1947); Yves Simon, *The Tradition of Natural Law: A Philosopher's Reflections* (New York: Fordham, 1965); Jacques Maritain, *The Rights of Man and Natural Law* (San Francisco: Ignatius Press, 1986); Leo Strauss, *Natural Right and History* (Chicago: University of Chicago Press, 1953); Janet Smith, *Humanae Vitae: A Generation Later* (Washington, D.C.: The Catholic University of America Press, 1991); John Paul II, *Veritatis Splendor,* 1993.

and family for the good of the polity in eugenic breeding or com-
munality of wives and children was too exalted for most people.
The more sober Aristotle simply maintained that it would not
work.

In modernity, whose will was to decide what was good, what
evil? Only two answers seem available in modernity: (1) Leviathan
or the General Will of the state selects by fear or autonomous reason to decree that whatever it decides is what is right or wrong;
(2) the will of the individual selects any good for himself, limited
by the capacity of all others to do the same. The purpose of society
is to make these "selections" possible for each human being, no
matter what they are in themselves. No objective judgment can
be made about their intrinsic validity.

Modernity can take many forms. The presumed demise of the
socialist ideology of the late twentieth century, if indeed the same
state socialism is not appearing in other forms, is not the end of
ideology. It is merely the end of one form of an intellectual position that, on the failure of one of its alternatives, is free to choose
any other alternative to achieve the same end. The project of modernity is that no norm or rule or standard exists except that
which man chooses and puts into being, subject to nothing but
himself. Thus the argument of modernity in its essential forms
must not be with itself, except as a kind of ritual combat between
differing positions based on the same principle. Rather it must
be with classical and medieval thought, which proposes that human nature is unchangeable, that in nature there is a reason, not
caused by itself, operative to make each being to be what it is. The
argument is that this reason in its integrity is better than auton-
omously willed reason of modernity.

7. What Is Valuable in Modernity?

What is good about the achievements normally attributed to
modernity? What is defensively good is based on reality, on nature
in the classical sense, not on the modern mind set free. What happens in the world does not depend solely on the configurations of
the human mind projected onto reality. It depends on the discovery by the human mind of an order of reality, in the light of
which it can act and do. No one doubts that in the past four hun-

dred years, vast improvements in the situation of man in the world have been discovered. More people live at a higher level of material well-being than ever before in history. It was Aristotle who observed that most men needed a certain sufficiency of material goods to practice virtue, that nature was not niggardly.

It would be foolish, however, to maintain that this development could have happened only the way it did. The crimes and horrors of modern history need not be denied to praise certain obviously valuable improvements in the human condition. Ideological solutions proposed as cures for the problems of modernity need not be recognized as the only possible solutions or contributions that have come forth. The work of intelligence to understand what remains good and what evil remains the essential task of the intellectual life.

Is the foundation for the good in modernity autonomous will? Is theoretical modernity the best position from which to accept what is good in the modern world? The argument is not about whether men are free or whether they have wills that can have an impact on the world. It is rather about the reasons man is a certain kind of being who can and ought to be *what he is*. If man is better made from nature than the alternatives proposed in modernity, we are left with a certain curiosity about why this might be the case. It could be an accident, of course, though a highly improbable one.

Man is not safe if his being is subject to nothing but a human will that has no grounding in anything but itself. The order and intelligence found in nature and in man would hint, at least, that something deeper is at work in man's own will. A consideration of the will itself, its results and claims, leads us to wonder what is incomplete in the will itself. We now know what the human will might produce if left to itself. On examining what this will did "do," when left to itself—and this is my purpose in recounting the history of the "brilliant errors" of modernity—we can reject the claim that the best regime is what has happened in modernity.

Modernity has produced regimes that were better than others. It has also produced the worst regimes in history. It has not produced any best regime. The disorders of modernity leave us with the question of their consequences and even of their punishments. Classical and medieval intelligence is a more reasonable basis for what is right about the modern world than the autonomous will. The results of modernity leave us with this possibility. Ironically, the nature of modernity is itself one of those questions that lead to questions beyond politics. The insufficiency of autonomous will incites us to a reconsideration of limited will, will limited by law not solely rooted in human will itself.

The result of autonomous will is the "context," as it were, of the "brilliant errors" that constitute the history of political philosophy. But how do such errors arise? It is not enough to say simply that they arise from pride and disordered intelligence in the service of autonomous will. This source, no doubt, does reveal the character of modernity and indeed of all human disorder. However, certain realities exist and must be accounted for rightly. Evil, death, and punishment are the natural contexts of all political philosophy that justifies itself in dealing with the human condition.

Political philosophy, to be itself complete, must pay considerable attention to these topics if it is to understand the forces and currents that flow within its own intellectual world. These realities are the most obvious issues that confront human life and must first be considered if we are then to approach the issues that lead beyond politics. It will be noticed that these issues, in their essential formulations, are already present in classical and medieval political philosophy. To these issues I now turn because they are essential to a full comprehension of the meaning and extent of political philosophy.

PART II

The Grounds of Political Realism

FOUR

Evil and Political Realism

> *"I [Boswell] talked to him [Samuel Johnson] of original sin, in conse-*
> *quence of the fall of man, and of the atonement made by our* SAVIOUR.
> *After some conversation, which he desired me to remember, he, at my*
> *request, dictated to me as follows: 'With respect to original sin, the in-*
> *quiry is not necessary; for whatever is the cause of human corruption,*
> *men are evidently and confessedly so corrupt, that all the laws of heaven*
> *and earth are insufficient to restrain them from crimes.'"*
> —*Boswell's Life of Johnson,* 1781[1]

1. *The Relation of Evil and Rule*

These blunt observations of Samuel Johnson about original sin
or the Fall, as it is sometimes known, are directed to the religious
doctrine that addresses the enigmatic nature and unsettling constancy of human evils in history.[2] Johnson did not begin with a
theological theory to conclude from it the fact that corruption
existed among men. Rather, he began from "evident" and "con-
fessed" facts about which everyone knew. G. K. Chesterton had
said something similar, namely, that original sin was the one
dogma the truth of which we did not need to "prove." All anyone
needed to do was to go out into the streets and open his eyes to
see what went on there. Aristotle himself, perplexed by the same
experience, wrote about those who thought they could deal with
disorders of property by a simple act of legislation:

1. *Boswell's Life of Johnson* (London: Oxford, 1931), II, pp. 423–24.
2. See Robert Sacks, "The Lion and the Ass: A Commentary on Books 1–10
of *Genesis* (Strauss)," *Interpretation* 8 (May 1980): 29–101.

Such legislation may have a specious appearance of benevolence; men readily listen to it and are easily induced to believe that in some wonderful manner everybody will become everybody's friend, especially when someone is heard denouncing the evils now existing in states, suits about contracts, convictions for perjury, the flatteries of rich men and the like, which are said to arise out of the possession of private property. These evils, however, are due to a very different cause—the wickedness of human nature. (1273b15–23)

Original sin as a doctrine may or may not explain the incidence of human evil. But this incidence, along with the related topics of death and hell, must be intellectually confronted. More than anything they explain the seriousness with which we must seek to understand human realities.

Whatever we may think of its cause, some fundamental disorder exists in human nature for which an account needs to be made both in theory and in practice. It is not only evil that causes disorder in human life and society; the search for an explanation of evil that does not make the evil worse can cause great discord. The effort to contain and understand the very reality of evil brings political philosophy beyond itself. We cannot maintain that absolutely *everything* human beings do is "good." So to affirm is either to equivocate about the meaning of what we understand by good and evil or to contradict or lie to ourselves.

The lack of order among men and within ourselves, which we call evil, then, provokes us, challenges us to limit it as best we can. It demands that we attempt to understand what it means. At no point do political philosophy, theology, and philosophy meet in more perplexing and tormented circumstances than in this question of the roots and causes of those disorders of action and heart whose existence we cannot (without embracing some philosophy or theology of illusion) deny. Such disorders are found in the most dire of circumstances but, perhaps even more frequently and more inexplicably, in the best of conditions. We deny the dignity of the poor, their claim to free will, if we maintain that they cannot and do not commit evil; and we withdraw from reality if we think that the rich and well off, simply by that fact alone, are good and happy or evil and rejected.

Government, whose most visible signs are often police, army, or tax collectors, does not, to be sure, arise exclusively from a need

to attend to the evils men commit against each other. Even supposing human beings never committed any evils, or to put it in
religious terms, even supposing there were no "Fall," an argument can be made, it was indeed made by Aristotle and refined
by St. Thomas, for the necessity of government from human nature itself. This is what Aristotle meant by calling man by nature
a political animal (1253a1).

This argument about the natural necessity of government
arose from the very freedom and intelligence of men, who can
discover a multiplicity of reasonable alternatives open to them on
almost any issue, alternatives that can be maintained without fault
or disorder. Among these alternatives, someone, designated as
"government"—whatever particular form that might take—must
choose to follow one course of common action rather than another.[3] Agreement to live together, and the need to spend time on
diverse things if they are to be well done, are natural and would
arise even if no disorder existed in the human soul.

Nonetheless, much of actual government, particularly its most
obviously coercive aspects, is occupied with counteracting the evils
men commit against each other—including, if possible, the evils
that come from the personal disorders of those individuals who
make up the governments themselves. C. S. Lewis put it this way:

> There are two opposite reasons for being a democrat. You may think
> all men so good that they deserve a share in the government of the
> commonwealth, and so wise that the commonwealth needs their ad-
> vice. That is, in my opinion, the false, romantic doctrine of democ-
> racy. On the other hand, you may believe fallen men to be so wicked
> that not one of them may be trusted with any irresponsible power
> over his fellows. That I believe to be the true ground of democracy.[4]

The doctrine of the Fall or original sin would insist that no body
of rulers can exempt themselves in principle from the dangers of
self-love and temptations to evil.[5] "Who will protect us from our

3. See Yves Simon, *A General Theory of Authority* (Notre Dame: University of
Notre Dame Press, 1980).
4. C. S. Lewis, "Membership," in *The Weight of Glory* (New York: Macmillan,
1965), 112–13. See also, on Lewis's political thought, Joseph Sobran, "Happy at
Home," in *Single Issues: Essays on the Crucial Social Questions* (New York: Human
Life Press, 1983), 156–89.
5. See Glenn Tinder, *Political Thinking: The Perennial Questions* (Boston: Little,

protectors?" has been a major concern of all practical political institutions.

Many instruments of government, from separation of powers to frequency of elections and even payment of legislators and bureaucrats out of government funds, were designed to counteract the dangers that arose from the possible corruption of government officials. It is one of the tenets of political realism that even these reforms are themselves subject to abuse and diversion from their intended purpose by perverse human will. Yet, without some government, conditions among men could be even worse: Plato understood that the very worst human condition would be a government itself totally corrupt. Constitution and law are, from this point of view, instruments designed to reduce the dangers to the governed that might arise from themselves, from foreign sources, and from the crimes of the governors, even those governors freely chosen by the people.

All theories of "political realism" seek to account for the propensity among men and rulers themselves to commit crimes and irregularities. Political realism does not deny the necessity of rule; it may indeed enhance it. Political realism posits at least these positions:

a. Serious political disorders regularly occur in all historical human societies of whatever criterion of race, nationality, gender, class, intelligence, or experience.

b. Government at its minimum—"that government governs best which governs least"—is established to lessen evils. Even when a government seeks to do good, there is still the threat of force and the prohibition of doing either good or evil, the danger of the government's adding to the very disorders it seeks to meet. Good will and good laws are by no means identical.

c. The anarchist thesis—that government itself is the main cause of evil, and evil would disappear if government disappeared altogether—would be, if put into practice, merely another way of quickly multiplying evil. The fact of evil that anarchist

Brown, 1974); Hadley Arkes, *First Things: An Inquiry into the First Principles of Morals and Justice* (Princeton: Princeton University Press, 1986); Herbert Deane, *The Political and Social Ideas of St. Augustine* (New York: Columbia University Press, 1966).

thought attributes to government lies in causes deeper than government can directly deal with. St. Thomas understood this clearly when he noted that civil law did not reach to those inner causes and choices from which all evil arose (I-II, 91, 4).

d. Government has the character of both a good institution required by men for their own completion and a necessary "evil" capable of confronting the extremes of crime and disorder that do occur in any polity. Force in all cases must be reasonable, designed to prevent greater evils.

2. *Crimes and Intelligence*

Samuel Johnson was an orthodox Christian. On the topic of why human beings do evil things, this orthodoxy meant that Johnson did not believe that man was by nature evil or corrupt, even though he was capable of doing many evil deeds. All being, including human being in all its given powers, as it exists, as it is, is good. This position did not mean that there was no evil proceeding from human beings. The evidence demonstrated that from human action there followed much evil, often evil of vast proportions. The teaching about original sin meant rather that the cause or source of this evil was not in the existence or nature of man, nor was it in any of man's given faculties or powers. Rather it was to be found in the perverse exercise of human freedom. This freedom, without which man would not have been the kind of being he was, was what made evil possible.[6]

For human beings to do evil, it paradoxically had to be possible for them not to do evil. Without this premise of the possibility of doing either good or evil, no such thing as responsible freedom (or, consequently, of real moral evil) was possible. Human beings were "rational" beings, even when they did evil. A connection thus existed between choice, reason, and evil. They did the evil they did for purposes that could be, at least to themselves, explained and justified in apparently reasonable terms (human beings always give reasons for the evil they do). Such rational explanation did not lessen the fact that what they did was both freely done and wrong.

6. For a basic account of the classic position on original sin, see *Catechism of the Catholic Church* (Vatican City: Libreria Editrice Vaticana, 1994), nos. 385–421.

Johnson stated an obvious if unsettling fact when he remarked that the "laws of heaven and earth were not sufficient to restrain men from their crimes." Arguing backwards from a survey of any historical political order, or of any human life, for that matter, Johnson was forced to conclude that crimes were not prevented by human or divine laws. This result did not mean that such human and divine laws were either useless or unnecessary; human and divine laws did prevent many crimes and disorders that might otherwise have occurred. Rather the fact of human disorders meant that human beings, in their freedom, could and did act against both human and divine laws.

Crimes and evils happened. No amount of rhetoric could obscure that fact. Some people in any era or polity were relatively good and honorable, saints even. Most people, who were a mixture of good and bad characteristics, as Aristotle observed, could recognize and do good things some of the time. But for the most part, crimes and disorders existed on a wide basis and had to be accounted for both intellectually—Why did they exist?—and politically—How to control or limit them? Not to address each of these questions, both the why and the how, indicated a failure to appreciate the seriousness and complexity of human life.

Johnson's words bring to our attention another permanent question arising in personal and political life, but one that in its overall meaning and implications seems to transcend politics. Johnson held that a Fall, or the effects of original sin, operated in the human condition and affected every human being. He also held that an atonement for such evil had to come from outside of purely human power. Yet this atonement manifested its effects within human life. Ultimately, the "reason" given for the death of Christ was specifically human "sins," as if to argue that even the Godhead recognized the need to account for human disorders.

Functioning within human nature or directed to it were spiritual or religious resources. These were real in themselves but invisible to, or beyond the reach of, politics. These resources, insofar as they too incited man to a right ordering of his soul, were the most important elements in the well-being of any political society. They explained why no human situation is, strictly speaking, irremediable. Invisible in themselves, they become visible and external in the deeds of men, though they can always be misunderstood or seen to be something other than what they were.

The truth of the doctrine of original sin and its visible results did not mean that human crimes made it impossible for human beings to hope, or to look beyond the reality of the crimes themselves, or even beyond the normal expectations of human nature. Johnson held that these evident crimes, which neither human nor divine laws were sufficient to prevent were committed by actual human beings who were not powerful enough by themselves to repair their own damage. They needed a "savior" to do what they could not do by themselves, because their crimes, bad enough in themselves, reached the divinity through the origin and dignity of human life itself.

Crimes and sins involved interaction not merely with those affected by them, and with the polity responsible to control them, but with the divinity who stood at the origin and end of each human being. Human crimes not forgiven or atoned for remained to cause resentment or vengeance that ended by corrupting both souls and civil order. Only forgiveness could stop the vengeance associated with crime.

3. Evil and Good Existence

In preparation for his famous proofs for the existence of God, St. Thomas Aquinas first listed the major objections that men have formulated against the possibility of God's existence. The first and probably most cogent of these objections is the "existence" of evil. Aquinas did not handle this objection to God's existence by denying that evil existed, as certain philosophies and religions have tried to maintain. Rather, he elaborated an ordered argument as to how both might exist.

But Aquinas did think that we must, if we be human, understand the implications of this problem of evil and its reality among men. The political awareness of evil and the capacity to counteract it depended upon a philosophic consideration that secured the topic from manipulation by a politics that itself claimed to be the sole source of the distinction between good and evil.

Aquinas recognized that, unless men are erroneously persuaded by a particular philosophic or religious argument to deny their experience, they will immediately acknowledge that some sort of evil exists in the world. If they are even more honest, they will recognize that it exists in themselves, as a product of their own agency.

Much may be said about the theoretical understanding of what evil might be. The intellectual consideration of this question is a necessary part of any examined life. It is clear, however, that the whole of the political world at one level is filled with a web of blame and anger that justifies itself by its opposition to the evil that occurs in any political order or in any individual life. That praise and blame exist, as Aristotle said, indicates that we recognize good and evil in our own and others' actions (1106a1).

We will consider (chapter 9) Aristotle's view of how evil was possible in our lives, how it arose in a rational being that sought happiness in his every act, even in his disordered ones. Likewise, in the discussion on hell (chapter 5) regarding the meaning of unpunished violations, the question will be asked whether violations of justice can be resolved finally so that the world can be considered morally and intellectually complete. The question of evil and its resolution arose in the contexts of justice and order. Some of the greatest of crimes known in human history and experience, moreover, have been perpetrated within and magnified by the political order, often by intelligent men, philosophers even, who claim to be seeking mankind's well-being. The scale of evil in the political order makes evil most obvious to us there. This is one of the reasons Plato called the civil society, in both its good and its evil, the individual writ large.

Political philosophy and political experience are assaulted on every side by questions involving evil. Evil again is one of those questions that arise initially in personal and civil life. But, in the pursuit of its intelligibility and restriction, it leads to deeper questions of philosophy and revelation.

No one can avoid the perplexity caused by evil. No one can fail to seek some accounting for it. No education is complete that does not at some point seriously confront the reality of evil among human beings. We should seek to understand evil, in its reality and varieties, lest we consent to do it. Preferably, our understanding would hinder us from doing evil, but as Aristotle has shown, virtue is more than knowledge: virtue includes knowing and doing (see chapter 9).

4. *"The Sword Not in Vain"*

The term "political realism" can be associated in differing ways with Thucydides, Augustine, and Machiavelli. Political realism was designed to account for what human beings did "do" in their lives and deeds. It also asked: who was responsible for counteracting or punishing deeds that were judged to be evil? Everyone was responsible, even in the worst society, not to do evil. This responsibility was the lesson that Socrates taught in *The Apology*, in the famous case of Leon of Salamis, when Socrates was required to cooperate in a deed he knew to be contrary to the laws. Instead of going forth to the illegal capture and execution of Leon of Salamis, Socrates went home. He did not cooperate. This refusal would have been sufficient to have had Socrates executed, he thought, except that the government fell before it could get around to his case (32B-D). The abiding teaching of Socrates was that it was better to suffer death than to do any evil.

The Gospel of Luke makes the same point in the following way. To a crowd of many thousands, Christ taught: "I tell you, my friends, do not fear those who kill the body, and after that have no more that they can do. But I will warn you whom to fear: fear him who, after he has killed, has power to cast into hell; yes, I tell you, fear him" (12:4–5). Both Socrates and Christ recognized that the death of the body is not the worst evil. The worst evil is spiritual. It is, either by word or in deed, to define what is evil to be good. The power to "cast into hell" is a power of persuasion that would justify as good what is in truth evil. That human beings have the capacity to choose evil grounds the seriousness of each human life. Human beings have the capacity to reject what is good, to reject a world fashioned in the light of this good, in order to place there instead one's own good at the heart of his actions and thoughts.

In the Epistle to the Romans (13:4), Paul said that the ruler "does not bear the sword in vain." That is, one of the duties of rulers was to prevent wrongdoing and even to punish wrongdoers. Evidently, some crimes (though not all) could be prevented by threat of punishment. The need for coercive government arose not from the nature of government but as a consequence of the Fall, as a result of human choice. It was possible to speak of the coercive side of government as necessary and even good without denying that evil ought not to be. That is, men ought not to choose the evil that necessitates coercive government. But once they do choose evil, coercive government, though even its officials can themselves do evil, becomes necessary and a potential servant of good actions.

Political realism points out the dangers of the utopianism that claims to know the sources of human evils and how to eliminate them by political or economic means. The modern intellectual, who claims to be able and obliged to refashion the world by his own thought rather than by discipline, grace, or metaphysics, has been the particular concern of political realism. Political realism maintains that evils can not altogether be removed from mankind, certainly not by purely human efforts. A certain living with at least certain types of evil might be required lest something greater be destroyed. Whereas on the one hand evil is evil and not to be done, nevertheless, not all ways of dealing with it are wise or permissible. It is quite possible to become evil in preventing evil. This ominous alternative forced political philosophy to confront the question of lesser evils and absolute standards.

5. The "Existence" of Evil

To return to our earlier question, does the fact of evil's existence make it logically impossible for God to exist? Aquinas answered his own question by citing Augustine: "God, since He is the highest good, in no way would permit anything of evil to exist in His works, unless God would be so good and omnipotent, that He might also bring good out of evil." Aquinas went on, in his own words, "It pertains to the infinite goodness of God, that evils be permitted to exist and from them good be brought forth" (I, 2, 3, ad 1). The word "permit" implies that certain possibilities cannot be avoided if other goods are to exist. The alternative is not between good and evil, but between good and nothing. The alternative to nothingness is fallible, finite being, being that can and often does err.

If a human being is to exist, he must be exactly and fully a human being, that is, a being with reason and a free will. Beings without free will exist, but they are not human beings. If a being has a free will, it must be permitted to be what it is, that is, free. Not even God can have it both ways. The omnipotence of God does not prevent this liberty when a naturally free being chooses evil. God rather brings good out of the good in which any evil must first exist in human choices and deeds. To be noticed in these responses of Augustine and Aquinas is, first of all, that evil is to be called nothing other than evil. The naming of evil—that is, its intelligibility—is what the human mind must strive accurately to accomplish. This naming is what mind is for. Accurate naming allows man the possibility of acting according to *what is,* of standing rightly with the given reality before him.

Next, what do we really mean when we designate evil as something that "exists" and must be accounted for? Evil is not an illusion or a figment of human imagination, as some philosophers have maintained. Yet Plato and Augustine (among others) held that, strictly speaking, evil is a "nothing." Evil does not "exist," as does a tree or a boat, but its reality implies something that fails to exist. If evil is merely a "lack" of what ought to be, what gives it its force or attraction, since we cannot be attracted by nothingness? Clearly it is not evil as such that is attractive; rather, what attracts us is our own power of choice to create a world in which only our will exists. That evil occurs requires that good things themselves exist previous to our will's own existence, good things that we can deliberately redirect to our own purposes.

When Aquinas observed that every act of sin or disorder or crime is rooted in pride, this is what he meant: all evil in human acts consists in the choice of the self against some higher purpose existing in things man did not make. Such an act includes the will to put into the world something exclusively of our own making with no dependence on nature or revelation. To be sure, we choose something good in every evil choice. But in the case of evil, our choice seeks to replace *what is,* what should be, with our own will. This choice is what God "permits" when He allows us to exist as free beings in the first place. His only other possible choice would have been not to create human beings at all.

This alternative is why Aquinas maintained that God will be

able to "permit" evil only if He can bring forth to its own fruition the good that is implicit in every choice of evil. Good can result from our evil actions because the good does not reside in our wills but in the reality found in the actions. We do not "create" from nothing in our actions. We act on what already exists, which is in itself good. Things, as such, are never evil. This fact is why the drama of reality depends on the relation of our wills to what ought to be, to what we ought to choose on the basis of *what is.*

The most dangerous way to "save" God from the charge of not being "omnipotent" (that is, since evil happens, God is not God) is to call what is evil precisely "good." The power to declare (but not make) "evil" to be "good" is at the very root of the political power and no doubt one of its principal dangers. This power was the essence of the account of the Fall in Genesis. This power was the central issue behind the trial of Socrates. Likewise, the Aristotelian notion that the theoretic order was superior to the practical order, of which latter order politics was the highest expression, was meant to limit or moderate the claims of politics to be absolutely sovereign over the distinction of good and evil.

6. *The Genesis Account*

In the book of Genesis, the question about why God permits the existence of evil arose in a somewhat different manner. The Fall of man occurred when, in picturesque language, Adam ate of the "tree of the knowledge of good and evil." This story expresses symbolically the phenomenon of human behavior wherein we claim the power to declare what is good and what is evil. That is, the classic prerogative of the divine power can also be claimed by men as their own right.

The subtlety of the Genesis account should not be overlooked. It recognized the root temptation to which every man in every one of his actions is potentially open. This temptation is for man, independent of anything but himself, to define the distinction between good and evil. In not accepting the divisions of good and evil as found in nature or revelation, men can propose their own alternate definitions of good and evil to suit their own purposes. They can attempt to carry them out in their lives and cities. History is the account of how they carry out their choices.

It is not enough to maintain that something disordered exists in human nature as a matter of fact. To this, we must add that this disorder has a certain striking intelligibility to it. This intelligibility identifies the nature and power of the human will to choose its own good, or at least what appears to be its own good, for it must live with the results of its own choices. The consequences of these choices, however, can and must be critically evaluated. Nowhere in either reason or revelation is it argued that men do not have to live with their choices, whatever they are. Even the final definition of hell is nothing other than living with our final choice of ourselves in the light of our own definition of good and evil. The consequences of human choices for good or evil, then, become themselves elements in our capacity to understand good and evil. To choose to see any evil consequence as something other than what it is, is always possible. Man's will is not determined even by facts.

If there were no nature and no God, human beings would evidently be free to accomplish this goal of following their own wills unhindered. The root of a theory of absolute human autonomy that leads to man's subordination of the distinction of good and evil solely to his own will is the prior intellectual elimination of God and an order in nature dependent on God. Human action is never wholly independent of human speculative thought about the ultimate order of things. At this theoretic level, atheism and tyranny are connected. If one grants the atheist thesis, nothing intrinsic can prevent the tyrant, of whatever form, even a democratic one, to seek to do as he wills.

The point is not, however, that all "atheists" are tyrants, but that nothing in principle prevents them from being so. Those who hold for God's existence obviously can also be tyrants. There are abundant instances of believers who have been tyrants. But this possibility—of a believing tyrant—in context at least requires the practical rejection of the theoretic limit that a definite understanding of evil places on the tyrant's activities. The religious tyrants of history generally do not seek to change the theoretic definition of good and evil, whereas the philosophic tyrant does attempt this very change.

The account in Genesis of the Fall is pertinent to the problem of evil in yet another way. The essence of the disorder in man attributable to the Fall is the claim on the part of man that he himself is the source of any distinction of good and evil. How can this power be reconciled with the notion that man cannot do any evil unless he pursues some good? The classical notion of "evil" was that evil was not a "being," was not a "thing" of some sort. Genesis had, in its own imaginative way, established this position when, in the account of creation, God looked on everything that He created and declared it good.

This position meant, contrary to dualist theories prevalent at the time Genesis was composed, that there were not two "gods," one the cause of good and the other the cause of "evil." Usually, in these theories, good was identified with spirit and evil with matter. The "better" we were, the less we would have to do with matter. In Genesis, however, the greatest danger to man's spiritual life came from the spirit, from denigrating matter to exalt spirit.[7] Spirit and matter were opposed only if man chose to place them in opposition to each other. In themselves, both were good and they belonged together.

The account in Genesis denied the position that pure spirit was, without qualification, nearer to God. The devil was pure spirit and was by far the more dangerous being. The highest forms of disorder were those that arose in the spirit. This position paralleled Aristotle's remark that the greatest disorders arise from philosophy (1267a8–18). Matter itself was declared in Genesis to be good. The distinction between good and evil did not arise essentially from the distinction of matter and spirit. If matter were evil, obviously God could not have become man, as Christian revelation later claimed. Neither could man, body and soul in one being, be as such good, which was the claim of Aristotle as well as of Genesis.

Evil was not a "thing," but nevertheless it seemed to have something directly to do with being, with real beings. Evil was the lack of something that ought to be in existence, that ought to be there, but was not. It was not "evil" for a dog not to have five legs, but it was an "evil" for it not to have at least four. Something that ought to be there was not there when it had only three legs. It was

---

7. See Denis de Rougemont, *Love in the Western World*, trans. Montgomery Belgion (New York: Schocken, 1983).

not an evil for men not to be "gods," but it was an evil for them to claim divine powers which they did not possess.

The right order of human action depended upon man's ordering himself according to what he was, something he did not make by himself. Again, man was the only being commanded to "be himself." He could choose to be not himself, that is, could choose not to be conformed to what man ought to be. He could choose against himself in both his thoughts and his actions, particularly in his decisions about what was good and what evil. The project of Socrates to "know thyself" had profound implications.

The location of evil had to be in something already good but which could act in such a way as not to recognize good as already in existence. The implication of the treatment of the Fall in Genesis is that evil arises in a good being who has a power to choose what it will do. Evil resides in the will, but only if man by his will chooses to erect a world contrary to the given world and its purposes that are ordered to man's end. The fact that man has a "will" always will be good even when a man uses his will for some evil end. The choice of "evil," the choice to put something into existence that ought not to be there, is not a choice independent of all other choices, but a choice implicit in them. Every action or choice has the deepest of overtones about our relation to ourselves, to the world, and to God.

7. *No Safe Social Order*

The intimate relationship between man's understanding of what his end or happiness is and his politics needs to be articulated. Man can reject any transcendent end proposed to him if he so chooses. He can logically conclude that his true grandeur is for him to enact in the world only that which he chooses on the basis of nothing but himself. The philosopher or believer who holds the existence of God with His order and the claimant who follows only his own will agree that some order in the world is to be established by man. What is different is the content of this order and its origin; that is, whether this order derives from the being and destiny that is given to man or from man's will alone.

From the tradition of political philosophy, the account in Genesis is particularly interesting, since subsequent theories that propose to eliminate evil by attributing it, not to will, but to the structure of property, family, or polity, are already foreshadowed in it. In Genesis, man's toilsome labor, woman's birth in pain, and the being cast out of the Garden wherein there was a harmonious relation between nature and man, were results—not causes—of evil. Evil originated in man's will and in his claim to establish the distinction of good and evil by himself. All theories of a this-worldly perfect society established by a reformation of property, family, or state (which positions have formed most of modern political philosophy) have here the reason for their actual and often tragic, bloody failures.

The ultimate cause of civil disorders does not lie in the structure of property (common or private), or in the structure of the family (wives and children in common), or in the state (its withering away or its complete control). No civil order will be content or ordered until its philosophers and politicians address the spiritual causes of why men choose, no matter what the civil order may be, to embody in their own political societies or in their own individual lives that which they formulate as their own good subject to nothing else but their own wills. This position does not deny that some regimes are better ordered than others, nor that some men are better than others in their deeds and proven character. It does assert that even the best order possible must still be willed into being.

The implication of this discussion of evil is that no political or social order is ever free from the possibility of human spiritual influence. This influence does not arise initially from the social order itself but from man's relation to *what is*. It arises from how man conceives himself to stand before God and the world. Men are not determined by their circumstances, nor is God absolutely limited by them. The suffering of the good man in any actual state means that the possibility of right order can appear in any state, no matter what its own disorders might be. Likewise, into the best of civil societies or families can come the worst men, because the distinction of good and evil runs through each human will.

8. *Evil Overcome by Good*

Yet to describe evil as merely a "lack" seems to lessen its force in human life. Evil seems almost personal. Indeed, it bears the character of an argument even when it is accurately described as a lack of a good that ought to be there. The "nothingness" of evil is why God is not responsible for it. God is responsible for the good and finite beings in which all evil must exist. God is responsible that something good besides Himself exists. This responsibility is the reason that God can permit evil and bring good out of the results of its disorder. It is to this realization, or at least its possibility, that political philosophy can lead the attentive thinker.

Evil is overcome not by evil, but by good. Evil thus is not an instrument of the good. Yet, if we speak of evil as such, that is, as the choice of a will, and not the effects of an action in the world caused by that will, we must say that the only way that evil can be overcome is for that same will to recognize that its effort to put its own order into the world is a failure. Evil always presents itself as a challenge, something to be debated. Its "personal" character arises from this constant "debate" that must go on between the claim that our autonomous view of the world is correct and the reality of a world given and created in a manner not under our control but addressed to us. Evil must be "justified," and in that sense it can be reasoned with.

No perfect state exists in this world, in part because of the abiding results of human evil. We must not expect perfection where it cannot be had. Recognizing this, we can avoid the dangers of a utopian theory. Utopian theory in its modern form depends only on itself for any understanding of what man and the world are like. It rejects any world dependent on God or nature. It would place into being only a world created by the human will. Political realism is based on the inability or unwillingness of men in practice to be good, on the fact that, in many respects, most men are not good. But political realism does not mean an undermining of intellectual standards so that we no longer recognize the distinction between good and evil.

Men are attracted to the good and ought to seek to know it and to put it into effect. Even if they choose not to do the good, they can do so only by choosing some other good outside of its proper order. The world can be fashioned to man's ends or purposes without at the same time identifying this legitimate endeavor to be man's final end. Political philosophy, for its own integrity, has to keep thinking about the question of evil. Evil is another of the experiences that, for its full intelligibility, requires serious thought and reflection but which, in the end, leads beyond itself, beyond the politics that often must deal with it.

If one of the natural origins of the "brilliant errors" of political philosophy arises from not dealing, or dealing inadequately, with evil, a second arises from the endeavor to think about the consequences, even ultimate consequences, of evil as an abiding reality. Classical political philosophers understood that consideration of the punishment of evil and the reward of the good did arise in political experience. The consideration of evil and the inadequate attempts to deal with it seemed especially fertile grounds of theoretical analysis. Plato knew the topic was so delicate that he spoke of it only in the context of myth, in the context of what we were likely prepared to hear.

The most intriguing and most unlikely subject of reflection in political philosophy might, at first or even second sight, seem to be hell. However, this topic provides grounds for a marvelously fertile consideration that ought not to be neglected merely because of its somewhat odd, anti-modern sound. If political regimes cannot punish all the crimes that arise in their confines, does this not imply that justice is necessarily imperfect? And what are we to do with the imperfections of justice? This consideration constitutes the next reflection about the brilliant errors that give rise to deeper considerations in political philosophy.

FIVE

Regarding the Inattentiveness to Hell
in Political Philosophy

> "Dr. Johnson surprised him [Mr. John Henderson] not a little, by ac-
> knowledging with a look of horrour, that he was much oppressed by the
> fear of death. The amiable Dr. Adams suggested that God was infinitely
> good. Johnson. 'That he is infinitely good, as far as the perfection of
> his nature will allow, I certainly believe; but it is necessary for good upon
> the whole, that individuals should be punished. As to an individual,
> therefore, he is not infinitely good; and as I cannot be sure that I have
> fulfilled the conditions on which salvation is granted, I am afraid I may
> be one of those who shall be damned.' (looking dismally). Dr. Adams.
> 'What do you mean by damned?' Johnson. (passionately and loudly,)
> 'Sent to Hell, Sir, and punished everlastingly!' Dr. Adams. 'I don't
> believe in that doctrine.' Johnson. 'Hold, Sir, do you believe that some
> will be punished at all?' Dr. Adams. 'Being excluded from Heaven will
> be a punishment; yet there may be no great positive suffering.' Johnson.
> 'Well, Sir; but, if you admit any degree of punishment, there is an end
> of your argument . . . for, infinite goodness would inflict no punishment
> whatever. There is not infinite goodness physically considered; morally
> there is.'"
> —Boswell's Life of Johnson, 1784[1]

The preceding chapter on evil, the following chapter on death,
and the present chapter on hell seem, at first sight, peculiarly odd
in a reflection on political philosophy. Yet, as I have suggested,
they lie at the natural origins of the "brilliant errors" that have so

1. *Boswell's Life of Johnson* (London: Oxford, 1931), II, pp. 554–55.

89

agitated the history of political philosophy. None of these topics is normally treated in any significant manner in political philosophy. Each looks to a different side of the unpleasant aspects of the human condition, however much each is related to man's being in the world. In revelation, hell and death are seen to be results of evil, even though they were not intended to exist from the beginning. But can a consideration of evil, hell, and death in political philosophy yield fertile results?

1. *The Political Element in Traditional Religion*

Patient reflection on this trio will, I think, bring much insight. Considered carefully, each of these subjects brings us a more profound reflection on the whole of reality, which, as I have indicated, it is the purpose of this book to present and clarify. The need to reflect on and confront evil is an obviously crucial aspect of political philosophy, as I have indicated in the previous chapter. The very power to choose evil makes each human life and choice potentially dramatic and full of ultimate risk. This power lies at the foundation of human worth.

The present discussion on hell appears in political philosophy not from religion, though it has its place there, but from the Tenth Book of Plato's *Republic*, where the rewards and punishments in actual political life are considered. Let me frankly admit that the title of this present chapter on the neglect of hell (as well as Johnson's response to Dr. Adams cited above) is deliberately provocative to the modern mind—to any mind, in fact. But nobody likes to speak of this controverted topic of hell unless enticed to do so by the suspicion that to neglect it will leave something basic out of consideration. Not to reflect on the topic seems like a voluntary closing off of something that ought to be wondered about, whatever we think of it in the beginning. I submit here that political philosophy itself forces us to treat this topic if we wish to reach a complete understanding of this discipline.

Leo Strauss cautiously touched on the importance of this topic in his *Thoughts on Machiavelli*:

The beginnings of men (in Machiavelli's view) were imperfect and low. Man is exposed, and not protected, essentially and from the beginning. Therefore the perfection envisaged by both the Bible and classical philosophy is impossible. But for the same reason for which perfection, and in particular the initial as well as the ultimate Paradise is impossible, there cannot be a Hell. Man cannot rise above earthly [*sic*] and earthly humanity and therefore he ought not even to aspire beyond humanity. Such aspiration merely leads to the most terrible and wholly unnecessary inhumanity of man to man.[2]

In Machiavelli's reasoning, ridding ourselves of hell was the way to prevent fanaticism in politics. It is the irony of this thesis, as Strauss hinted, that what was once thought to be beyond politics— the ultimate punishment for violation of right—returns to the political order with the denial of this punishment, but now deprived of any transcendent check on the tyrant, who is freed to create a hell on earth because he is not limited by any principle of right and wrong except his own success.

In this light, hell is a topic that advances the discussion of the relation between politics and the transcendent order of things. Here again a question begins in politics—Why are not all unjust deeds punished?—but cannot find its ultimate resolution there. Political philosophers have been accused of having overlooked everything from Plato to Nietzsche, from the decline of socialism to the rise of ecology, from the neighborhood to the reconstruction of the whole world. But few, I suppose, are conscious of having neglected anything so esoteric as hell. Yet it is a neglect and one worth some considerable reflection. This reflection is as much political as theological, if only because some of the most absolute passions that occur in the political order are those that are incited in us when we witness the heinousness of extreme violations of human dignity—the gulags, the mass executions, the various genocides, not to forget the pre-born who are also of our kind.

Hell, besides being a mild cuss-word, is a concept so versatile that it can be taken to mean its very opposite. In the *New Yorker* (March 2, 1987), for instance, a delightful cartoon by Stevenson placed us in the midst of a wild Roman orgy, with everyone in toga sitting around and splashing in pools, wine-ing, yelling, leering. Sitting somewhat confused, but happy, with a lovely lady, toasting the crowd over his head, one toga-clad, slightly befuddled

2. Leo Strauss, *Thoughts on Machiavelli* (Glencoe, Ill.: The Free Press, 1958), 167. See Sebastian de Grazia, *Machiavelli in Hell* (Princeton: Princeton University Press, 1989.

gentleman turned to another reveller to remark, "I forget who our cult actually worships, but we have a hell of a good time." This idea of hell has incorporated into it all the things ever forbidden to us, as if "hell" were that in which a good bash, not to say a good life, consisted.

The incentive behind these remarks on hell was not supplied so much by this wonderful cartoon in the *New Yorker* identifying, for our amusement, hell with orgies and a Nietzschean-like forgetfulness of the gods. Rather it came from Hannah Arendt's perceptive remark in her *Between Past and Future*, that "the most significant consequence of the secularization of the modern age may well be the elimination from public life, along with religion, of the only political element in traditional religion, the fear of hell."[3]

Several things are to be noticed in Hannah Arendt's observation. She identified the modern age, or modernity, with secularization, that is, with the idea that this world is all there is. Since there was no other source, man could only act on the basis of his own autonomy or norms. This was likewise the implication of Strauss' remark about hell in Machiavelli.

This identification of modernity with secularization involves, furthermore, the elimination of any religion that still holds—not all, unfortunately, not even all versions of Christianity, do—that there is a transcendent relation to God through or apart from the world. Finally, Arendt remarked that the fear of hell had a political purpose. Without this fear, we might expect some radical disorder in a polity because nothing could control man's evil propensities. In this sense, the elimination had unintended and dire consequences in politics itself. The theoretical understanding of this connection cannot but be of great concern to political philosophy seeking to understand its own scope.

Recall that an apparent difference exists within Christianity between Augustine and Aquinas on the question of whether government among men has its origin in evil (the Fall) rather than in a good human nature fulfilling its own purposes. For Aquinas, the ultimate origin of government was in nature, but coercive government was due to the Fall. In the view of St. Augustine, follow-

3. Hannah Arendt, *Between Past and Future: Six Exercises in Political Thought* (New York: Viking, 1961), 113.

ing the Stoics and St. Paul, the sword was given to civil rulers for our punishment. The fear of eternal punishment is parallel to the fear of the justice of the king or emperor. Human beings are prone to commit evil deeds. The sword is given as a kind of remedial good lest evil things happen. Hangmen, soldiers, jailers, and police are "necessary evils." They ought not to exist in a perfect order, but, in religious thought about politics, they are found necessary. Given the fact of ill deeds and actions among men, coercive governmental institutions are good insofar as they control or lessen the disorders caused by human choices of evil. (The extent to which such fear of punishment lessens disorder is a matter of experience.) A wide variety of coercive measures designed to establish a more peaceful society can be found. Punishment, temporal or eternal, and government, from this point of view, find their origins in human disorder or evil.

2. *The Case for Coercion*

Aquinas did not disagree with this analysis by St. Augustine, that governments needed to exercise coercion because of evils that needed to be confronted. Neither Aquinas nor Augustine thought that human nature was inherently corrupt. This latter was the position of a Machiavelli or a Hobbes, but would have been contrary to basic Christian doctrine. Some writers find a connection between Augustine's pessimistic conception of what men do and Hobbes' description of man in a state of nature as evil and at war with one another.[4] In fact, nothing is found in Machiavelli or Hobbes about men's evil actions toward one another that is not already also described objectively by Augustine, or in Aristotle and Aquinas, for that matter. The former approve what the latter still understand as evil even when they know its existence.

St. Augustine, a Christian, had read Genesis. He understood that no actual thing in this world is, in its existence, evil. Evil is the lack of a good that ought to be there, but is not. Evil is located in the finite but free will, not in finite, existing being as such. Evil comes from choosing something in a disorderly fashion. It does not come from the power of choosing as such; that power is an

---

4. Herbert Deane, *The Political and Social Ideas of St. Augustine* (New York: Columbia University Press, 1963), 236.

essential element in the being of man and therefore in itself good. To exist, to exist in a limited manner, is itself good, although such finite existence cannot fully cause its own being and goodness. Aquinas, following Aristotle, argued that because of this natural goodness of human beings in particular, man was by nature a political animal. The state would have existed even without the Fall, that primordial disorder described in Genesis that clouded our desires to do good.

The so-called "coercive state," the one with the sword and army, however, arose because of the disorder of the Fall. This dis-order was, in each of us, radically theological. It needed to be confronted not merely by political means—that is, as Aristotle saw at the end of *The Ethics,* by coercion of the young men whom their fathers could not handle (1179b11–30)—but by spiritual means, by virtue and grace. Nature was not able to achieve its own ends because men did not will to choose the good they were capable of doing.

This conclusion suggested that coercion exercised by the state need not be evil itself if it must be used to protect the innocent against the injustice of others who by their own choices are not good. Coercion as coercion is not intrinsically evil. Otherwise, it could not be recommended or used at all. What is evil is the hu-man being using his will to act against the innocent and the good. Coercion, in its legitimate sense, is designed to enable responsible people to protect the innocent against the unjust acts of others who initiate destructive action. Nothing requires us to multiply evil by renouncing the use of force as a principle. Our intelligence is given to us, in part, to figure out ways to reduce evil. The mul-tiplication of evil is the result of human choice. It is not a natural necessity. Coercion is not, in the present order of things, itself always evil, though it can be so used. Evil and coercion should not be identified.

3. Fear of Hell and Fear of the Leviathan

For Hobbes, at the beginning of modern political philosophy, each person's fear of violent death was supposedly man's most basic passion. This fear explained how the Leviathan, the state, could use absolute coercion against anyone as a means to attain its own end. Fear of punishment was to eliminate arguments, particularly those of religion or philosophy, that might lead to unrestricted warfare. The fear of violent death, by an almost scientific argument, led to the granting of all power to the state. Power was to be used as an instrument to eliminate religious and philosophical ideas from the public order, since such ideas were held to be the main causes of civil disorder.

From this perspective, "peace" was preferable at any cost, even at the cost of truth itself or of any discussions about it. In such a political theory, the death of Socrates and the death of Christ would have been routine, legitimate acts of power. Truth was rendered innocuous by eliminating it from the public order as dangerous or irrelevant. The cost of peace was the denial that truth had meaning in the public order. Tolerance, not prudence, became the highest practical virtue.

However, when Hannah Arendt maintained that the elimination of hell from the public order may be the most significant aspect of modern secularism, she did not add that the fear of hell was, in practice, replaced by the fear of the Leviathan. That is, hell, which had formerly been something beyond this life, came to be located in this life in the unrestricted power of the state. Political hell, in the form of gulags or concentration camps, came to be instruments of public power. The most dire, hellish punishment followed opposing the Leviathan's will to establish its own definition of peace. Through its concentration camps and use of drugs—modern "hells," in other words—those who disagreed could be "refashioned" or eliminated. A Socrates, who did not fear death, could not have lived in a Hobbesian state. His death would have had no meaning in its terms.

A state with absolute power and no restrictions on its use imitates the fear of hell, in that it forces most men to capitulate to its threats. The most disturbing character of modern tyranny is its often-plausible claim to be doing good through the use of unlimited force. As a result, no distinctions but political ones, ones backed up by the absolute power of the state, could have any human meaning. This is not to disclaim the fact of fanaticism of various sorts. But fear of fanaticism is no basis on which altogether to exclude identifiable truths and human goods. Limited force may be quite necessary in many instances. In political philosophy we should not fail to ponder the reasons for the rise of absolute states with unlimited coercive powers. Is there any connection between the decline of religion in the public order and the rise of hell-like political entities?

How would one go about exploring this perplexing topic? Both Flannery O'Connor (in her introduction to *A Memoir of Mary Ann*) and Walker Percy (*The Thanatos Syndrome*) found that some connection existed between murder and compassion, between tenderness and holocaust. This connection will seem surprising. Yet it is worth thinking about, since modern political ideology has been a search for a way to use state power to eliminate evil from the world, in the name of compassion for the suffering.

In this search, modern ideology has sought to define who is good and who is evil, in some almost manichean sense, in order to eliminate what could be called evil. Guilt and punishment are no longer personal issues to be placed for judgment in the hands of a merciful yet just God. All problems are politicized. The very existence of certain classes or races or nations or genders or other abstractions, not individual free will, is considered to be the "cause" and location of evil. The newer abstract political evils—racism, sexism, genderism—are offshoots of this theoretical consequence of mislocating the causes of evil.

Modern totalitarian absolutism incites many thinkers to inquire further into this issue: Why or how did a good God make a world in which evil could exist? Some would hold that the evils of men are to be identified with the God of creation, who is said to be at fault for making such a world in which identifiable "hells" can exist. This thesis, that evil was caused not by men choosing wrongly but by the very structure of the world, would justify a rebellion against God on moral grounds. Ironically, the possibility of our freely doing evil deeds enables us to defend the possibility of our existing at all. Not to be able to do evil deeds means that we cannot do good deeds either. To have neither of these possibilities, which cannot be separated, would mean that the kind of being we are could not exist. The theoretical problems that arise from the political horrors of the twentieth century—or any century, for that matter—are more than political in origin.

4. *The Classic Context*

No doubt, the classic location for any discussion of hell in political theory goes back to the *Republic* of Plato, to the problem of justice. In the *Republic,* in a famous scene in Book II, the young potential philosophers Adeimantos and Glaucon called Socrates aside to tell him that they wanted to hear justice praised for its own sake, not, like most people's opinions about it, for any rewards or punishments that might come from being just or unjust. Socrates was impressed by the honor and sincerity of these two young men in not caring for anything but the truth of the topic itself. He admired their ability to state the case for evil but still feel that it was not a correct argument. Their souls and their heads were in conflict, so to speak. Only after the whole argument of the *Republic* had taken place, after we knew what justice was in itself and why we should practice it for its own sake, could we take up again the topic of the rewards and punishments of our actions.

Christians in particular will note that the doctrine of the immortality of the soul, which is not directly a Christian doctrine, arose in a political context. It arose in political philosophy to account both for the evils that could not be punished by the polity and for the rewards that could not be fully recognized by purely political means. The polity was limited in what it could reward and punish. Higher questions crop up in every human life, questions, in part, of justice. These questions would destroy the polity if it tried to resolve them by itself; they must ultimately have a transcendent resolution beyond politics, which frees politics of the divine burden of righting every wrong. But that some ultimate resolution was demanded by the dynamic of unresolved justice was within the logic of the analysis of the human condition. Mercy, equity, and forgiveness were addressed to the limits of justice.

For Plato, a punishment after this life taught that we should live rightly in the one life we are given, a position in substantial agreement with the revelational teachings. This point was found in the final "Myth of Er" in the *Republic*. No one who was not from the beginning well disposed to select it could choose the good. Also, there was no "second chance": this life was of ultimate significance.

A similar notion is found in the Gospel of Luke, in the story of Lazarus and the rich man. The rich man, after a disordered life of neglecting his neighbor, finds himself in hell. He wants Lazarus to be sent to warn his brothers back on earth not to do the same thing that he did, but he is told that a gulf exists between him and Lazarus in the bosom of Abraham. Abraham reminds the rich man that his brothers "have Moses and the prophets; let them listen to them." The rich man knows better and objects, "No, Father Abraham . . . if someone from the dead visits them, they will repent." To this proposal, Abraham replies, "If they do not listen to Moses and the prophets they will pay no heed even if someone should rise from the dead" (16:29–31). Human life, rooted in free will, is free to choose what it wants even when it knows the consequences. Love of self, not fear of hell, is the most radical problem of the human spirit.

Looking at the proposal for an ultimate punishment, St. Augustine realized that the Platonic position on hell was an entirely legitimate one. Hell, ultimate punishment, was a real possibility for evils not punished by the state or in any way repented. The modern solution was that, since all truth was relative, no real evil except that defined by the will could exist. If there was no evil in principle, however, there could be no ultimate or transcendent punishment, no hell. If this be so, everything, including ultimate rewards and punishments, must be accomplished in this life. This proposition meant that, in the final analysis, either no right or justice existed, or the task of eliminating evil must belong exclusively to the state. The former alternative is the origin of modern political relativism, the latter of modern totalitarianism.

Both of these positions are philosophically intelligible and justified by the failure to think properly about the location of ultimate punishment for evils that are perpetrated by men in living polities in a definite time and place. Nothing is to be gained by denying the tragic depths of the record of human evils, a record that seems to be exponentially multiplied when man sets out to reform himself and to achieve the highest good through politics. Augustine's solution still seems to be the most pertinent: that men's desire for the City of God (or, if you will, for "The Republic," which after all bears the original name of Augustine's idea) is quite legitimate. The question of the location of man's best regime cannot be suppressed as a philosophic or religious or political issue without dire consequences to human worth itself and to the civil order.

5. *The Non-Contingency of Evil*

Leszek Kolakowski, in a famous essay, "Can the Devil Be Saved?" asked whether evil was contingent. Could what was defined as evil ever, by a change of situation or culture or mind, become good? Was evil, in both its definition and its frequency, persistent through time, or was it capable of being reversed into its opposite? Who was to decide this possibility? These questions, under other forms, are behind what is currently known as "cultural relativism" in the academies. Kolakowski himself did not think evil was mutable.

Flannery O'Connor had come to the same conclusion when she remarked on the difference between the South and the rest of the country. In her view, the South when she wrote still understood original sin. This meant that the disorder we observe is radically in our hearts, and not primarily in our institutions. No amount of rearranging of the institutions of property, family, or state will eradicate evil.[5] In even the best polity or family, evil can appear. In the worst polity, good can appear, a point Solzhenitsyn made about the gulags. This sudden appearance of good or evil is possible because of the nature of human freedom, the source of all human action in the world.

"The Christian tradition," Kolakowski wrote, affirms "that certain effects of original sin are ineluctable and that there can be salvation only through grace."[6] Against this truth, we can either rebel and attempt to create a wholly manmade world, or we recognize that politics is limited. Certain things politics cannot do. Rather politics, as Aristotle saw in the *Ethics*, is bound to the distinctions between good and evil already existing in human nature. This conclusion means that genuine risk is found in the world. This risk was and is an intrinsic part of every human action. If

5. *The Habit of Being: Letters of Flannery O'Connor,* ed. Sally Fitzgerald (New York: Viking, 1979), 302–3.
6. Leszek Kolakowski, "Le diable peut-il être sauvé?" *Contrepoint* (Paris), no. 20 (1976): 136.

we try to remove our possibility of choosing evil, we end up ourselves either subject to an absolute state that makes the distinction
for us or dwellers in a world in which no choice really means anything. If we allow for our being able to choose evil, however, we
cannot fully account for its final consequences. We must leave
these rewards or punishments to the transcendent order, to what
St. Augustine called "the City of Man" or "the City of God."

Raïssa Maritain, in her lovely *Journals,* wrote, to this point:

I am coming to take humanity quietly—for what it is. Without excla-
mations—regrets—sighs—and groans. In a way quite different from
that of Leibnitzian optimism—all is the best. *God knows what he permits.*

He is not like a man who regretfully permits what he cannot prevent. He has let men go their own way armed with their freedom—
and they go it. They go, gamble and work, risk everything—win more
or less, and perhaps will end by winning everything. God has simply
reserved for himself in humanity one Man who is his Son.[7]

Everything related to the ultimate question of final rewards and
punishments concerns the free answer of men to what constitutes
their final happiness. But this answer is manifested in actions that
bear in themselves a possibility of choosing against reality, a
choice that, in its final consequences, traditionally goes by the
name of hell.

6. *Hell and Ultimate Meaning*

Men can and do, no doubt, choose wrongly. However, the enterprise of living a single human life in each of its moments is of
utmost seriousness. Without the realization of this risk, of the seriousness of this freedom, human life would be trivialized. Paradoxically, the final cost of the denial of the existence of hell is the
denial of ultimate personal meaning. Human life with no real ultimate worth in each human being would be subjected to a polity
that itself defined, in lieu of something higher, both what was the
worth and the punishment for human deeds it decided to recognize. Justice, on such an hypothesis, would mean no more than
this conformity to a political judgment based on nothing but itself.

7. *Raïssa's Journals,* ed. Jacques Maritain (Albany, N.Y.: Magi Books, 1974),
365.

The neglect of the doctrine of hell in political philosophy, however odd that phrase might sound, has the serious consequence of mislocating the context and the final importance of everything we freely do. The orthodox religious teaching about hell does not claim to know whether anyone is actually in hell. Our status is reserved to God. However much we might want to consign someone there for terrible deeds done against individuals or against mankind, we ourselves in our finiteness do not know. Forgiveness is as much a reality and as much an ambiguity as hell. Yet we do know that this doctrine graphically calls our attention to the importance of each human action that can have ultimate consequences at any moment of its choosing.

St. Augustine was right to see that Plato posed the right question. In our embarrassment with the real dilemmas about evil and its punishment that arise in our polities and in our lives, we end by creating something at first sight more comforting. We conclude that hell does not exist because, after all, nothing is of such importance as to warrant so drastic a consequence. We conclude this argument only to find, philosophically, that by it we have allowed something much more dangerous to take over our lives, namely, the power of the state or some other human power to decide the distinction between good and evil. We are inattentive to these questions, I think, at our own peril. We live in a world in which risk is of the very essence of our dignity. The doctrine of hell guarantees that what we do with our lives is of more than passing importance. Nothing else can quite make that point to political philosophy so graphically.

The consideration of hell is an extension of the consideration of evil. Indeed, it is its final consideration. Both evil and hell cause us to discuss the significance and ultimate importance of human life in its highest activities of knowing and choosing. We are, according to an ancient saying, to call no man happy until he is dead, as if there is a relation between a capacity to choose and a capacity to live. Albert Camus, in *The Rebel*, wrote:

Men are never really willing to die except for the sake of freedom: therefore they do not believe in dying completely. . . . Those who find no rest in God or in history are condemned to live for those who, like themselves, cannot live: for the humiliated. The most pure form of the movement of rebellion is thus warmed with the heart-rending cry of Karamazov: if all are not saved, what good is the salvation of one only?[8]

In this context, no one can forget Ivan Karamazov's other remark, that "if God did not exist, all things would be possible." That is, there would be no distinct right and wrong. Camus wants to be his own savior and that of others, but savior from what? Can we be saved from what we choose by anything but choice—by a choice that recognizes a standard according to which choice is good or evil? We cannot force all to choose rightly.

Death, that final statement of our freedom and our passage, the topic to which I next turn, is to be seen in the context of Socrates' discussion of immortality, of the final punishment for real deeds chosen against the good, of a punishment that does not permit the good to be called evil. Camus's plea to save those who will not be saved, his Promethean claim, rings untrue in the light of the opposite passage of the New Testament: "What doth it profit a man to gain the whole world and lose the life of his soul?" (Matthew 16.26).

Camus wants to save all, no matter what the status of their choice, evidently as if individual choices made no difference except their own uniqueness. Each would be saved no matter what, a position that implicitly justifies, with Thrasymachus in Book I of the *Republic*, the worst regime. In this context, someone who chooses in fact a good life, because it is good and will remain good, will be seen as alienated from all the others who did not so choose. I shall say something further of this position in the discussion of friendship (Chapter 12). What is to be emphasized here is that the place of freedom and human worth in political philosophy involves directly the position we take on evil, hell, and death itself.

8. Albert Camus, *The Rebel: An Essay on Man in Revolt*, trans. Anthony Bower (New York: Vintage, 1956), 291, 304.

SIX

Dwellers in an Unfortified City
Death and Political Philosophy

> *"Against all else it is possible to provide security, but as against death all of us mortals alike dwell in an unfortified city."*
> —EPICURUS, *Fragments*, Vatican Collection, no. 31

> *"For no sooner do we begin to live in this dying body, than we begin to move ceaselessly toward death. For in the whole course of this life (if life we must call it) its mutability tends towards death. . . . Our whole life is nothing but a race towards death. . . ."*
> —ST. AUGUSTINE, *The City of God*, XIII, 10

> *"Rather proclaim, Westmoreland, through my host, / That he who hath no stomach to this fight, / Let him depart; his passport shall be made, / And crowns for his convoy put into his purse, / We would not die in that man's company / That fears his fellowship to die with us."*
> —SHAKESPEARE, *Henry V*, IV, iii, ll. 34–39

1. A Complete Political Philosophy

Eventually, virtue and friendship, happiness and salvation must be accounted for in political philosophy. Before treating these central subjects, however, it has been necessary first to see the "brilliant errors" in which political things have been propounded. In addition, the natural context of those errors, the perplexing realities of evil and hell needed to be understood to see how these issues do bring us to the heart of basic issues in human dignity and worth.

Human death is a third of these dire issues that begin with enigmas and realities in the human lives in any polity but whose understanding transcends the civil institutions. Death is an unavoidable topic, yet it is one that is too seldom treated with any direct purpose in political philosophy, even though there is a long traditional reason for doing so. Death brings up the question of the permanence of friendship, a subject of the greatest importance in political philosophy, one that relates to the ultimate status of the good and the evil.

Aristotle, in the *Ethics,* understood the virtue of courage, the first of the cardinal virtues, to mean that death was the highest act of this virtue. It upheld human worth. Courage upheld the good even if no one chose it. No one was to be called happy until he was dead. Salvation included salvation from death. Death did appear in political philosophy. The beginnings of political philosophy are found in the death of the philosopher Socrates and are reproposed in a new way in the death of Christ. At the beginning of the *Republic,* in the very introduction to political things, Socrates talks to an old man to find out about the road we all must travel and how we must prepare for death by squaring away our violations of justice (327C–331D).

In 1769, James Boswell, not unmindful perhaps of Socrates' remark that philosophy itself is a preparation for death, mentioned to Samuel Johnson that two days previously he had seen the execution of two criminals at Tyburn. What struck Boswell about this scene was that "none of them seemed to be under any concern." Johnson was not surprised at this apparent indifference to death. "Most of them, Sir, have never thought at all," he bluntly replied. Boswell persisted, "But is not the fear of death natural to man?" Johnson agreed, "So much so, Sir, that the whole of life is but keeping away the thoughts of it." Boswell continued:

He (Johnson) then, in a low and earnest tone, talked of his meditating upon the aweful hour of his own dissolution, and in what manner he should conduct himself upon that occasion: "I know not (said he,) whether I should wish to have a friend by me, or have it all between God and myself."[1]

---

1. *Boswell's Life of Johnson* (London: Oxford, 1931), I, p. 394.

Execution by the state at Tyburn, no less than any other "aweful hour of our dissolution," ought to cause us to think about the meaning of death, even if we are not so prone to reflect on it.

This frank passage in Boswell causes us to ask ourselves whether or not this same reflection needs to be applied to the discipline of political philosophy. Do political philosophers too spend their whole lives "keeping away" thoughts of death? Does the fact that death is something between God and oneself mean that some kind of intellectual separation between church and state prevents us from even broaching the subject of the relation between political philosophy and the meaning of death within the earthly regimes of men?

If we understand political philosophy as a special branch of philosophy, the branch that deals with the meaning and arrangement of our civil life together, death does not appear to fall much within the purview of the political philosophers. Death seems more metaphysical. Yet, to repeat, the discipline of political philosophy began with a death, with the death of a philosopher, Socrates. Contrary to Johnson's worry, though without denying his point, to avoid the thought of death is to ignore the very beginnings of political philosophy. Unless the polity is rightly ordered, which no existing ones are, it seems that philosophers (seekers after truth) and politicians (seekers after order) are on a collision course in any actual state.

2. *Politicians Kill Philosophers*

The understanding of the conflict between truth and politics was the first act of *political* philosophy. One of the significant tasks of philosophy was to render politics benevolent to philosophy's own needs and nature. The task of politics, for its part, was to tame the philosopher so that he would not overturn the polity. The fact that the best of the ancient polities killed its philosopher, its best man, ominously suggested that "success" in politics often necessitated the death of the philosopher.

No one has articulated this view of the presumed philosophic incompatibility of politics and philosophy better or more ominously than Machiavelli. Modern political thought is founded on this very premise. In Book V of his *Florentine Histories,* Machiavelli presented a theory to justify the use of cruelty to rule, a theory he had advocated in *The Prince*. Reviving cyclic thought that was needed to undermine the linear implications of the doctrine of creation, Machiavelli observed that things pass from decay to perfection and back again:

For virtue gives birth to quiet, quiet to leisure, leisure to disorder, disorder to ruin; and similarly, from ruin, order is born; from order, virtue; and from virtue, glory and good fortune. Whence it has been observed by the prudent that letters come after arms and that, in the provinces and cities, captains arise before philosophers. For, as good and ordered armies give birth to victories and victories to quiet, the strength of well-armed spirits cannot be corrupted by a more honorable leisure than that of letters, nor can leisure enter into well-instituted cities with a greater and more dangerous deceit than this one.

This was best understood by Cato when the philosophers Diogenes and Carneades, sent by Athens as spokesmen to the Senate, came to Rome. When he saw how the Roman youth were beginning to follow them about with admiration, and since he recognized the evil that could result to his fatherland from this honorable leisure, he saw to it that no philosopher could be accepted in Rome.[2]

For Aristotle, the transcendent end of the city was leisure, the contemplative life, prepared by the practical virtues acquired by good choices through the polity. For Machiavelli, who sympathized with the politicians who accused Socrates, letters and leisure were most grave worries for a statesman, since they threatened to corrupt the virtues necessary to defend the city.

When Cato, the traditional example of sober Roman virtue, saw the youth running after the philosophers, he excluded the philosophers. Civil ruin could, presumably, be prevented by insisting that the philosopher never enter Rome or any other city. At his trial, Socrates affirmed that he could not choose banishment and still be a philosopher in another city, because in that case, the same thing would happen to him in Thebes as was happening to him in Athens. Roman statesmen understood this possibility. The military virtues dealt with the worthiness of death for the sake of the city and the good life, that is, the life of this city,

---

2. Niccolo Machiavelli, *Florentine Histories*, trans. Laura Banfield and Harvey Mansfield (Princeton: Princeton University Press, 1988), 185.

Thebes or Rome. These practical virtues for the Romans were not subject to the contemplative virtues and ends, to the ones that determined the place of the military virtues in the first place. The primacy of life over good life began here where death threatened the philosopher and forbade him to enter the city. Even Cicero wanted the philosophic republic to exist as the actual Roman Republic.

3. Death and Life before the City

Socrates died reminding Crito to offer a sacrificial cock to Asclepius, the god of healing (*Phaedo* 118). Christ died asking the Father to forgive his executioners for they did not know what they did (Luke 23:34). Death "cured" Socrates, while death gave Christ the opportunity to explain in what this healing might consist, that is, a remedy for the limits of justice and the limits of mortality itself.

In *The Gay Science*, Nietzsche commented on this incident of Socrates' last request before his death. He asked that a sacrificial cock be offered to Asclepius, the god of healing. Nietzsche maintained that he "admired the courage and wisdom of Socrates in everything he did, said—and did not say" (no. 340).[3] Nietzsche wished, however, that Socrates had remained silent in this last moment instead of acknowledging this particular god. Nietzsche maintained that what Socrates meant by this request to Crito was subversive to life itself. "This ridiculous and terrible 'last word' means for those who have ears: 'O Crito, *life is a disease*'." Death was the cure of a sickness called life. The normally cheerful Socrates, in Nietzsche's view, overturned all that he stood for in these last words. Socrates, it turned out, merely "suffered life." He did not appreciate it.

Socrates revenged himself on all his subsequent readers who might think he was not a "pessimist." Nietzsche could not forgive Socrates:

Socrates *suffered life*! And then he still revenged himself—with this veiled, gruesome, pious, and blasphemous saying. Did Socrates need

3. Friedrich Nietzsche, *The Gay Science*, trans. Walter Kaufmann (New York: Vintage, 1973), 272.

such revenge? Did his overrich virtue lack an ounce of magnanimity?—Alas, my friends, we must overcome even the Greeks!

This overcoming the Greeks, however, this accusation that Socrates looked upon life as a disease that needed a cure, proposed the conquering of death to which, as Augustine said, we are rushing daily. Some being other than those who die is proposed as the center of attention and action. The intellectual heart of subsequent totalitarian theory lies here. The reality and dignity of personal death—which each person, as a mortal, has to face—become obscured in the ridicule and the arrogance that would promise something more by means of man's own power. Camus's wishing to save everyone, no matter what they do, is but a version of this promise of man's self-proclaimed power to save all.

Death appears in all polities existing in time or in speech. "Let us imagine a number of men in chains, and all condemned to death," Blaise Pascal wrote in his *Pensées*, "where some are killed each day in the sight of the others, and those who remain see their own fate in that of their fellows, and wait their turn, looking at each other sorrowfully and without hope. It is an image of the condition of men" (no. 199).[4] Every polity has the fact of death in its various forms ever present as one of its justifying purposes. Either to protect or punish, police and army are organized around the possibility and fact of death caused by human injustice.

Yet a polity is primarily this-worldly, about life, not death. Police and army arise only out of what ought not to exist. Even when a state legally decides to inflict death for crime, something mysteriously beyond politics remains, to recall the conversation of Boswell and Johnson. The execution of even the most heinous criminal still forces our attention, as it should, to the mystery in which we all share. The point of a "public" execution is the realization that law and duty are encumbent upon everyone. All are responsible both for the execution and for the fact that the crimes that happened in the polity destroyed innocent citizens.

4. *Pascal's Pensées and the Provincial Letters*, (New York: Modern Library, 1941), 73-74.

4. Death Limits Politics

The fact of death can and should serve as a limit to politics. No death caused by civil action is justified unless it upholds justice, unless it protects us from our own crimes and aggressions and those of others. A polity that sees or fears nothing beyond itself claims that complete self-sufficiency that exempts it from answering for those of its actions that lead to death. The dignity of death before the polity, the political point of both Socrates and Christ, consists in the fact that the polity is itself not the highest thing to which man can be subject and destined. Given a choice between polity and truth (a choice that in fact happens in existing polities), right order of the soul requires that truth be preferred to power that acknowledges only its own definition of civil theology or order. A state does not form some sort of corporate "being" with a substance of its own; states are composed of individual mortals who die. Polities exist over time only through replacing individuals who die with other individuals. The effort to immortalize the deeds of citizens in lasting polities is not the same as the question of the immortality of the soul of these same individuals. For political philosophy, the question of death does hint that the desire to perform immortal deeds and say lasting words of truth is itself subordinate to the question of the destiny of the individuals who compose a polity. These two questions are related to each other, but they are not the same question. Immortal words and deeds that last until the polity itself declines and falls do attest to that desire for permanence that arose with the problem of the immortality of the individual soul.

The frailty of polities is less obvious than the passingness that greets each individual human being at birth. Sometimes states and empires are destroyed by their enemies. Sometimes they become corrupt and dispirited over philosophical and moral issues. They do not display energy sufficient to reproduce themselves and their way of life. A few civil societies last two or three hundred years under the same form, but rarely. The relation of soulcraft, the chosen virtues and vices that form what each human being is in himself, and statecraft, the order of regime, is close. The spiritual condition of citizens ultimately decides the worth if not the permanence of their polities. The form of polity, nevertheless, can make virtue more possible or promote the ease or incidence of vice.

5. *Things More Shameful Than Death*

The monuments to the dead, as Pericles explained in his "Funeral Oration," are the words or deeds of the once living. These monuments indicate what virtues a civil society thinks should be preserved and imitated. They memorialize what the polity wants to emphasize when it recalls its dead. They define its present in terms of how the polity remembers the deeds and men of its history (II, 4).

Pericles continued:

They [those who fell in the War] gave her [Athens] their lives, to her and to all of us, and for their own selves they won praises that never grow old, the most splendid of sepulchres—not the sepulchre in which their bodies are laid, but where their glory remains eternal in men's minds, always there on the right occasion to stir others to speech or action. For famous men have the whole earth as their memorial: it is not only the inscriptions on their graves in their own country that mark them out; no, in foreign lands also, not in any visible form but in people's hearts, their memory abides and grows. It is for you to try to be like them. Make up your minds that happiness depends on being free, and freedom depends on being courageous. Let there be no relaxation in face of the perils of the war. The people who have most excuse for despising death are not the wretched and unfortunate, who have no hope of doing well for themselves, but those who run the risk of a complete reversal in their lives. . . . Any intelligent man would find a humiliation caused by his own slackness more painful to bear than death.[5]

Death is not, in this description, the worst of evils.

Contained within this famous passage from Thucydides (which should be compared with almost an identical sentiment in Lincoln's "Gettysburg Address") are the essential terms of the problem of death and polity: the idea that the death of the well-placed and the well-educated is the most difficult to bear. Their good

5. Thucydides, *The Peloponnesian War*, trans. Rex Warner (Baltimore: Penguin, 1966), II, 4, p. 121.

fortune is found in the record of noble deeds. The worthiness of their deeds addressed all mankind. Some things are more shameful than death. In preferring death to shameful deeds, death upholds the order of virtue and piety. The same argument is found in Socrates: "In every kind of danger there are plenty of devices for avoiding death if you are unscrupulous enough to stick at nothing. But I suggest, gentlemen, that the difficulty is not so much to escape death; the real difficulty is to escape from doing wrong" (39). The dead continue to live in the city, which abides without them. The city is a place in which deeds and words are remembered in order "to stir" other noble words and actions, as Pericles put it.

6. *Mortality and the City*

We are the mortals, the beings who die and who know that we die. In the universe, what is immortal—ideas, species, the heavens—all attest to the ongoing presence of objects and ideas that transcend the life of individual human beings. Socrates dies, executed by his own polity for not believing in its gods and for corrupting its youth. As he himself noted to the jury, because of his years Socrates might have died soon anyway. But his judges chose to destroy him rather than let him die of old age. The mystery of death, whether through old age or by state execution—as Cicero's account of Cato and Plato's memory of Socrates indicated—seemed to entail different sorts of thoughts about death. The jurors, now through Plato's Dialogue immortalized as those who killed the philosopher, thought that he was corrupting their own city. They held him worthy of death. The city is to be defended against its enemies internal and external. The life of Socrates suggested that one city at least should not exist, namely Athens, the existing city in which Socrates was born. The philosopher, Plato intimated, was more important than the city.

A conflict to death between the philosopher and the city always seems possible. The fact that it does not often happen that philosophers are killed by the state does not disprove that perhaps philosophers still corrupt existing states by confusing the potential philosophers about virtue and truth. The normal course of life, if left to itself, ends life. But life before it ends may beget other life. Man wants to leave both his offspring and the memory of his particular self in the polity of his allegiance. The noblest, indeed, have a claim to be recorded in all polities—Pericles, Socrates, Christ, Cicero, Dante, Lincoln.

Civil society is designed to enable us to live well, even though it claims to have the duty to destroy us when our lives or, in some places, our thoughts threaten its good or viability. This claim is, however, in the name of life. We should want to be punished when we do wrong. We can threaten and destroy other lives. The polity can require us to defend it, its common good.

The polity is necessary to live. It transcends mortal lives by inciting questions that are beyond politics. This further questioning was characteristic of the contemplative life, that life which was rather "divine" and not proper to man insofar as he was mortal (1177b25–30). Socrates in death, however, made his city live in a way that it could not have lived had he been pardoned or banished.

Not just any sort of life is worth living. Socrates solemnly affirmed:

If on the other hand I tell you that to let no day pass without discussing goodness and all the other subjects about which you hear me talking and examining both myself and others is really the very best thing that a man can do, and that life without this sort of examination is not worth living, you will be even less inclined to believe me. (37)[6]

If the only life worth living consists in such daily philosophic discourse, very few human lives have been worth living. Even the life of the philosopher—in what sense is it "worth" living?

7. Death and What Is Right

In the *Gorgias*, a dialogue of ominous proportions, the Stranger who converses with the younger Socrates confronts Callicles, the politician who also had studied philosophy in his youth (485). The very character of Callicles alerts philosophy to the dangers that lie in the education it gives to its potential philosophers and poli-

---

6. Unless otherwise indicated, citations from the Dialogues on the Death of Socrates are taken from *The Last Days of Socrates*, trans. Hugh Tredennick (Harmondsworth: Penguin, 1969).

ticians. Callicles thought that the young ought to study some philosophy. A good liberal education required it. But when these sons were older and had the charge of the city, they could not afford the witty conversations of the philosopher, who only talked in corners with yelping boys. More serious things needed doing. Callicles finally refused even to talk philosophy with the Socratic Stranger. The Socratic Stranger was aware that the refusal of the politician to talk over his principles with the philosopher meant that philosophy had no chance in the polity. The philosopher's life was at risk from that moment.

The philosopher always had to prepare for death when he failed to engage the politician in serious conversation.

> SOCRATES: So to be disciplined is better for the soul than lack of discipline, which is what you yourself were thinking just now.
> CALLICLES: I don't know what in the world you mean, Socrates. Ask somebody else.
> SOCRATES: This fellow won't put up with being benefited and with his undergoing the very thing the discussion's about, with being disciplined.
> CALLICLES: And I couldn't care less about anything you say, either. I gave you these answers just for Gorgias' sake.
> SOCRATES: Very well. What'll we do now? Are we breaking off in the midst of the discussion? (505).[7]

The refusal of Callicles forced Socrates to continue the discussion as a monologue. This denial of the philosophic method of dialogue meant that the politician, for all his youthful philosophy, which he admired, could not be drawn into the essential questions of truth when it came to ruling the actual city. These profound disquisitions were not questions the politician could afford to ask or allow to be asked. The death warrant of Socrates was signed when the politician refused to discuss anything further with him, just as Christ's was sealed when Pilate asked cynically, "What is truth?" (John 18:38).

If no objective truth existed, or if the very pursuit of it was dangerous, it follows that Callicles, those who voted for Socrates' death, Cato, and Pontius Pilate were all quite correct in their positions on the supremacy of politics over truth. But we must not

7. Plato, *Gorgias*, trans. Donald J. Zeyl (Indianapolis: Hackett, 1987), 85.

argue that objective truth exists because we need it to uphold our polities. Polities must be upheld because truth does exist and does exist properly within them. The philosopher ought not to be killed solely because he is a philosopher. The essence of philosophy is not argument for argument's sake. Both the politician and the philosopher can be benevolent to each other only when both in their own way seek a common truth.

The appeal of liberal education has always been, of course, that there are things that ought to be known because they are true in all polities. A city of mankind did exist. Cicero remains the best expositor of this position.

If he sees nothing unnatural in wronging a fellow-man ... , he is taking away from human beings all that makes them human. If ... he concedes that this ought to be avoided, yet still regards death, destitution, and pain as even more undesirable, he is mistaken. He ought not to concede that *any* damage, either to his person or to his property, is worse than doing wrong.

So everyone ought to have the same purpose: to identify the interest of each with the interest of all. Once men grab for themselves, human society will completely collapse. But if nature prescribes (as she does) that every human being must help every other human being, whoever he is, just precisely because they are all human beings, then—by the same authority—all men have identical interests. Having identical interests means that we are all subject to one and the same law of nature; and, that being so, the very least that such a law enjoins is that we must not wrong one another.[8]

What is evident here is the force of the argument that death is not to be preferred to what is right. The right is the foundation of civility.

8. *The Politician's Refusal*

On the last day of Socrates' life, his wife, Xanthippe, was sad because, as she said, this would be the last day during which Socrates could converse with his friends (60). Socrates' friends, however, were not much better than Xanthippe when it came to controlling their tears. Socrates expected more of the philoso-

8. Cicero, "On Duties," III, Chapter III, *Selected Works*, ed. Michael Grant (Baltimore: Penguin, 1967), 168.

pher, because this self-control was the nature of his profession, the preparation for death. What amazed the men who remained with Socrates, however, was his calmness. He did not wail and shout and blame others, as the jailer told Socrates had been his general experience (116). The calm of Socrates was caused by his philosophy, by what he talked about in this cell provided by the state for his death, almost as if to say that the only place for true philosophy, for the search for the truth in the polity, was the antechamber of death. This was where Socrates had his "second trial," not before the city but before the potential philosophers who could follow his arguments about immortality.

What did Socrates talk about? He talked of the immortality of the soul. Socrates was sure that death was not the worst evil. He was quite convinced that the soul was immortal (105, 608). If this was the case, if this was the fruit of his philosophic knowledge, he was freed from that power of death threatened by the politician. The politician's power to execute could be used to coerce Socrates to do what he did not think it right to do. Callicles knew this quite well. This is the reason he would not discuss anything further with Socrates. Cicero likewise understood that death was not an excuse for preferring what is advantageous to what is right. This conclusion suggests that the reasons men give for which they die are the reasons that limit the state from completely defining their own lives.

Death limits politics not merely because the polity must articulate the reasons for which the taking of life is permitted or necessary, but because the polity must remember those who have died in the defense of its continuing life. If the polity remembers no philosopher, if the greatest deeds and words are only those spoken in the polity about its own continuance in existence, then the education of the youth must ever keep out those disturbing questions that death proposes, questions concerning what life is about in all its dimensions, including the happiness and salvation that can come with death.

If death is merely an instrument of rule, it is primarily a means to retain power. In this sense, Cato was right. We must keep a philosopher or a St. Paul out of Rome if we would preserve the city as it is constituted. The philosopher who spends his life preparing for death engages Callicles the politician up to the point at which the politician will no longer talk. This silence on the part of the politician is threatening. It cuts the philosopher off from the discourse that makes his words come alive and mean something outside of himself. The power over life and death that lies in the hands of the politician claims to subordinate philosophy, the search for truth, to the needs of the polity. When this happens, the philosopher is the noble, the politician the monstrous figure.

But the politician knows that the philosopher may choose against the good. In his youth, the politician too has read Plato and recalls that the philosopher can give persuasive arguments against justice. Aristotle explained how to be a successful tyrant; in his explanation, the instruments of force and surveillance were already presented in their classical form (1313a34–14a29). It was because Adeimantos and Glaucon in the *Republic* were so capable of arguing against justice but not in believing their own arguments that Socrates was taken with their honesty and zeal (368). This charming attention to the intellectual sincerity of these young potential philosophers incited Socrates to construct the city in speech, the only one in which the philosopher might, in keeping faithful to philosophy, live and not die for political reasons.

As a young man Plato beheld the circumstances surrounding the death of Socrates, the Philosopher, his teacher. He spent the rest of his literary career bringing Socrates back to life in various ways, to determine whether he had had to die and, if so, who was responsible for his death. No doubt, this concern of Plato gave us political philosophy. Sometimes, Socrates justifies his method by claiming that he is wiser than others among the Greeks because he knows that he knows nothing. Death is often pictured as the return to ashes, to nothingness. If political philosophy returns to its roots, does it return to naught? If it seeks to relate its treatment of the polity, the science of living well, to death, does it end up merely in perplexity and frustration?

Nietzsche, who despised the instinct of mere self-preservation as unworthy of man and as the work of merely consumptive scholars like Spinoza, wrote: "The wish to preserve oneself is the symptom of a condition of distress, of a limitation of the really fundamental instinct of life which aims at *the expansion of power* and wishing for that, frequently, risks and even sacrifices self-preservation" (no. 349).[9] The point of this passage for political philosophy, however, is that death here is seen as preferable to merely staying alive. In this Nietzsche is not different from Socrates. But risking death to "expand power" is Machiavellian, not classic order. Nietzsche's alternative—that is, to expand power— is the attempt to overcome death and man by superman. It is the result in modernity of the specific rejection of the Socratic discourse on immortality and the Christian doctrine of the resurrection. Nietzsche was right. The growth of the state based on successfully expanding power limited by nothing but itself is the result of denying the limits defined by classical philosophy and revelation.

9. *The Discourse of Political Philosophy on Death*

The discourse of political philosophy on death is no neutral or indifferent one. Whatever one might argue about the "normal" dealings of any polity with the facts of death among its members, including those deaths caused by the polity itself in the pursuit of its own legitimate purposes, the greater problem concerns what limits the polity to be itself. The definition and terms of this limitation of politics are the great themes of political philosophy. This effort is the intellectual enterprise that seeks to know where politics falls within the scheme of the whole of being. Implicit in Callicles' refusal to speak further with Socrates about the purposes of political rhetoric was the affirmation that death bore no meaning. Death implied no judgment, no meaning other than its fact. The philosopher had no significance.

In his conversation with Boswell, Samuel Johnson, as we saw, had remarked that at that "aweful hour of his own dissolution," he was not sure whether he would want to be with a friend or to "have it all between God and myself." In the *Discourses* of the Stoic slave-philosopher Epictetus, he likewise pictured himself at his hour of dissolution.

"Who shall tend me?" God, and your friends. "I shall lie on a hard bed." But you can do it like a man. "I shall not have a proper house." If you have one, you will be ill all the same. "Who will give me food?"

9. Nietzsche, *The Gay Science*, 291–92.

Those who find it for others; you will be no worse off than Manes (a slave) on your sick-bed. And what is the end of the illness? Nothing worse than death. Will you realize once for all that it is not death that is the source of all man's evils, and of a mean and cowardly spirit, but rather the fear of death? Against this fear then I would have you discipline yourself; to this let all your reasonings, your lectures, and your trainings be directed; and then you will know that only so do men achieve their freedom. (III, 26)[10]

What I wish to suggest is that Johnson and Epictetus, however much their language seems to be the same, represent almost diametrically different views of death. Johnson was a believing Christian, and his relation to God was personal, one of accounting for his life before God at death.

For the Stoic, the fear of death was what counted. Man showed his superiority, his self-sufficiency, by not being touched by those natural fears that arise before death. These needed to be controlled. Cato was right to keep the philosopher, who might see some higher order to the passions, out of the city. As with the Epicureans, the fear of the gods prevented the sufficiency that is due to man. Man is unsettled, they thought, by the gods who exist only because of irrational fears. The removal of the gods is the condition of peace. If the gods are the "opium of the people," as a famous follower of Epicurus on this topic once wrote—Marx wrote his dissertation on Epicurus—the overcoming of the fear of death is the justification for the supremacy of politics in the world. Political philosophy becomes not ethics but metaphysics, a metaphysics that grows not out of being as it is received in nature but out of that sort of being that can be put in place by man, the maker even of polities.

"Our whole life is a race to death"—words of St. Augustine, who agreed with Plato that the philosopher must build the city in speech. He disagreed with Plato only about its possibility and its location. The City of God remains the basic and central answer to Nietzsche, who maintained that Socrates ought not to have offered a sacrificial cock to Asclepius, the god of healing, because mankind was not sick unto death. Nietzsche wanted to risk even death for power. Socrates suffered death by political power. When

10. "Discourses of Epictetus," in *The Stoic and Epicurean Philosophers*, ed. Whitney J. Oates (New York: Random House, 1940), 405.

told to behold their king, the people present shouted to Christ, "We have no king but Caesar" (John 19:15). Even if this king be a philosopher, he will be killed in all existing cities, as Socrates thought.

The limits of politics begin where Cato and Callicles will allow the philosopher in the city. The dignity of politics to be itself depends on whether man can find a complete happiness that includes the friendship of the gods and of men. This happiness would have to be, as Aristotle said, in a complete life, a life that would include body and soul, in the wholeness of which we are composed. If he cannot, he will look to politics for his alternate answers, answers that depend only on himself and are not related to *what is*.

"The physical fact of death, in a hundred horrid shapes," G. K. Chesterton wrote, "was more naked and less veiled in times of faith or superstition than in times of science or skepticism. Often it was not merely those who had seen a man die, but those who had seen him rot, who were the most certain that he was everlastingly alive."[11] The dwellers in an unfortified city confront the physical fact of death at the limits of science and skepticism. These are the very limits of political philosophy itself wherein, as St. Augustine suspected, the Republic, the city built in speech, the unfortified city, meets the City of God. Against all else, as Epicurus said, it is possible to provide intellectual security.

11. G. K. Chesterton, *Fancies Versus Fads* (New York: Dodd, Mead, 1923), 175, cited in *The Quotable Chesterton* (San Francisco: Ignatius Press, 1986), 83.

PART III

At the Limits of Political Philosophy

SEVEN

The Death of Christ and the
Death of Socrates

> *"Almighty God, heavenly Father, who desirest not the death of a sinner,
> look down with mercy upon me, depraved with vain imaginations and
> entangled in long habits of sin. Grant me that grace, without which I
> can neither will nor do what is acceptable to Thee. Pardon my sins,
> remove the impediments that hinder my obedience; enable me to shake
> off sloth, and to redeem the time misspent in idleness and sin, by a dili-
> gent application of the days yet remaining, to the duties which thy prov-
> idence shall allot me. O God, grant me thy Holy Spirit, that I may repent
> and amend my life; grant me contrition, grant me resolution, for the
> sake of Jesus Christ, to whose covenant I now implore admission,* of the
> benefits of whose death *I implore participation. For his sake have
> mercy on me, O God, for his sake, O God, pardon and receive me.
> Amen."*
>
> —SAMUEL JOHNSON, Prayer, Easter Eve, 1757[1]

1. From Errors, to Questions, to Answers

The first two parts of this book set down the context in which
political philosophy arises, its historical setting and the "the
grounds of political realism," those naturally perplexing issues of
evil, punishment, and death that are found in every human life
and every human polity. The following two parts deal not with
those darker and unsettling realities of human life, but how these

1. Samuel Johnson, *Rasselas, Poems and Selected Prose,* ed. Bertrand Bronson
(New York: Holt, Rinehart, and Winston, 1958), 32–33 (italics added).

123

issue into some sort of higher resolution, a resolution that the accurate reflection on these questions seems to have suggested.

Moreover, it is not merely the more disturbing sides of human life that lead to questions of the contemplative and revelational orders, but likewise those aspects of human life whose reality is not evil. Happiness, virtue, law, and science do not in themselves express a disorder in human nature, but its ordering, its perfection, even though these remain realities of a finite, fallible being that man remains in his essence.

Evil, punishment, and death challenge every order, to be sure, including those that are in themselves good. But in its own way, virtue must ask what it is itself "for," in its own goodness. We want to know the meaning of the truth we do discover in science and philosophy. We wonder about our limited but sometimes relatively good polities that we have organized by our laws. Above all, we wonder about our friendships.

Although we find these matters discussed in many fields, all of these issues are found in their deepest forms also in the political philosophers. Yet, often they are found there unreflected on or unanalyzed for their more profound implications. Just when the really perplexing issues arise—why friendship at its best most unsettles us—we are left with no further comment. Perhaps no topic more naturally and easily enables us to pass from the history of political philosophy to the natural context of its errors, and on to the good but somehow incomplete side of human nature than the classical treatments of the deaths of Socrates and Christ at the hands of the best states of their time.

These trials and deaths are the twin fonts of a claim on truth and universality that seeks to reach the particular depths of each individual and to the right order of each polity. No political philosophy will be finished or adequate that neglects them. By reflecting on them, the path beyond the brilliant errors through the tragic side of our nature will take on a new clarity. The answers that each presents will be possible answers, studied here not so much for themselves, but for the curious way they respond to questions accurately posed first in political philosophy.

2. *The Two Political Deaths*

Nowhere do the questions and tentative answers of the philosophers meet in a more graphic manner than in the accounts of the trials and deaths of Socrates and Christ. Nowhere do reason and revelation appear more vividly before each other and before the city. Here are graphically illustrated the themes of virtue, friendship, evil, hell, death, happiness, and salvation.

The individual deaths of Socrates and Christ, in their accounts from Plato and the Gospels, have an especially central and fruitful place in the ongoing philosophical reflections on politics. They naturally follow on a discussion of evil and death and mysteriously transcend both in their very telling. Yet the issues raised by each are intelligible in terms of political philosophy.

No exercise in political philosophy is more rewarding than a consideration of these two deaths. But these respective considerations are sobering ones. They reveal something not merely about abstract human nature, or about the characters of ancient Greeks, Jews, and Romans, but also about our own hearts.

These ancient narratives become disturbingly alive when they are again pondered by the student, by the potential philosopher, or by the ordinary man to whom they are likewise addressed. "Nothing can be great which is not right," Samuel Johnson wrote in *The Rambler,* on December 24, 1751.[2] Both the death of Socrates and the death of Christ bear in their unfolding a sense of greatness and a sense of rightness that confront the reality of each human being who reflects on them.

In religious environments, the death of Christ will be studied and meditated upon with little reference to Socrates.[3] In academic circles, though this practice is difficult to justify in principled intellectual terms, the death of Christ is treated less frequently than the death of Socrates. About the death of Christ will hang for the most part a kind of ominous silence. Few students will be asked

2. Ibid., 136.

3. See however, Romano Guardini, *The Death of Socrates: An Interpretation of the Platonic Dialogues,* trans. Basil Wrighton (New York: Sheed & Ward, 1948). See John Paul II on Socrates and Christ, *Crossing the Threshold of Hope* (New York: Knopf, 1994), 82–83.

to consider its circumstances and meaning; they will more often be asked to reflect on Socrates. The origin of this neglect almost invariably lies in politics or in intellectual bias.

This academic neglect of the death of Christ as an issue in political philosophy is unfortunate. No full understanding of political life can be claimed if either of these deaths, each with its particular theoretical and historical implications, is neglected. Traditional political reflection as we know it originates in these deaths. No two events in human history serve better to confront the question of the limited nature of the state and whether human life is completely defined and absorbed by the political.

The accounts of both deaths are easily available. These historical and philosophical narratives form basic poles of our literature. They confront issues that help us meet the full implications of the human condition in any era or polity.

3. Before the Civil Tribunal

Socrates and Christ were each in their turn executed by local civil authorities after a public trial. Though no doubt each trial contained minor irregularities that good lawyers of the time might question, each trial was technically legitimate in its own right. Neither Socrates nor Christ was an anarchist who in principle denied the need for and power of civil authority. By their words and actions, they acknowledged the validity, or at least the inevitability, of the legal processes against them. Both explicitly affirmed the legitimacy of political authority. Socrates was pleased to have been raised by the laws of Athens (*Crito*); by His answer to those who sought to entrap Him, "Render to Caesar the things that are Caesar's; and to God, the things that are God's" (Matthew, 22:22), Christ accepted the nature of political authority.

Both trials, while legally correct, served in their turn to condemn those who, it seems, irresponsibly brought them about and participated in them. Something was radically amiss and paradoxical in each trial; otherwise, we should never have heard of either trial. The narratives of the trials of Socrates in Plato and of Christ in the Gospels were themselves instruments to rectify the injustices undoubtedly perpetrated by their executions.

The legacy of these trials for every subsequent generation, the fact that men knew of them and reflected on them, served to limit political aberrations. Books, in other words, can redeem and restore justice and decency, if not to those judged unfairly, at least to their legacy among those who reflect on them. Subsequent legal codes can be formulated to try to prevent abuses found in these classical trials.

In the terms of political philosophy, the trial of Socrates is the easier event with which to deal. Socrates himself claimed a divine vocation, a voice that guided him, that was operative at his trial. The voice's silence indicated that Socrates was to go forth with the legal proceedings in peace. But Socrates did not see himself to be a god, nor did anyone else. Socrates was the philosopher.

Plato, through his dialogues, taught every subsequent potential philosopher to experience in his soul the drama of Socrates. He taught students to wonder whether the trial of the philosopher had to end this way. Was the conflict between philosophy and the city perennial, unavoidable? Would the city always kill the philosopher? But did not the philosopher disrupt the city's peace with his strange questions? The politician has his duty. There were false philosophies, false prophets. Or were all politicians cynical men like Callicles seemed to be in the *Gorgias*?

Christ, however wise, was not a philosopher. Both Plato and Christ taught in myths or stories or parables in which the most profound of philosophic and religious reflections were hidden.[4] The myths or parables both obscured the truth from the dangerous political authorities and enabled the truth to be grasped by the humble or by the wise. Christ, like Socrates, can be treated as a good man. In both cases a good man was brought to trial because there was a claim for truth involved in his being (in the case of Socrates) a philosopher or (in the case of Christ) the man-God.

Many writers and thinkers, after Socrates and Christ—Dostoyevsky is perhaps the most famous—have suspected that should their lives and trials have been repeated in other times or in other historical polities, the same thing would have happened to them. The study of the trials of Socrates and Christ is a study in the constancy of human nature.

---

4. See Leo Strauss, *Persecution and the Art of Writing* (Westport, Conn.: Greenwood, 1973), 22–37.

Socrates acknowledged this possibility, that his fate would be played out anywhere he went. He refused at his trial, when offered the chance, to accept banishment from Athens. He suspected that the same thing would have happened to him in Thebes as in Athens if he had insisted on philosophizing there. The deaths of Socrates and Christ revealed something disordered in human nature as such, something that required powers greater than politics to heal. The accurate, sober recounting of the deaths of Socrates and Christ is the fundamental exercise that a young potential philosopher must re-enact in his own mind and heart if he is to begin and progress in political philosophy as it relates to the highest things.

4. *The Fate of the Good Man*

Salvador de Madariaga wrote that each European student, about the time of his graduation from the university, should be given two books, one the dialogues on the death of Socrates as found in Plato and the other the descriptions of the death of Christ as found in the New Testament.[5] These books were to be given as testimonials from the ages, sobering gifts to inform those coming of age that their predecessors did know what human nature might do and how it might reflect on its deeds.

These young students, potential philosophers all, were to be given these accounts first to remind them of the depths of their own souls and second to keep them in touch with the central experience of Western, indeed of universal, civilization. In lieu of their actual presence at the trials and deaths of Socrates and Christ, these students were to reflect on the accounts we have of these trials because men, including themselves, were free. They were not determined to repeat these trials in every generation, but could very well do so. They could examine the causes that led to these trials in their own souls.

Neither Socrates nor Christ wrote a book, though the primary way we know of their lives and deaths is through books that testify to the reality of what they did, taught, and suffered. Both Socrates in his philosophy and Christ in his teaching intended to reach not

5. Salvador de Madariaga, "The Europe of the Four Karls," *The Tablet* (London) (June 23, 1973), 580–81.

just Athenian Greeks or Jewish or Roman politicians, but all men.
Even those who would not listen they sought or conversed with.
They claimed a universality that reached to the core of what it is
to be human. These experiences and teachings were not products
of one civilization. They were the foundations of civilization itself
against which all cultures and cities of all ages and places must
be judged and compared. These trials are not isolated incidents
of long ago. Both trials and deaths, together with their consequences, claim the attention of every person. They are the foundations of a universal philosophy and revelation.

In *The Republic* of Plato, we find an unsettling discussion in
Book Two of the fate of the good man who might appear in any
existing city. This brief but penetrating insight immediately followed the equally disturbing explanation of the ring of Gyges.
This latter story argued the prevailing opinion, common to most
men, that anyone in any society would do evil if he could. The
only thing that prevented anyone from doing evil was fear of de-
tection and law, not one's internal virtue. The young potential philosophers wanted to hear justice praised for its own sake. This is
why they sought out the philosopher.

The contrasting presentation to the myth of Gyges dealt with
what would happen in any existing state if a really good man suddenly appeared in it. In terms of the death of Christ, which took
place some four centuries after Socrates, these lines, written by
Plato, spoken by Glaucon, seem almost prophetic. Common opinion everywhere, in Glaucon's view, estimated that if a good man
were to appear in any existing state, most people would expect,
"that the just man who has such a disposition (of being actually
good) will be whipped; he'll be racked; he'll be bound; he'll have
both his eyes burned out; and, at the end, when he has undergone
every sort of evil, he'll be crucified and know that one shouldn't
wish to be, but to seem to be, just" (Bloom, 361e-62a).

These lines, in some reflective way, have served to connect Socrates and Christ through events and theories arising out of considerations proper to political philosophy. What Glaucon worried
might happen, did appear to have happened in the case of Christ.
Perhaps it is only coincidence; still, it is a fertile one in political
philosophy, not to be excluded out of hand as if the coincidence
could not bear fruit.

We need not consider Plato to have been a "prophet" of future events for writing these lines, though many believers (from some of the Fathers of the Church to the philosopher Eric Voegelin) have suspected something of revelation in the work of Plato. Rather, Plato was possessed of such an acute insight into abiding human nature that he could understand what it might do in extreme circumstances. Evidently Plato knew already that the response of men to the good, to a good man or to good acts, would not necessarily be good.

Men are not automatically good or bad because of their circumstances, societies, education, or the living examples of those among whom they live. Individual goodness and badness always remained the result of personal choice. Otherwise, the good man who appeared in any state would have called forth only a positive response of change or repentance, which, as Plato foresaw, was not necessarily the case. The good could occasion resentment, envy, and hatred by actually being good.

A parallel incident in the life of Christ is the case of the man with the withered arm. The Gospel of Mark gives this account, in which certain specific and hostile Pharisees were watching Christ to see if He would cure the man on the Sabbath,

so that they could bring a charge against him. He said to the man with the withered arm, "Come and stand out here." Then he turned to them: "Is it permitted to do good or to do evil on the Sabbath, to save life or to kill?" They had nothing to say; and looking around at them with anger and sorrow at their obstinate stupidity, he said to the man, "Stretch our your arm." He stretched it out and his arm was restored. But the Pharisees, on leaving the synagogue, began plotting against him with the partisans of Herod to see how they could make away with him. (3:1–6)

These few plotting Pharisees—not all Pharisees were so hard-hearted, of course—represent something that can exist in every human being. No one questioned the fact that the arm was restored or the marvel of it; but the response to something that was unambiguously good was not one of awe or rejoicing as we might have expected. It took the form of a plot to destroy someone who could do such a good deed. Plato's estimate of the fate of a good man in any existing society and the reaction of witnesses to an actual good, evidently miraculous, deed in the case of Christ seemed to correspond.

Men could and did, it seems, choose evil in the very face of the good. Both of these accounts serve to ground a realism that is essential to political philosophy if it is to deal with what actually can happen in human nature and history. If we do not understand that such reactions to good people or deeds are possible, we are not fit to deal with the actual human beings in existing cities where such things do occur.

5. Before the Hemlock and the Cross

In Aristotle's treatment of how we choose to do evil, we note that some good, however convoluted, is chosen in every evil act (Chapter IX). "There is some soul of goodness in things evil," we read in Shakespeare's *Henry V,* "would men observingly distill it out" (IV, i, ll. 4–5). In the death of Socrates and in the death of Christ, the people involved in carrying through the deed to its bitter conclusion manifest a kind of reluctance before what they do.

Socrates was given every chance to escape his fate. He could have chosen banishment or a small fine or begged mercy. The Athenians were annoyed that he "forced" them to execute him by leaving them no easy way out. They insisted on thinking that he mocked them when he proposed as the proper penalty for his presumed crime free room and board at the town expense. In his view, he had by his philosophy only benefitted the city. He saw no reason for punishment of any kind, however mitigated.

Pilate, the Roman governor, wanted the crowd to prefer Christ to Barabbas. Pilate wanted to execute a known criminal rather than one he himself and probably most others by comparison thought to be innocent. It was almost as if neither Socrates nor Christ really wanted to escape his fate. Nor did either want to let the judges and juries out of their own logic. Certainly neither would escape if it meant doing something wrong or refusing to do God's will in order to save his life.

Saving one's life at any cost meant that nothing higher than merely keeping alive was of any worth. Neither Socrates nor

Christ stood for this position that reduced all worth merely to staying alive. Both stood for the worth and validity of things higher than mere life. Both were courageous in the classical sense. But neither denied the worth of life itself.

Socrates did not desire to perish by the hemlock, nor Christ by the Cross. Neither wanted the responsible Athenian, Roman, or Jewish officials to act in the way that they did to force this conclusion. Yet, no one could legitimately treat either Socrates or Christ as a sort of public "suicide" because of the failure of the mechanisms of escape offered to each. Both would have been content had the judgment in their respective trials gone in their favor.

Socrates expressed surprise that he received as many votes for acquittal as he did and felt that he would not have been found guilty had not all three politicians—the poet, the craftsman, and the lawyer—joined in his accusation. Christ hoped that the agony would pass from Him. But He realized that He was to drink the chalice the Father gave to Him (Matthew 26:39). Christ told the disciples to put away their swords but implied that heavenly forces were available to Him though He did not choose to employ them (Matthew 26:52).

6. Responsibility for the Deaths of Socrates and Christ

In the examination of the deaths of Socrates and Christ, the first question needing clarification is that of the guilt of those responsible for their deaths. The case of Socrates seems clearer, because every member of the jury had to choose for or against him. Socrates thought that the particular three who accused him and prosecuted the trial, along with those who voted for his condemnation, were guilty.

Socrates added in *The Crito,* however, that this fact did not justify him in not observing the laws of Athens even when they condemned him to death. Only by obeying the laws of Athens, even in accepting execution by hemlock, could Socrates prove the superiority of philosophy to the city. Philosophy was a daily practice of death, Socrates taught. If he did not know whether death was good or bad, but he did know that ceasing to carry out his vocation was wrong, then—given a choice between death and doing something evil—the philosopher should choose death. Death, as Socrates reflected in the *Phaedo,* may have brought the finest of blessings.

In the case of Christ's trial and death, implications of some sort of "collective" guilt are to be avoided. In human affairs no such thing as "collective guilt" exists. All guilt must pass through the knowledge and will of some particular person. Obviously, important individual Romans and Jews of the time were directly responsible for the execution of Christ, whether He be judged innocent or guilty of the charges against Him. We know their names—Pilate, Judas, Annas, Caiphas, no doubt a few of the Roman soldiers and Sanhedrin members, and at least some in the crowd who called for Christ's death. Some of these latter evidently thought Him guilty of violating a religious claim that in local law, rightly or wrongly, carried the death penalty. There were cries from the crowd before Pilate to "crucify Him" (Matthew 27:23). To others, some of the leaders especially, this legal aspect seemed more of a pretext than an honest examination of the man's position. Some simply wanted Him out of the way.

Pilate bore responsibility for the justice and legality of the trial itself. He did not think Christ was guilty of trying to subvert Roman jurisdiction or authority (Luke, 22:22). When he asked those crowded about the Praetorium in the scene with Barabbas whether he should "execute their king," they cried back, "We have no king but Caesar" (John, 19:16). This affirmation was not the real position of most of those present, who in fact did not recognize Caesar as their king.

Pilate, for his part, did not present Christ as someone who threatened to undermine Caesar, the almost invincible political and military power in the area. Pilate found no fault in Christ, no political ambitions. But even should He have had such ambitions, He had no armed forces at his disposal that could be any threat to Rome. Thus Pilate tried to wash his hands of any personal responsibility for what happened. No one who follows these episodes thinks this action of Pilate exempted him from responsibility for the deed.

Josef Ratzinger wrote of Pilate's inner conflict with himself about what to do with Christ:

The truth often makes people uncomfortable; it is probably the strictest of teachers in the process of learning unselfishness and real freedom. Let us take the example of Pilate. He knows for a fact that the accused Jesus is innocent and that according to justice, he should acquit him. He even wants to do so. But then this truth begins to conflict with his position; it threatens him with inconvenience, of even the loss of his post. Public disturbances could arise; he may be made to appear in an unfavorable light with Caesar and similar fears. And so he prefers to sacrifice the truth, which neither cries out nor defends itself, even if its betrayal leaves behind in his soul the dull ache of failure.[6]

Pilate, the politician, knew the truth, but this truth conflicted with his position. His position led him to compromise the truth, though one of his duties was to uphold it (for the Romans stood for justice and fairness). Politics and philosophy crossed.

Christ was executed by crucifixion, a terrible penalty whose infliction the Romans, for reasons of state, reserved to themselves. (Jewish law executed by stoning, as happened to St. Stephen [Acts of the Apostles 7:58].) Crucifixion was a particularly effective form of deterrent and required the Roman governor's consent to its use in executing criminals dangerous to the Roman power. The Roman governor was more or less equivalent to a governor of a minor outlying state within a federal union.

Before this particular crucifixion, which was foreshadowed in Plato, Pilate discussed with Christ the nature of both Christ's and his own authority, particularly the authority over life and death that is in the hands of political rulers. The discussion was not over whether capital punishment was morally right or not. Neither Christ nor Pilate nor the Jewish leaders—nor Socrates, for that matter—questioned whether capital punishment was legitimate if it was legal, justly tried, and followed a public purpose. Christ affirmed that Pilate had authority.

7. The Extent of Public Authority

The real question was whether Christ claimed a political authority that would threaten either Jewish or Roman power. When Christ refused to answer any more of Pilate's questions because He evidently thought the Roman official to be either weak or dis-

6. Josef Ratzinger, "Focus: Some Perspectives . . . ," *30 Days* (February 1990): 49.

honest, Pilate asked Him if He did not know that he, Pilate, had the power of life and death over Him. Christ responded in a phrase which has become classic in political philosophy, namely, that Pilate would have no authority at all over Him were it not given to him by His Father. Christ evidently was silent not because He did not understand the mechanics of politics but because He did. Pilate's problem was not theoretical, but whether he would actually be just in the case before him.

The Romans could claim with some justice to have been the fairest and wisest of the ancient conquerors. Their reputation for justice was why St. Paul, later on in the Acts of the Apostles (22:22–29; 25:12), would prefer to let his own case be tried by the Romans rather than any other tribunal. Christ was not interested in the theoretic question of whether Pilate, as a Roman governor, held legitimate political authority in Palestine. The Romans, as had the Greeks before them, controlled this area by conquest. Christ acknowledged that Pilate had de facto political authority, and He expected him to use it justly. But would Pilate uphold the Roman reputation for justice?

When Christ told Pilate in his interview that His "kingdom was not of this world," it was sufficient to convince Pilate that Christ, whatever He taught, did not threaten Rome with political subversion. This incident with the Roman governor is the foundation of a long subsequent discussion about the meaning of those things "not of this world," the things to be rendered to God. The things not belonging to Caesar became of central importance to every man to free him from the invalid claims of the state or other institution (Acts 4:19–20). Christ told Pilate that he, Pilate, would have no authority at all over Him if it did not come from His Father. He recognized both that political authority has its justification in human nature and that Pilate was engaged in a specific act involving this same political authority.

This passage in the Gospel of John (19:11) about political authority, together with Paul's remark in his Epistle to the Romans (13:1–7), that all authority comes from God and so we should obey the emperor, parallels the Greek argument that man is by nature a political animal. Man needs a polity to be fully what he is in his givenness. But this scriptural account adds to the Greek idea of the naturalness of political authority the notion that this authority ultimately stems from an intelligent and willed source in the Godhead. Political authority is not merely an abstract principle or form. Political authority and hence political life are not merely philosophically justified but religiously grounded. Neither of these foundations contradicts the other, but in fact they are directly related as complete to incomplete.

The breaking of moral laws, acting against virtue, is not only a violation of some abstract rationale or system. It is a rejection of human nature and of the personal cause of human nature. This is why virtue as a philosophic concept implies something more than itself. The "rebellion" against the goodness of *what man is* that we have seen to exist in human nature finds its ultimate root here.

Evil, in its medieval and modern understanding, has much greater depth than it did among the Greeks because its consequences are more visible and more grounded. Human disorders are "sins," not just rational errors or psychological quirks, because they involve a chosen disorder of a personal nature. The deep seriousness of human life is manifest in every responsible action. Each action in principle reaches the cause of personal being itself, a cause that also bears the marks of personhood.

8. The Essential Teaching

Socrates had defined philosophy as but a preparation for death. The highest act of life arose at the very moment when life ceased. The burden of philosophy was to tell us this truth. Socrates spent his last day in jail talking with his friends, who were amazed at his calmness. This last day has sometimes been called Socrates' "second trial," the one demanded by the potential philosophers not satisfied with the reasons given before the public jurors. What did they all talk about? They talked of a subject that surprised Socrates' companions—the immortality of the soul. The soul was immortal, not just in the sense that our deeds lived on after us in the polity, but in the sense that some specific, personal existence continued after death.

If in death, however, we would be rid of those impediments that prevent our understanding the right order of things, we would be rid of those "ills" that prevent us from busying ourselves with the highest things as our normal lot. The freedom of death, in the Greek view, caused us to be rid of the bodily impediments that prevent us from knowing in its highest forms.

In this analysis, political things can lose their ultimate focus when they are not seen in the light of a preparation for death. The moral and political injustices we commit in our polity cause us at least to worry, as did Cephalus in the First Book of *The Republic*, about how we should atone for our evils. We must inquire whether it is possible for us to atone by repaying our debts or offering sacrifices.

The New Testament teaches that by ourselves we cannot forgive our own sins or evils, though they can be forgiven when acknowledged for what they are before those who have the "power" to forgive sins, a power always conceived to be not merely human. Forgiveness implies an unchangeable standard against which we measure our actions. In a relativist or historicist morality, where evil is contingent and subject to change, no forgiveness is possible, only a change in the definition of evil or of what is to be forgiven.

The teaching of *The Republic* was that we have one life to live. It should be lived rightly the first time. We will not recognize real good if we deflect ourselves from it in our choices. Socrates held that we should seek the good in speech. Christ taught that we should first "seek the Kingdom of God" (Luke 13:31). Right order toward the highest things alone made the order of worldly things to be intelligible and capable of being rightly situated among human priorities.

Neither Socrates nor Christ intimated that the life of man in this world was in itself evil, though separation from matter seemed for Socrates to be the way to avoid evil. But neither professed to find in existing political life the highest things for which human beings were made. Both Socrates and Christ taught these lessons to the world because they both once appeared, however reluctantly, as public figures in their own polities. Without their polities, we would not have known of them. Without the traditions and books in which these events were recorded, we would not now be able to ponder them as guides to the highest things.

9. Forgiveness

If there is any striking difference between the death of Socrates and that of Christ, it is found in the doctrine of forgiveness. "The discoverer of the role of forgiveness in the realm of human affairs was Jesus of Nazareth," Hannah Arendt wrote.

The only rudimentary sign of an awareness that forgiveness may be the necessary corrective for the inevitable damages resulting from action may be seen in the Roman principle to spare the vanquished—a wisdom entirely unknown to the Greeks—or in the right to commute the death sentence, probably also of Roman origin, which is the prerogative of nearly all Western heads of state.[7]

Pilate, in the case of Barabbas, sought to exercise this power to commute, or at least exchange, a death sentence.

The notion of forgiveness is of particular force in political philosophy. Forgiveness is directed to the limits of justice, the primary political virtue and concern. Christ taught that we should love our enemies and do good to those who hate us. He did not, to be clear, deny that justice is a virtue nor that we might have "enemies" whom we should identify as such.

No doubt, as Plato observed in the First Book of *The Republic*, we could confuse our enemies for our friends and our friends for our enemies. The fact is, in experience, that not everyone loves us and some would even hate us. The most difficult teaching of the New Testament concerns the love of our enemies. The love of enemies was not a naive blindness toward those who would harm us or others, nor was it an unwillingness to admit that there could be and often were those who hated us for no just cause, nor was it a doctrine of pacifism preventing us to protect ourselves or others.

Christ asked His Father to forgive those who executed Him "for they know not what they do" (Luke 23:34). The question of the guilt of those who executed Christ must be seen in this light, without denying that some basic crime was committed in killing Christ (Acts 3:17). The whole of the New Testament begins in Mark with a doctrine of repentance and forgiveness (1:5, 15).

---

7. Hannah Arendt, *The Human Condition* (Garden City, N.Y.: Doubleday Anchor, 1959), 214–15.

This doctrine does not teach that we are so weak that we can do nothing right, but that we are so strong and autonomous that we can do evil to others if we will. This doctrine can hold true only if there is something to repent and if there is someone to whom our deeds, particularly our evil deeds, made any difference. One cannot "repent" principles. We can only prove them right or wrong.

Christ was continually in trouble for His claim to forgive sins. This power was considered to be, and is, a divine power. The claim was either blasphemous or implied that Christ was God. Christ often used miraculous incidents to call attention to or to prove His power to forgive sins. In such actions, evidently He did claim to be divine. Forgiveness meant that the experience we have of the unending disorder caused by our evil actions could be stopped, but not by ourselves alone.

An action that began in family or civil life, with consequences in either family or polity in the lives of others, could not be totally confronted by political means. Here again, reason and revelation are strangely juxtaposed. A problem that arises in experience and a solution that is proposed in revelation confront each other in an intellectual context in which it looks, at least, as if they ought to be related. One possible solution, forgiveness for admitted moral disorders, appears to exist. But the solution cannot be considered intellectually until the problem of the consequences of evil are confronted.

The harshness of justice indicated that there should be a power to mitigate its strict demands in the name of some higher public good. This necessity is why Aristotle has a virtue called "equity" in the Fifth Book of *The Ethics,* to deal with the cases where the letter of justice is too harsh. The Greek polity itself was designed to stop the unending sequence of vengeance. With no political judgment or coercion to stop the cycles of vengeance, punishment follows punishment unceasingly. In *The Republic,* Plato stressed not law but the wisdom of the philosopher-king to prevent disorders. Complete justice needed to concern itself with the particular, not only the general case, in order that everyone's total life might be accounted for.

Perhaps we need not look to rightness or wrongness, but to expediency. Thucydides, in the famous debate about Mytilene

(*Peloponesian Wars* III, 2), held that the questions of politics are not decided primarily in terms of justice or guilt but in terms of what course of action might be best for a state to follow for its higher good. This political approach, however, did not directly address itself to what was at issue in the case of forgiveness. Repentance and forgiveness are two sides of the same coin. One cannot be forgiven without repentance except in the external political sense. No doubt even if someone who offends us does not repent, we can still forgive him in our hearts. The real test arises when the admittedly guilty party repents and asks for our forgiveness. Do we always insist on justice, the problem Shakespeare presented in *The Merchant of Venice*?[8]

Guilt involves "knowing what we do." If those few who saw to it that Christ was crucified for a political crime "did not know what they did," as Christ Himself said of them (Luke 23:34), were they then guilty of nothing? What they did not know was who Christ was in the fullness of His being. Even if Christ was only human, they were still guilty of an unjust act. But, as we suggested, the formalities of the law were followed in the instance of Christ's execution. This point indicates the difference between external legality and morality. But if Christ were a fraud, which some probably held, then "we have a law and according to that law He must die" (John 19:7). Subjectively, some of these people could have been acting justly.

10. *The Limits of Justice*

The full implications of the doctrine of forgiveness can only be seen in terms of the limits of justice. Justice has a certain infinity about it. The quid pro quo of justice, the eye for an eye of the Old Testament, leads from one act that seems unjust to another in revenge that seems equally unjust. No stopping the actions of justice is possible unless something intervenes to interrupt its multiple retaliations. What can this intervention be? It is clearly forgiveness.

Aquinas argued that revelation was necessary because of the limits of natural reasoning (Ia-IIae, 91, 4). By ourselves we could

8. See Allan Bloom, "On Christian and Jew: 'The Merchant of Venice,'" in *Shakespeare's Politics* (Chicago: University of Chicago Press, 1964), 13–34.

reach a high notion of justice, but human law could not regulate our inner thoughts and plottings, from which real evils flow. Revelation tells us not merely not to kill, but not to plan to kill, not to formulate disordered ideas and musings.

Real disorder in the world originates not in the actions of men as such but in those practical thoughts from which actions followed. Since the law of the state and the capacity of men to judge others did not reach to the interior of a person's thoughts, the only way these thoughts could be ordered would be by a divine admonition or law, the effect of which was to challenge or incite the person to order those thoughts of his that might lead to civil or personal disorder. Revelation remained contingent on freedom for its effects in the world, but it did address the problem of the origins of human disorders. There was a congruence between the problem as it appeared in political life, when properly formulated, and an answer suggested by revelation for free men to consider.

11. *The Location of the Best Regime*

Plato came to hold, because of the death of Socrates, that "The Republic" could not be located in any actual city, such as Athens. Nor could it be in Rome, as Cicero had taught it might be. Was it illegitimate, therefore, to ask the question about the location of this "Republic" or, in terms Christ used with Pilate, of "the Kingdom" of God (John 18:37)? St. Augustine was enthralled by Plato's endeavors to articulate the city in speech.

The question of the best city arose naturally and logically from the existence of differing cities of different qualities, good and bad. But Plato found that the best city existed only in speech, only in argument or dialectics. As a reader of the Old and New Testaments, St. Augustine was a realist in his treatment of ultimate things. St. Augustine held that Plato was not wrong in seeking the best regime, but only in thinking that its location in speech, however valid for the pursuit of dialectics, would satisfy men.

The "City of God" (a phrase found in Psalm 87) for St. Augustine had an existence and a real population composed of all those intelligent beings who would choose to love God above themselves. Those who chose themselves had their own city of man, which included only themselves. The loving oneself, for St. Augustine, meant the placing of one's own ideas of blessedness, good, and evil over any consideration of what God had established. The members of this latter "city of man" were those who, in the words of Genesis (2:17), ate of the "tree of the knowledge of good and evil." It was composed of those who lived out their own definitions of good and evil, not the ones that came from God through nature and reason. Philosophy reached exalted heights but could not satisfactorily answer its own question about the location of the best regime and its inhabitants. But philosophy knew the question was a legitimate one.

St. Augustine called Cicero, the great Roman philosopher, to witness to the inadequacy of the answers of the philosophers:

The blessings which men crave (in this life) are not invariably bestowed upon them, lest religion should be cultivated for the sake of these temporal advantages, while it ought rather to be cultivated for the sake of that other life from which all evil is excluded. Therefore, also, does grace aid good men in the midst of present calamities, so that they are enabled to endure them with a constancy proportioned to their faith.

The world's sages affirm that philosophy contributes something to this—that philosophy which, according to Cicero, the gods have bestowed in its purity on only a few men. They have never given, he says, nor can ever give, a greater gift to men. So that even those against whom we are disputing have been compelled to acknowledge, in some fashion, that the grace of God is necessary for the acquisition, not indeed of any philosophy but of the true philosophy. And if the true philosophy—this sole support against the miseries of this life—has been given by Heaven only to a few, it sufficiently appears from this that the human race has been condemned to pay this penalty of wretchedness. And as, according to their acknowledgement, no greater gift has been bestowed by God, so it must be believed that it could be given only by that God whom they themselves recognize as greater than all the gods they worship.[9]

St. Augustine was not content with a solution to the problem of the City of God that included only a few philosophers, none of

---

9. St. Augustine, *The City of God*, XXII, 20–22; see translation by W. Oates (New York: Random House, 1948), 641–46.

whom could have reached the true solution to his own problems by himself alone. In this sense, revelation re-proposes the conflict of poetry and philosophy to encompass a destiny that might include all men, even the nonphilosophers, though this solution again was not political in its primary purpose.

This conclusion meant that the highest things were intended for more than just the philosophers. The doctrine of forgiveness joins the realism of actual politics, for it is clear that very few if any in actual regimes are perfectly good. The doctrine of forgiveness is not addressed to the reformation of civil regimes, though it can indirectly affect them. Rather it is directed to the condition of most men who are sinners or fallen, to human beings who actually do evil deeds which call forth revenge or justice. Forgiveness can stop the actions of revenge. But forgiveness is the sole possibility for most men, non-philosophers not the least, for reaching the highest things.

From the dialogues of Plato, we know that Socrates argued that his soul was immortal. As we will see in discussing the classic teaching on friendship, something was inadequate about this teaching, because the soul was not the whole Socrates. The death of Christ was followed by the resurrection. The death of Christ was followed not by a philosophic teaching in which His thoughts were preserved, though this preservation was also done by Church and Scripture in His case, but by an announcement and witnessing that He was risen, body and spirit.

In New Testament teaching, all men were destined for completion in a manner beyond Socrates' immortality of the soul. The resurrection of the body restored the human being to his created fullness, body and soul. But the status of each would depend on his free choices, on his repentance, and on his being forgiven. Nothing was nonpersonal in the highest things; it was precisely a "communion," a city, an interchange. Their "city" was decided by their thoughts and actions, but the whole of the person was to remain, no matter which way the choice was made. Resurrection was of both the just and the unjust. The New Testament teaching on forgiveness did not hold that everyone would be saved, but it did hold this as a possibility. It could do no more, because a free being had to choose to act well or ill. The reality of what it was to do evil or to do good remained to define the moral world in all times and places, including in what came to be known as heaven and hell.

The enigmas that political philosophy confronted, both in the doctrines of the limits of justice and in the rewards and punishments connected with justice, found their possible solution in the revelational teaching of forgiveness, salvation, resurrection, and freedom. But political philosophy had also treated the more classical issues to which the teachings of Socrates and Christ gave rise—those of happiness and of virtue and vice, issues that now must be considered in more detail, for they are the theoretical background within which the incomplete feelings of political philosophy had their origins.

The surprising horizons of political philosophy thus include not merely questions dealing with the origins and meaning of evil, punishment, and death, but also questions dealing with man at his best. Even more strikingly than the questions connected with the natural origins of the bitter and brilliant errors of our thinkers do the philosophic reflections on happiness and the worth of virtue lead beyond themselves, all the while containing within themselves the roots of the realities on which they are based.

Unless these questions are asked in the beginning and formulated in political philosophy, it will not be clear why certain answers stand in the otherwise enigmatic form that they do. Political philosophy has the distinction of treating such questions and realities as its own questions, even as they open up onto vistas that, while not expected, still appear worthy of consideration. The deaths of Christ and Socrates, paradoxically, are events in our history that, more than any others, can guide us to considerations not only of evil and death, but also of virtue and friendship, to the things of uncommon importance that lie at the limits of political philosophy.

EIGHT

Happiness and Salvation

"Every man is sufficiently discontented with some circumstances of his present life, to suffer his imagination to range more or less in quest of future happiness. . . ."
—SAMUEL JOHNSON, *The Rambler*, April 3, 1750[1]

"Mrs. Knowles. 'The Scripture tells us, "The righteous shall have hope in his death".' Johnson. 'Yes, Madam; that is, he shall not have despair. But, consider, his hope of salvation must be founded on the terms on which it is promised that the mediation of our SAVIOUR *shall be applied to us,—namely, obedience; and where obedience has failed, then, as suppletory to it, repentance. But what man can say that his obedience has been such, as he would approve of in another, or even in himself upon close examination, or that his repentance has not been such as to require being repented of? No man can be sure that his obedience and repentance will obtain salvation.'"*
—*Boswell's Life of Johnson*, 1778[2]

1. The Contrast of Happiness and Salvation

In this chapter and the one following, I will continue to discuss the relation of questions in Greek philosophy and in revelation. The context will be a clarification of a curious incompleteness (or, better, an openness) in finite things even when they are doing what is proper to them. This incompleteness is provocative. We cannot leave it alone. In Aristotle's *Ethics*, the end and purpose of

1. Samuel Johnson, *Rasselas, Poems and Selected Prose*, ed. Bertrand H. Bronson (New York: Holt, Rinehart, and Winston, 1958), 65.
2. *Boswell's Life of Johnson* (London: Oxford, 1931), II, p. 223.

all human activity, including virtue and friendship, is called "happiness." In the revelational tradition we read of "eternal happiness," but it is described as "salvation."

Since both words, happiness and salvation, describe that for which human beings exist, the clarification of these two understandings will serve to make more precise the meaning of subsequent topics in political philosophy. With the trials of Socrates and Christ, we have already seen that central issues of philosophy and revelation do relate intriguingly to political philosophy. Here I would add that political philosophy is most fascinating when it deals with its own highest topics because of the way these topics remain unfinished, almost as if they stand before the horizon at dawn waiting for further light.

Happiness is what we desire to achieve by and in our living. Without being "selfish" in any pejorative sense, happiness is intended to be what we want for ourselves according to the level and kind of being we find ourselves to be given. Our own happiness and the happiness of others ought not to be conceived as if they were intrinsically contradictory to each other. Being by nature a political and social being means just this recognition of a proper place for every different person in a common whole.

In principle it is not necessary, at the heart of why we exist, to posit some struggle or need. The diversity and orderedness in our being was the teaching of Plato in the *Republic*, where the philosopher-king was to see the proper place for everyone in the whole. Mutual love means that our happiness includes the happiness of another. The fact that this love can be denied does not obscure its central teaching. Roughly, this is what St. Augustine said when he remarked that "two loves built two cities."

When happiness is conceived in principle to be at the expense of another's good, it is difficult to see how we can speak of the happiness of all. But if happiness has no objective content, no objection can be proposed to the seeking of one's own happiness at the expense of another's. Even though our own activities can and do contribute to or interfere with the presumed happiness of other human beings, the happiness of one human being does not in itself take away from the happiness of anyone else, at least not without the other's consent or our own disorder. This personal status before some good given to us is why the problem of evil

must be included in political philosophy. Happiness is not opposed to the good unless some choice is involved which puts them
into conflict.

Happiness is the subject matter of the Greek notion of the ethical and political life, whereas salvation describes what the religious man seeks above all. The classical Greek authors sought to
spell out the experience of every person in any place or time that
would cause him to ask the questions, "What is happiness?" "How
can I attain it?" The religious man asked rather, "Can I be saved?"
But was it possible to be happy and not to be saved? Or could
someone who was not happy still be saved? On whom or what did
happiness or salvation depend? On ourselves? On other human
beings? On society? On God?

The philosophical question of happiness was concerned with
the essence of happiness, with what it was, rather than with the
factual question of whether anyone actually attained it—though
for the Greeks, knowing what it was, was itself an essential part
of its reality. What happiness was, which was the subject matter
especially of Books I and X of Aristotle's *Ethics*, seemed to be a
vital and necessary question to ask even if no one actually ever
attained it. Questions could be formulated that seemed to have
no answers. Yet, even Aristotle insisted that happiness was an activity, not something merely intelligible or abstract.

Salvation was concerned with the given individual, even the
worst sinner or criminal, in his ultimate status. The question of
salvation seemed to defy the assumptions of philosophy and politics. Salvation promised something that neither philosophy nor
politics could claim to provide.[3] The happiness described by the
philosophers seemed either fleeting or incomplete. Certain para-
doxes in philosophic and political life made each life seem incomplete in the very experiences in which each life was most itself.
Neither political happiness, in which all the practical virtues were
able to be activated, nor theoretic happiness, devoted to understanding the highest things, guaranteed an individual's concern
about his own status.

No philosopher or saint would deny that happiness and sal-

---

3. The most complete and accurate notion of salvation as it is found particularly in the Catholic tradition is described in *The Catechism of the Catholic Church*
(Vatican City: Libreria Editrice Vaticana, 1994), nos. 122, 124, 161, 169.

vation, in their own ways, addressed questions intrinsic to every human life, addressed questions, indeed, that initially arise, at least in part, in family and political life. Happiness is that purpose or end for which we do all that we do, including the living of human life itself. Happiness pervades every action that we perform through the human capacities we receive from nature. Happiness has no meaning if it is not something that properly belongs to us, something that is ours. No doubt, the discussions of happiness by Aristotle in Books I and X of his *Ethics* remain classic texts for any consideration of this topic.

We arrive at the meaning of happiness when we critically reflect on ourselves, on our activities. We can distinguish within ourselves the different capacities and the actions flowing from those capacities. We can see the objects of our capacities, their particularities, their fullness, and even their failures. Happiness includes the reflective intellectual ability to discover and elaborate what happiness itself means and that this elaboration is a concern we find in ourselves. The "unexamined life" that was not worth living, as Socrates noted at his trial (38A), was one that made no effort to arrive at a true understanding of what happiness meant for a human being.

The very challenge of human life includes the power, indeed the obligation, to find out what this life is about. Happiness looks to ourselves to bring it forth. Yet, what it is in itself is not totally of our own design or making. This element of givenness in happiness, that it is not totally ours to define or make for ourselves, is the best thing about it. This givenness indicates that we are designed for more than even we could anticipate or conjecture. This superabundance is not just a wish but the perceived tendency in nature as it relates to us.

Salvation relates to something outside of ourselves that we want but which we cannot give to ourselves. Salvation would seem to imply that when we know all we can know about happiness, there is, because of what we learn about it, something missing, something incomplete. The good philosopher is the one who is the most perplexed by salvation and what it implies.

Happiness indicates a dignity that we must accomplish in ourselves by activating the potential of our nature. But we must achieve this completion on the basis of what we already are and have. Our finiteness makes the happiness we do achieve seem insufficient. But if there is to be a completion, we want it for ourselves. Neither happiness nor salvation can mean anything if somehow we become someone else or some other sort of creature. The question of happiness arises within us, for it asks the ultimate question of what it is we are about in the particular lives we lead.

Happiness thus means nothing if it is not ours. Happiness is something we want for ourselves. We cannot not want happiness whatever it is. Even when we think that we reject it, we seek it in the very act of rejecting it. Those who despair do not deny it. What they deny is the existence of any way for them to achieve it.

Our active seeking of happiness is not to be seen as separate from our individual choices to do this or that particular thing. Rather, each thing we do, on reflection, is an attempt to achieve the sort of happiness we finally decide will constitute the meaning of our particular lives. Each particular life has an objective meaning that arises out of its own pursuit of the happiness it seeks for itself. Happiness, moreover, seems to be multipliable. Happiness indicates an unsuspected abundance in the universe about the highest things.

2. *The Elements of Happiness*

Happiness, what it is, even though we must still choose it when we know it, is discovered, not made by ourselves. Human beings have many activities that are under their rational and voluntary control. The differing powers and the activities flowing from them, as we shall see later, define the differing virtues found in us. These activities should be brought forth from the potential capacity that is given with human nature itself from its beginnings in conception and birth. Man appears in nature as already man, a certain kind of being who eventually can reflect on what he is and know what is not himself. His reflective activity is his evident purpose in being and the activity through which he comes to know himself.

Man can know himself only by first knowing something that is not himself. We are not direct objects of our own intelligences. We depend on the existence of a world of things not ourselves even to know ourselves. In knowing something else, not ourselves, we are reflectively aware that it is we who know something that is not ourselves. Only if he recognizes that he already is human, a certain kind of being with his own reality given to him, can man properly begin to understand himself. We need to identify the differing activities open to man and to posit their relative relationship to each other. The relative hierarchy of the virtues, the relation of the active and contemplative virtues, the relation of the active virtues to each other, are essential elements in our understanding of happiness and how it is to be achieved.[4]

Aristotle called happiness the appropriate activities of all the virtues. These virtues were acquired habits to guide us easily and with purpose in doing the right thing at the right time and in the right circumstances in those areas—our fears, pleasures, wealth, anger, manners, thoughts—in which we could and should rule ourselves. When he came to give a more complete definition in Book X of the *Ethics,* Aristotle said that happiness was the activity of the virtues, and, if there was a highest virtue, the activity of that virtue, presupposed to the others, in a complete life. Happiness included the practical and the theoretical virtues. Happiness contained something both from nature and from our own rational and voluntary use of what we have been given in that particular human nature that causes us to be what we already are.

The technical terms "first nature" and "second nature," terms often used in discussions of human virtue, were meant to clarify the distinction between being and action. The first expression referred to our being human beings and not, say, toads or sharks. The second indicated what it was we did with that given nature under our immediate control, whether we made ourselves into good or bad human beings in our choices and thoughts. Our dignity in the chain of being, in our relation to plants, animals, and gods, was due to first nature, which caused us to be human beings. We ourselves had nothing to do with this nature being given to us. Our worth, our stature was due to our second nature, that over which we had control by virtue of our reason and will.

Second nature referred to what we did with our capacities. We were the beings whose very nature and purpose it was to complete themselves by themselves through living in a world of others like

4. See *Josef Pieper—an Anthology* (San Francisco: Ignatius Press, 1989), 27–87.

themselves. Without human presence, the world was not "finished." It did not fulfill its real purpose unless men themselves became what they were intended to be. The world itself became actively intelligible and articulate only through man. This articulateness and intelligence demanded on man's part some kind of further response. This response is called "gratitude" if man accepts what he is as good. If he does not, his response takes the form of "rebellion."

3. *The Order of Things*

If we contrast the notion of happiness with that of salvation, we can see how the two notions are related to each other. The consideration of happiness in its most complete meaning leads us to a further analysis of salvation for the one who is philosophically happy. Happiness and salvation have very different but not contradictory origins and purposes. Their intellectual challenge is whether they can be reconciled.

Happiness focuses on our own activity, while not neglecting the objects of this activity—indeed, delighting in them. Each activity we find in ourselves has some objective relation to what is not ourselves. We have fear as a power of our given being, but what frightens us comes into our lives from outside ourselves, or at least from outside our own intelligence and will. This characteristic is true of the other objects of the virtues.

Ancient Epicurean philosophers maintained that fear of the gods was what caused our unhappiness. To eliminate our fears, we should get rid of the gods. These Epicureans were attempting to use philosophy itself to remove discontents that seemed to arise outside of ourselves. This radical solution failed in its very premises because philosophy did not demonstrate that the gods did not exist, nor did it reveal that fear of them was simply irrational. It even appeared that fear was itself a good and constituent part of our being as such, so the question was not to remove the gods but to ask why fear was given to us as a good of our being. Thus, in Ecclesiastes (1:13) we could even read, in the revelational tradition, that fear of the Lord was the beginning of wisdom.

While it is something we desire for ourselves, happiness is not dependent on ourselves as the Epicureans thought. Rather we recognize that what is not ourselves contains the secret to our happiness. We are beings who have our own limited autonomy and independence, yet we are incomplete. We cannot wholly give to ourselves that which would make us most ourselves. The Platonic conclusion to the existence of a Good-in-Itself or the Aristotelian First Mover was conceived to be the highest content that philosophic happiness could attain. It was a constituent element of happiness to know *all that is*, including the reality of God insofar as the human mind could know it.

Happiness, to be complete, included the possession of what causes us to be happy. We could not really be happy if we knew of the existence of something that seemed the center of meaning, yet a something that had nothing to do with us. Aristotle spoke of the fact that we were not, by ourselves, "self-sufficient," by which he meant that we needed more than ourselves to complete or fulfill what we actually were. The world and its goods that we needed if we were to live at all, let alone live well, were there for us to understand and to work on for our purposes.

These goods or things, moreover, were there before we were, though it is our intelligence that identifies what they are. It is our hands and wills that enable them to be fashioned into human purposes. Human happiness included the notion that the re-forming of the world by human hand and understanding for man's purposes, from the most ordinary to the highest thing, was what the world was for. The things lower on the scale of being than man—animals, plants, minerals—are themselves, what they are. But also they exist for those beings who exist knowingly for their own sake, for human beings. This is why the struggles with ecology and environmentalism are also philosophical and theological struggles that deal with the nature of man as such, with whether he is merely an accident in the universe or intrinsically related to its own purpose.

The world indeed became a better and fuller world because of the fact that it was the proper object of human intelligence and action following on it. The relationship of world and mind was not itself unthinkable. This relationship did not mean that man in his own proper activities could not abuse nature by this same human capacity. But it did indicate a potential harmony in all existing things, which was manifest most graphically by man's ca-

pacity to understand and use things for his own purposes because
he could understand their purposes.

The world could be a better world because of the existence of
man in it. But it could also become a worse place. This realization
was why Aristotle would say that man, at his best, is the best of
beings, but at his worst, he is worse than any of the animals, because his intelligence allows him to multiply the effects of evil far
beyond any natural defect or insufficiency.

4. *Philosophic and Political Happiness*

Human happiness, as Aristotle taught, was of two kinds or levels quite directly related to each other. The highest happiness,
contemplative happiness, had to do with the philosophic understanding of the highest things, with that power of understanding
that seemed to be the highest faculty in man. This philosophic
activity included the question of the soul's immortality. Through
philosophy, man realized that he was made for something more
than a practical life.

Practical happiness, on the other hand, referred to man's life
on earth insofar as he was on earth, during the years of human
life before death. This practical life was that of the composite single whole. Practical happiness, the life of mortal man on earth,
was real enough and could not be neglected, for it made possible
the leisure required for philosophic activity. It consisted first in
reason's ordering each of man's faculties to himself, then to others
in a family and in a civil society. Finally, reason looks to its own
order. Its highest function is to know the highest things.

Practical or political happiness meant that man's personal "insufficiency" was overcome in the polity or civilization. What was
necessary and abundant for the physical and moral life of man
could be formed and put in order by human activity over time.
To do this was one of man's purposes, why he was a political being
whose nature it was to erect an order in which he could live well.

The possibility of moral life itself depended on man's own free
choices and on his technical activities from his mind and his
choices. These activities, in turn, led to questions that were no
longer simply moral, to realities that did not fall into man's own
control. Moral life was designed to leave men free clearly and hon-

estly to wonder about the sort of world that they lived in and their place within it. Conversely, when men did not properly understand the kind of world they were in and their place in it, the chances were that they could not live a moral and complete human life, because they did not know what they were or the nature of the happiness for which they existed.

Neither Plato nor Aristotle thought that most men would reach a high degree of practical virtue. They held that most civil orders would be imperfect in some identifiable degree. Both nevertheless recognized virtue's possibility or meaning. Even though it was difficult to know virtue without being virtuous, it was possible and indeed right to know what virtue implied, even if it was not fully practiced. Experience did show that, along with confused or even corrupt thinkers, some genuine philosophers existed, though few if any really good cities existed in actual history.

The failure of most men and most cities to reach the happiness that could at least be understood as desirable caused great moral and philosophical perplexity. It indicated something radically wrong with the world or man. How was it possible to formulate the conditions of happiness, even to the extent of maintaining that the world could be fashioned to allow a human being to complete himself in his temporal life but still find it true that not many men could achieve this happiness? Even in those few cases wherein some genuine happiness—according to the description of the philosophers—might have been achieved, it was fleeting. It applied to such a few people, and these difficult to recognize, as the case of Socrates or Christ demonstrated, that some radical disorder appeared to exist in human nature and in the world.

To remedy this distortion, several avenues seemed open. One was rebellion against those norms or natures that existed in the world. Instead of "following nature," the rebellious philosopher wanted to replace it. Replace it with what? He usually sought to replace it with his own alternative world, a world dependent on the only intelligence he knew, that is, his own. Happiness would be subject to nothing other than man's own rules.

Aristotle had already hinted in his *Metaphysics* (982b29), that man's bondage, his awareness that he is the least of the intellectual beings, gave him an incentive to rebel against the sort of being he found himself to be. This rebellious attitude implied that hap-

piness was not found through the examination of man's powers
and their proper activities, because these seemed to be the origins
of the failure to achieve happiness in the first place. Rather, happiness would be achieved through the replacement of these natural ends and capacities by man's own criteria and purpose. The
defiance of the gods was, in this sense, seen to be the real source
of human nobility, since the gods were presumably responsible
for the dire conditions in the world.

5. *The Limits of Philosophic Happiness*

Happiness and salvation are most clearly related to each other
at this very point. The argument about the nature and conditions
of happiness as formulated by the philosophers seems to be
proper and valid. The controversy in classical thought did not
necessarily end in a theory of rebellion, though it could have.
Happiness was seen to be so infrequent an event among living
human beings that in practice it applied to no existing human
beings. The account of happiness by the philosophers was both
accurate, attractive, and grounded in understanding. Human nature protected its dignity not by actually finding examples of
happy lives but by finding philosophers who understood what it
was. However noble, this infrequency of the incidence of actual
happiness did seem rather odd and unsatisfying.

Two difficulties about happiness were striking. The first was
that practical or political happiness, the life of the virtues, the
good life, required a long time in preparation and was rarely, if
ever, perfectly achieved. On reaching old age, men often experienced a long period in which nature itself interfered with its
appreciation. The treatises on old age, such as that of Plato in
Book I of the *Republic* or Cicero's *De Senectute*, witnessed to the
rarity of the philosophers ending their lives happily. No human
life, even the longest one, lasted very long, though apparently it
lasted long enough to accomplish what human life was for.

Plato did not think reliving life would make any difference.
Nor did he think that lengthening old age was the solution, since
the problems of old age depended on our character and not on
the amount of time we lived. But to identify the sort of happiness
that we could understand philosophically with that life of man as

he lived it on earth, even in good circumstances, was not possible. Philosophic happiness, also, was itself uncertain and difficult to attain in this life. Insofar as it referred to the life of the soul as separate from the body, it was like no happiness that most people could recognize.

Neither practical nor speculative happiness, however brilliantly described by the philosopher or politician, was the lot of most people who ever lived, including most philosophers and politicians. Both Plato and Aristotle, along with many classical philosophers, recognized that the philosopher could most likely be a tyrant, or at least someone who betrayed his own vocation. The deepest disorders in any society came not from the ordinary people of mediocre virtue but from the errant philosophers with great capacity, but capacity used for the wrong purposes, for vice.

What was one to make of a world in which there was a brilliant definition of happiness but little actual complete happiness? One alternative we have seen, in the chapter on modernity, is metaphysical rebellion. In this view, we must cease to consider the classic search for happiness to be proper. We should construct an alternate happiness, which would manifest itself as a projection of a world in which all men could achieve a form of happiness that was confined to the limits of human nature in its incapacity to achieve the good on a general scale.

The other alternative, once granted that men cannot be happy in the philosophic sense by their own powers, is found under the heading of salvation. Salvation rises to the surface in religion before it is encountered in philosophy and politics. Salvation addresses what is perceived to be a failure or incompleteness in politics and natural reasoning. Salvation is not indifferent to men's deeds and thoughts in the world. Its question is whether each person can reach the highest reality no matter what sort of polity he lived in, even the worst. The doctrines of repentance and forgiveness are, unlike friendship, addressed not to the successes of philosophy, but to its failures.

6. Repentance, Salvation, and Politics

Ancient cities were modeled on the order of the gods or cosmos. The order of the world, the order of the city, and the order of the soul were to be in harmony. Not forgetting Prometheus, who stole fire from the gods to aid man, the notion of a city with no order but itself is largely a modern idea. But the idea that the modern city has no gods is deceptive. For what has taken the place of the order of the gods is the order of the ideologies. Functionally at least, these have taken the place of the gods as models for the civil order. It is difficult, however, to see how man can be at all happy if he is not well oriented to the world that is not himself but from which, as man, he came forth.

The idea that the city ought not to be ordained directly to the gods, however, was Christian, not pagan, in origin. Unbelief in the traditional gods caused the ancient Romans to look upon Christians as atheists. Like Socrates, they were unbelievers in the gods of the city. When addressing the state, Caesar was said by the Christians to have "things" which were legitimately "his," while God has His own claim (Matthew 22:22). Salvation appeared, to the Romans, to undermine the importance of politics. The city was necessary to complete the insufficiency of the individual citizens, their moral insufficiency in particular.

But Christians wondered whether the moral or practical virtues were enough even if achieved? This worry was the main question that the condition of all existing cities presented to political philosophy. Political philosophy had to address this perplexity: could the truth of the philosophical doctrine of happiness be maintained (a) if man is not made for happiness in this world alone, and (b) if happiness is not exclusively something of human making?

The difference between the philosophic and revelational traditions had to do with repentance and forgiveness. Socrates, for instance, did not "forgive" those who were responsible for his death. Rather, they were condemned by Socrates' words and Plato's recording of them. All men would remember them as those who killed the philosopher, an ignominy. Even though Plato understood that we should choose to undergo the punishment that our crimes deserved, and that we should not get caught in the cycle of doing wrong in the first place, he did not recognize that it was possible for our evil deeds to be forgiven if we acknowledged them as offenses, not just against one another, but against God. Both our dignity and our significance are much greater if our thoughts and actions reach not just their immediate objects but, through them, the Godhead Itself.

Forgiveness implied that there was something to be forgiven. Repentance was the self-reflective awareness that since we had created disorder in the world and in ourselves by our own choices and deeds, we needed to acknowledge this disorder and, if possible, to stop its consequences. What needed to be forgiven included the sins or faults that were described by the natural moral philosophers and understood by our own reason.

All sins or faults that happened were necessarily actions or thoughts following upon choices of individual persons and so known by them to be disordered. No collective guilt existed. The fully accurate description of the world was not that of the philosophers defining happiness, however valuable this was. Rather it was the account of actual human beings about their own mostly disordered actions, the majority of which did not lead them to any proper happiness, even as understood by the reasonings of the philosophers. What was worthy about such lives?

7. Salvation and the Status of Good and Evil

Political philosophy leads to philosophy and philosophy to revelation. Reflection on human life poses questions that must be asked but do not seem to admit of adequate answers once properly posed. In the case of salvation and happiness, the question is formulated over the quest for happiness that is found in each human being as something that he seeks for himself in all that he does. Happiness is intended to be the individual's happiness. It is intended to be complete.

This happiness manifests its content through examination of the various powers and capacities found in each human being from nature. These capacities can be completed through their activities, which are then more deeply settled into each human being as habits, as virtues and vices. Many of these virtues need to be completed by something beyond the individual, whereas the vices usually so affect others that some authority or coercion must be employed to enable others to be minimally virtuous before the actual vices of others.

Everything in the discussion on friendship, which is the locus

of the relation of ourselves to one another and to God, would indicate that the experience of love and friendship implies a permanence that includes everything that we are. Obviously, we
cannot provide this permanence by ourselves. Friendship requires that we remain human beings, the particular human
beings that we are. It would seem to be possible to have friendship
with God only if God manifested Himself in human form so that
the bridge between man and God, of which Aristotle rightly
spoke, could be passed over.

The treatises on happiness and friendship lead to questions
about which revelation has responded. These responses, from the
point of view of the philosopher, are only "possible" but unlikely
solutions. From the viewpoint of revelation, they require, in addition to certain philosophical grounds, faith, but a faith that is
based on certain events that happened in history. The doctrine
of salvation presents itself not as a theoretical impossibility but as
a possible solution to philosophical enigmas that actually arise in
human conditions.

From many angles, we require a completion that we cannot
provide for ourselves. But we seek a completion that does not in
principle so transform ourselves and our world that we cease to
be ourselves. Polities generally outlast the lives of the individuals
who compose them, though not always. But polities do not exist
as something apart from the individuals who compose them. The
"reality" of polities must be grounded in the prior reality of human beings and their destinies. If human beings are destined to
pass away, so also are polities. But polities might pass away and
something of human life be permanent.

The question of "salvation" differs from that of philosophic
happiness. Salvation is not concerned with perfection in this life,
either in individual or in corporate life, though it does not think
it an unimportant consideration. Politics is a necessary, practical
preparation for our understanding of the highest things. But salvation is concerned with the lives of actual human beings who are
by no means perfect and who do die.

Salvation thus is addressed not only to the ontological question
of the immortality of the soul and the theological question of the
resurrection of the body, but to the moral question of the distinction of good and evil as lived and recognized by the individual

human being in all his metaphysical depths. We can say that we want to be "saved" from the conditions of our lives without denying the goodness of the human life or condition itself. We can recognize that we have a direct relationship to the source of all being without claiming that we are ourselves divine. Rather, we wish to remain ourselves, even in our sins and faults, though we wish them to be rendered harmless.

The doctrine of salvation of each individual retains the notion that good must remain good and evil remain evil. Salvation does not and cannot change the meaning of good or evil. But it does include a way for those who commit evil to restore the good according to the exigencies of their own nature. Salvation does not pertain only to the philosophers or to the most intelligent, though it does not leave them out either. Salvation looks to the permanent status of that particular human life, begun in a real place and definite time, in which happiness has been sought.

Salvation is concerned with what a given human life has defined or manifested about itself in its own actions. It subsumes the philosophic teaching about happiness. But it recognizes that the solution to the enigmas that have arisen about individual permanence and imperfections, about the individual relation to God, do not find solutions in philosophy, even though philosophy can recognize that its own questions are being answered in some, to it, curious and surprising manner.

This working out of happiness and salvation was, as we saw, nowhere more graphic and intellectually visible than in the trials of Socrates and Christ, trials that served to link the highest issues that are pondered by mankind. But to understand more fully how these issues are related, we must still consider the meaning of virtue and vice as related to these trials, to their indications of the meaning of happiness and salvation. The proper questions to be asked at the limits of politics are seen most clearly in the classic discussion of virtue and vice. Aristotle said at the end of Book I of the *Ethics* that happiness was simply the activity of the virtues, as if there were a certain relationship between living well and the perplexing problem of whether this very living well is limited to this life, even when it is achieved. Such is the context of the consideration on virtue and vice that follows this reflection on happiness and salvation.

NINE

Virtue and Vice

The Rule of the Self over the Self

"The fallacy of that book [Fable of the Bees] *is, that [Bernard de]
Mandeville [1670–1733] defines neither vices nor benefits. He reckons
among vices everything that gives pleasure. He takes the narrowest system of morality, monastick morality, which holds pleasure itself to be a
vice, such as eating salt with our fish, because it makes it eat better; and
he reckons wealth as a publick benefit, which is by no means always true.
Pleasure of itself is not a vice. Having a garden, which we all know to
be perfectly innocent, is a great pleasure. At the same time, in this state
of being there are many pleasures vices, which however are so immediately agreeable that we can hardly abstain from them. The happiness
of Heaven will be, that pleasure and virtue will be perfectly consistent."*
—SAMUEL JOHNSON, April 15, 1778[1]

1. The Meaning of Virtue and Vice

The classical authors provided adequate yet somehow insufficient definitions of what was meant by human virtue. They asked:
What is virtue? Is it its own reward? Does it lead beyond itself by
being itself—to happiness, say, or even salvation? The clearest
and most authoritative discussion of human virtue and vice is
found in Aristotle's *Ethics* and *Politics*, though one cannot forget
either Plato or Cicero, Augustine or Aquinas. Aristotle simply
said that happiness is acting virtuously. St. Thomas added that
virtue was the "ultimate potency," by which he meant that virtue

---

1. *Boswell's Life of Johnson* (London: Oxford, 1931), II, p. 221.

is the actualization of all the capacities given to man to perfect in his life.

Since virtue leads in a particularly graphic manner to the limits of human actions both personal and political, I think it important here to devote some time to restating what is perhaps familiar, yet too often neglected in reflections arising from political philosophy. Our primary understanding of the very notion of rule comes from the rule of ourselves. All political rule is analogous to this initial sense of rule. The very discipline of reflecting back on our own powers and acts remains the intellectual grounding for our realization that, even at its best, human virtue is not just for itself.

To live a "good" human life means to rule by our own discipline, understanding, and choice our given capacities and to cause them to do what we ought to do through them. All human virtue has two origins. The first is from nature, by which we are what we are, that is, human beings. The second is from our own internal powers and will, by which we activate our given capacities from our nature to know, to fear, to delight, to be angry, to be truthful, even just to be pleasant to our neighbors. Sometimes these are called, as we previously noted, "first" nature and "second" nature, to distinguish the reality of what we are from what in ourselves is the result of our own particular choices and actions.

Aristotle's position remains that foundation in common sense and in philosophy against which the "brilliant errors" are examined and on the basis of which anything found on the further horizon of political philosophy must be compared. I will proceed with a rather detailed statement of Aristotle here. He reminds us of realities within ourselves, about whose meaning he is still the best teacher. He also best suggests those questions about the ends of virtue with which we continue to grapple in considerations of political philosophy.

An interrelated order exists among our given human capacities. Each separate capacity or power we possess is related in its own way to man's two highest powers, his capacities to know and to choose. Man is not like other animals, which are complete by being born and following instinct. He must complete himself by acting in the world with what he is initially given. Man's coming into being does not depend on himself, but his completion, his happiness, in some fundamental sense does. Otherwise he could not properly be said to be capable of his own particular happiness.

Man's action in the world passes through his rule of himself. We cannot understand political philosophy, either the brilliant errors of its history or a sane analyses of virtue and vice in human beings, without constantly recalling Aristotle's discussion. I propose this reflection on virtue and vice here primarily as a guide to that horizon of meaning to which virtue in particular leads us. We have previously indicated the problems connected with vice, though I will touch on that too.

According to Aristotle's teaching, virtue and vice are acquired by particular acts of virtue or vice. Thought is not enough. To be just we must both know what justice is and actually do a just act when occasion demands. To be cowardly, we must perform a cowardly act. What is given to us is not virtue or vice itself but a capacity or power to act this way or that. The words "virtue" and "vice" refer to what Aristotle called habits. A habit is a specific modification of a given capacity.

A habit enables us to do easily and almost automatically what we want to do, whether it be throwing a ball or acting generously with our wealth. Every act, however, is attributed not to the capacity or power to act but to the whole person who acts. It is Socrates, not just his will or reason, who acts and who is just or unjust. We are responsible for our habits, because they exist in us through our own chosen, human acts. We are brave or temperate in our actions, not simply because we can define bravery or moderation. As Aristotle taught, it is not enough to know the definition of brave things, we must do brave acts.

Aristotle taught that all virtue stood in the middle or mean between two vices, one vice too much, one too little. Courage, the guidance of our fears, stood midway between rashness and cowardice. Aristotle was not simply "postulating" that such extremes existed. Rather, his written work was intended to direct our attention to what went on within us. The raw material of Aristotle's book exists within us, where we must first recognize it if we are to understand ourselves or his argument.

Every virtue with its two opposite vices has its own "subject" matter. The subject matter of bravery or courage, for instance, was our own interior fears or pains in all their varieties. Not to have fears or pains would mean that we were not human beings. The virtue of bravery or the vice of cowardice was formed within us by continual acts of bravery or cowardice. The only way we could acquire the virtue of bravery or change it to the vice of cowardice would be by particular acts of ruling or not ruling our fears or pains. Through our particular acts, we ruled ourselves. We were responsible for the form of rule that we placed in our characters. These habits and choices define the sort of happiness we choose for ourselves in each of our acts.

2. *Virtue, Vice, and Political Philosophy*

Aristotle's insistence that virtue or vice is acquired only by specific acts of the virtue or vice in question is in part his criticism of a theory of Socrates, who held that virtue was knowledge. Aristotle realized that to know the definition of justice, for example, however necessary, was not in itself sufficient to make anyone just. Our billfold was not safe if our neighbor knew the definition of justice but did not form himself with a proper habit to be just in all his acts. Our security and peace depend on the virtue acquired by others. Aristotle's first concern was that we actually have virtue as something properly our own, that is, as something known and chosen by us. Our character is the particular combination of virtue and vice that make up each of us.

A clarification of Aristotle's discussion of virtue and vice is useful here. In Books II, III, and VII of his *Ethics,* Aristotle considered the way we could habitually stand to our own actions. Though we might act this way or that in the beginning, we came to do or not to do certain things on a regular basis. While we might do otherwise in a particular case, after a certain point in our lives we usually did not act in a way contrary to our habits and character.

Aristotle listed six possible ways we could rule ourselves in relation to our own actions. We could be (a) superhumanly virtuous, (b) virtuous, (c) continent, (d) incontinent, (e) vicious, and (f) bestial. For Aristotle, most people with regard to most virtues and vices were either continent or incontinent. Only rarely did we find human beings who were superhumanly virtuous, or totally bestial.

But such persons do exist and need to be accounted for. Few human beings were fully virtuous or wholly vicious; their character was perfectly formed to do always the right thing or always the wrong thing when the occasion arose.

The "continent" person for the most part did the right thing but was on occasion capable of doing the wrong thing. The incontinent person usually did the wrong thing but might still on occasion do the right thing. He was not wholly vicious; that is, he was still aware of the attraction of doing the right thing. In these observations, Aristotle implicitly acknowledged that most people, most of the time, were imperfect. Their weak or disordered actions were factors in the world and could not be ignored.

Aristotle accounted for the rarity of the worst and the best without compromising the validity of the best. Aristotle did not say, as Thrasymachus in the *Republic* maintained or as Machiavelli was later to advocate, that what men did "do" was the only criterion of their virtue. The philosopher and the good man were, in fact, rare. Aristotle affirmed that an objective standard of the human good is something given in reality in each human act, whether we choose to do it or not. Ethics and politics were valid practical sciences independently of our putting into being their highest or lowest norms.

This truth is no doubt one of the most perplexing ones in political philosophy. The criterion of what it was to be a good person was not subject to the human artistic capacity of making or doing, as if the rightness of human actions could be conceived independently of the givenness of human nature. Though we could and did act wrongly, we could not avoid the fact that some things were wrong independently of our making them so.[2] Human dignity and its capacity for nobility depended upon defending this insight that the good was good even if we did not accomplish it in ourselves.

3. Law and Punishment

Whether we accept or reject Aristotle, his treatment of this topic of human action and its conditions remains that against

2. See Gertrude Himmelfarb, "Of Heroes, Villains, and Valets," *Commentary* 91 (June 1991): 20–26.

which we must understand our nature and tradition. His teaching is the quickest and most easily accessible way to the heart of questions that are properly those of political philosophy and of philosophy itself. The treatment of the virtues and vices forms the intelligible core of the nature and limits of politics.

Implicit in Aristotle's treatment of virtue and vice is a teaching about law and punishment that classifies character and polity based on more or less grave deviations from the good. These deviations can be understood even if we do not put them into our own being, character, or polity. Aristotle defined law as "reason without passion" (1287a32) to indicate what it was that mostly interfered with our seeing the truth of our actions, namely, our passions (Chapter XI). Along with ignorance and force, extreme passion will be one of the legitimate reasons to mitigate or remove our moral responsibility for our actions. Though we should control our passions, Aristotle recognized that even the best men could not always completely do so.

Punishment was designed in part to prevent wrong actions when reason or habit did not suffice. Fear of punishment in many instances prevented bad actions and therefore the creation of bad habits. But beyond the hindering of evil acts, Plato taught that punishment should even be desired, because in it we recognize the disorder we put into the world by our evil actions. The acceptance of legitimate punishment acknowledges the objective wrong in our evil actions; it also allows us to acknowledge that we know the results of our wrong actions and wish to repair the resultant disorder.

After their unsuccessful plot to kill Henry V was discovered in Shakespeare's play, Sir Thomas Grey and the other conspirators said to Henry (II,ii, 161–65):

> Never did faithful subject more rejoice,
> At the discovery of most dangerous treason
> Than I do at this hour joy o'er myself,
> Prevented from a damnèd enterprise.
> My fault, but not my body, pardon, sovereign.

And Henry did forgive him his fault, but not his body. Henry's reasoning on how to punish turned precisely on what it would have meant to the realm had the actual crime been carried out.

> Touching our person, seek we no revenge,
> But we our kingdom's safety must so tender,
> Whose ruin you have sought, that to her laws
> We do deliver you. (ll. 174–77)

The relation of punishment to forgiveness becomes another of the transcendent questions posed by politics to political philosophy.

4. *The Capacity to Do Evil*

Does not the difficulty of acquiring virtue imply something intrinsically wrong or even evil about human nature itself? Or, if not (as it did not for Aristotle or Aquinas), what is the justification for human nature as it is? This justification must deal with the metaphysics of evil as it appears in ethical and political life. Theoretically, we could deny that evil is evil, which would betray our experience of human actions. Or we could propose a cause for evil exterior to ourselves, which, when it was defined, we could seek by our own powers through some political or economic program to eliminate. This latter is the utopian or "modern" solution. Finally, we could seek to understand how the possible and repeated performance of evil acts is located in the human power of choice, itself good.

How is it that we do evil? Aristotle's explanation of this problem, found in Book VII of the *Ethics,* was called the "practical syllogism." It presupposed his discussion of the voluntary and the involuntary, which appears in Book III. He stated that if an action could not properly be attributed to our own agency because ignorance, passion, or fear interfered, the action did not proceed from human choice. Knowledge and choice were both necessary elements in those variable, free actions, deserving of praise or blame that we put into the world.

Aristotle recognized that we always act with some reason. We can always explain why this or that action of ours was done "rightly," even when we know it was wrong. We recognize that we had a choice of logic or premise in most of our actions. While we always act to be happy in everything we do, we can and do choose how we argue this happiness in particular acts. In each of our acts, even our evil ones, a distinct good is achieved. Paradoxically, we cannot do anything wrong unless we also do something right.

Something that belongs to someone else, for example, may also be good or desirable as, say, food or clothing. We can argue that we ate or took the thing because it was tasty or warm, which it was. But at the same time, we avert our gaze from the proposition that would consider the same action as including the property of someone else. We commit evil by refusing to consider the whole situation in our act. What we want takes precedence over the objective situation. Evil was incorporated in our action because we knew that we were not permitting the whole reality of the object to be included in the immediate reasoning process that produced our particular action.

We always can and do justify our action because some good element was in it. But we do not admit that we were aware of other circumstances that we chose not to consider. This deliberate avoidance of the whole picture is where our fault came into being, into our being, and why we can be blamed for our actions. A virtuous act has the same structure as an evil one; in that case we are aware of the possibility of doing something wrong or doing something less good or noble in our actions, but we choose to act properly. The implicit possibility of acting wrongly is what gives acting rightly its dramatic and ethical status.

5. The Intellectual Capacity

Aristotle's *Ethics* and *Politics,* in spite of some difficulties with our present texts, form a single whole designed to discuss the implications of human action. Aristotle wanted to know about human actions insofar as we ruled ourselves, our family, and the polity in which we, as an organized group of human beings, lived. The very basis and model of our notion of what it is "to rule" was the rule of ourselves over ourselves, in those areas over which we had some rational control, that is, with our practical intellects and wills. Following Plato, we could look upon ourselves as a kind of small kingdom over which we had the obligation to rule well.

The single mind that each human person possesses as a constituent part of his own given being, when used to rule himself, to guide him to achieve some purpose or project, was called the "practical" intellect. When the same intellect was used, not to know for the purpose of action, but simply to know the truth or falsity of anything, it was called the "speculative" or "theoretic" intellect or mind. We could act not for some practical purpose, but for the act itself, for its own sake—knowing was such an act. The drive of our minds to know is caused by wonder about what is there before us in the world through no cause of our own. What is not ourselves is there before us. We want to know the answer to "What is it?"

We can desire to know something for no other purpose than just to know. But we ultimately want to know *all that is*. Aristotle defined the mind as that power capable of "being all things." What was not ourselves—the rest of creation—returned to us through our power to know. We became "more" by our knowledge without changing anything in creation but ourselves. Our perfection was not just to be or to act in our own limited arena, but to know all that was not ourselves. We encountered what was not ourselves as already made, already there. It became ours when we proceeded to know it, without ceasing to be what it was. To act correctly, Aristotle argued that we should know these things about ourselves, about our ways of knowing and acting in the world. This was the burden of Book VI of his *Ethics*.

6. *Kinds of Human Acts*

In his ethical and political books, Aristotle dealt with those activities that proceed out of human beings insofar as each person forms a whole in which both mind and matter belong together as proper ingredients in a single human life. What Aristotle treated in his ethical-political works was man as he is in this life, someone who comes into being at conception and passes out of life at death. Man is not two "beings," body and soul, as Plato seemed to say, but one being composed of both body and soul. Whether this same human being had a pre-existence (as Plato sometimes thought) or an immortal soul was not directly relevant to these considerations of the practical life, though the questions were important, even practically.

Those activities that included both our intelligence and our passions were the specific subject matter of ethics. Such activities made the human being the kind of person he was ultimately to be, for they were all ordered to that end, that happiness, according to which each one defines himself by his own proper actions, his own choices.

Speculative or theoretical questions were of the highest order in Aristotle. Practical life, which included politics as the most important of the practical sciences, was itself ordained to the speculative life. The ability to think correctly presupposed the right ordering of the capacities and the virtues. The philosopher's vocation was the noblest. But Aristotle did not think that the philosopher should also be king. He recognized two different and legitimate roles. This recognition is why in Aristotle there are books both of metaphysics and of ethics and politics.

In the area of human action, two broadly differing possibilities can be identified—things to be made and things to be done. The arts and crafts dealt with the things to be made; prudence guided and ruled the things to be done. The purpose of the arts and crafts was to make a good object, say a handsaw. A craftsman knew what a saw was. The craftsman formulated his idea and specifically ordered his material and his work so that he could fashion a saw that existed outside his mind and did what it was supposed to do, that is, saw wood. Only at that point was the craft work properly accomplished. St. Thomas would state this Aristotlian principle as "the right order of things to be made."

Not just any object would saw wood, but only a properly made saw. The purpose or nature of a saw was to do what it was designed to do. But this instrument could not have existed without some human being to put it into being. Saws do not appear in nature. It is a perfection of nature, both human and nonhuman, that human art and craft can fashion things for human purposes. Nature can be improved by craft. Yet, since all things made by craft are also results of human purpose or design, art and craft are ruled in their turn by prudence, which subsumes them into the order of human action. The craftsman does not cease to be a man. He always needs a proper understanding of what he is, how he relates to the world and to others.

We can make paintings and artifacts. We can produce beautiful things to exist outside of ourselves, things that go on after our making action ceases. We can also turn back on ourselves to recognize that there are things in us that can be ruled or guided by our own intellectual and voluntary efforts. When we rule ourselves in those things that we find in us capable of being ruled, we are said to be using practical intellects as directed to ourselves. One of the main goals of life is properly to rule ourselves in those areas over which we have some direct control, in those areas for which we are praised or blamed.

7. *Happiness and Human Activity*

To live virtuously or viciously meant that a human being, looking inwardly at those things over which he had the possibility of self-rule, managed to rule himself well or ill. For Aristotle, virtue and vice depended on the prior consideration of happiness, the subject matter of Books I and X of the *Ethics*. Happiness meant that there was an ultimate reason or aim in all that we did. Happiness defined the sort of being that a person chose himself to be—both how the person saw the world and how its meaning related to himself.

The ultimate distinction of human beings is not according to race, nation, or talent; rather, it is according to what they consider to be their good and what, on the basis of this good, they choose to do or not do in their actions. Everyone's evil is a function of what is his good. This good will be subject to the criterion of philosophy, that is, to a rational examination about what is the true good in relation to the chosen good.

Aristotle observed that we do everything we do in order to be happy. But we had to reflect on what happiness might mean. We had to sort out the different claimants for it that men usually demonstrate in their actions and theories. We as individuals or members of polities could err in what the definition or reality of actual happiness was. Happiness was not whatever we thought it was. A criterion of happiness existed according to our nature; we were not free to alter it, but only to discover it. Our freedom consisted in doing what we ought to do, not in doing what we could do with no other criterion than our own choosing.

On the basis of observation, Aristotle listed the general answers that men by their actions gave to this question of happiness. Some acted as if happiness were identical with wealth, others with pleasure, others with political honor, others with the self's own choice, and others with truth or contemplation. Human beings had themselves to decide to what purpose they oriented their own particular actions. They had to select what purpose they had in mind when they acted. They were free to choose their end, but not free to make any arbitrary end the real purpose of human living as such. They lived under the doom, as it were, of making wrong choices, or the glory of making right ones.

Families and cities were groups of people living together for the same purposes—wealth, honor, liberty, pleasure, or truth. Families and polities manifested the external pattern of choices that took place in the hearts of individuals. Regimes or constitutions reflected the character of the citizens. The forms of regimes or constitutions were ways to improve and secure the sorts of happiness the citizens had chosen for themselves. An "oligarchy," for example, was a regime composed of people who had effectively chosen wealth as the end or purpose of human living. These people, with the same ends, had organized themselves under a constitution whose order enhanced and fulfilled this end, which they identified with human happiness as such.

The real problems of ethics and politics lie not in external forms or institutions but in human choice. Nothing will ultimately happen for better or worse except at that inner level. This position was not "individualism" in the modern sense, but an effort to see the individual in terms of his actual nature and composition in relation to himself and others. Political regimes and institutions reinforced or fostered these choices, good or bad, made in the hearts of citizens.

The invisible inner life of the individual was the primary location of a kind of motion or activity that was unique in the universe. Its status was above natural activities not subject to human choice. Man was not only a being from nature but also a being whose activity made himself more fully what he was or, if he chose, to deviate from what he ought to be. Man was both the worst and the best of living creatures because of this capacity to choose how he would form himself in his actions and deeds. In one disturbing sense, the distance between virtue and vice was not very great. The same person could chose either a good or bad form of life. Yet the distance between virtue and vice was the greatest chasm in the human universe, since the distinction between good and evil was, as such, absolute.[3] Heaven and hell, in whatever form they might appear, are reflections of our need to maintain the fundamental nature of this distinction.

8. *The Proximate Norm of Human Action*

Aristotle examined those areas within or about each human being over which he had some control or self-guidance. Aristotle was very quick to recognize that if we are to call this an ethical or political "science," we must be aware that the subject matter of a science decides the degree of certainty we can expect from it (1094b12–15). Aristotle was willing to speak of an ethical or political "science," provided we realize that the subject matter of this science was itself intrinsically variable, because of human understanding and choice.

The ethical and political sciences were engaged in putting actions and relationships following from them into reality. Until an action is actually performed, the plans for it can be "otherwise," can proceed in some other way. Until actually done, no action need exist at all. Then, once done, the action is eternal, unchangeable.

No single human action can be identical with another because each action proceeds from a different person, in different times, places, and circumstances. But this particularity and uniqueness of each existing action does not mean that these actions were either "subjective" or defective in their own order as compared with the speculative sciences, whose objects cannot be "otherwise." Variability is of the essence of ethical and political things. It is due to the very nature of human choice and the variety of circumstances that surround every human deed or action. This variability in itself is a good, not an evil.

Aristotle did not maintain that the "subjective" judgment of our activities was what justified them. He proposed rather that in our every action, what we should do is what the "good man would do" in the same circumstances (1143a38–42). This norm was the proximate criterion of the goodness of our own actions. The im-

---

3. See James V. Schall, "A Latitude for Statesmanship: Strauss on St. Thomas," *Review of Politics* 53 (Winter 1991): 126–45.

port of Aristotle's position should not be missed. Aristotle was saying that we should each be the philosopher-king in each of our everyday actions. Aristotle knew that most of us would not reach this exalted position. But he wanted to insist that there was an objective good possible for us in each action or deed we performed, whether we ourselves could find it or not, whether we ourselves admitted it was there or not, whether or not we did the act or not.

This criterion of what the good man would do in any particular circumstance was not a substitute for our own intelligence. Aristotle was trying to promote, not denigrate, worthy actions. If, on every occasion in which we wanted to do something, we had to rush out to find out what a "good man" advised us and automatically do that, we would be failing the ethical duty given to each of us to act ourselves. The action was to be our action. We were to realize that there was possible to us an actual good that we ought to do in these particular times and circumstances, even if we did not in fact do it. This is why Aristotle told us to "deliberate" before acting (1112a19–13a11).

When Aristotle said that we should do what the "good man would do," he meant that we could find in every possible action a right thing to do. We should recognize and act on this norm because it was the right thing to do, at the right time, place, and circumstance. But if we did not see it was the right thing to do— even though it was in fact what the good man would do and was in fact the right thing to do—we should not, subjectively, do the right thing until we did see it was right. Moreover, if we did the wrong thing, thinking it to be right, the disordered consequences of the wrong act would still have their effects in the world.

9. *The Four Moral Virtues*

Aristotle, in Books II–V of the *Ethics,* wanted to distinguish the different virtues and opposing vices. A human being in his uniqueness included his capacity to rule himself in those areas of his being over which he had some control. We were to do acts of virtue "virtuously." This peculiar, but well-chosen phrase meant that we were to rule ourselves not because of custom, law, or force, but because we put them into effect in the right way, at the right time, in the right circumstances. We did this because we saw this was the right way to act. Aristotle held that there was a different virtue for every area over which we had some possibility of practical control.

Classical tradition distinguished the major and the minor virtues. The major virtues, sometimes called moral or cardinal virtues, are four—bravery, temperance, justice, and prudence. The minor virtues were control of our anger, of our wealth, of our speech, of our manners and wit in interaction with others. A virtue was found for every area in us over which we did have some control. We needed to form ourselves so that we could rule ourselves for our highest end. This self-rule required deliberation, decision, effort, and practice. Self-rule was often recognized to be the most difficult area of control that most people would ever encounter. The virtues were themselves needed to enable us to reach our end.

Each virtue had two opposite vices. The object in us over which we ought to have some control for the virtue of bravery, for instance, was our fears or pains. We could be cowardly or rash. But what we could and ought to do was to rule our fears or pains so that they did not rule us or deflect us from our proper duties and goals. This rule of self would be more difficult in some than in others, but everyone had some problem and needed to gain control over his own particular fears or pains. In the light of their peculiar strength in him, each person was to judge the degree of effort needed to guide himself in the face of their presence to accomplish what ought to be done or achieved in life. Fears and pains, while having their own functions in keeping human beings safe or well, still needed to be subsumed as far as possible under self-rule. This self-rule did not deny that some especially dire fears or pains made self-rule most difficult or impossible. But when these extreme passions or circumstances happened, it was recognized that the person was no longer a true moral agent.

Temperance or moderation dealt with the pleasures, in particular, the enjoyment of food and sex. Aristotle recognized that pleasures of hearing and smelling and touch existed but that, for the most part, these did not cause much aberration. For Aristotle, pleasures were not in themselves bad or evil. They were good, necessary elements given in human nature. However, they could be and often were abused, and they presented most people with some sort of difficulty in ruling themselves. These pleasures could be ruled in us, more or less, if we chose to rule ourselves. We were to rule them according to our end, to place them in the service of our happiness so that we could be free to choose what we ought to do in all the variable circumstances of our lives. Temperance is our rule of ourselves over our pleasures, at the right time, in the right place, in the right circumstances and spirit.

Justice is discussed in Book V of the *Ethics*. It was the first virtue that did not look solely within ourselves for its primary object. Justice had to do with our voluntary or necessary relations to others. Aristotle began his treatment of justice by speaking of what he called general as opposed to particular justice. General justice (or what was sometimes called legal justice) simply meant that the act of any virtue, say, temperance or bravery, could also require and include an act of justice.

For example, a father who had a difficult time controlling his fears would still be obliged in justice to save his child in danger of attack or death from fire or assailants. He would have to overcome his fears and perform an act of justice because of his relation to his child. This act would be one and the same act, not two acts, but there would be in it both an act of bravery and an act of justice, one of overcoming his fears, one of fulfilling his obligation to his child.

Special justice, in contrast to general justice, was divided into commutative and distributive justice. Justice was the virtue that most caused us to enter into public and political arrangements, most caused us to get out of ourselves. Unlike temperance and bravery, whose objects were within us from nature, justice was outside of us, existing in our standing toward or in our relationships with others. Commutative and distributive justice were based on the famous definition of justice, that is, to "render to each his due." Some relationships arose between individual persons because of their exchanges or promises; others arose as a result of a fault or crime. These issues were dealt with under the heading of commutative or "rectificatory" justice.

Thus, if we borrowed one hundred dollars from someone, we owed the hundred dollars. The rightness or unbalance was restored or rectified when the money was paid back according to the terms of the agreement. Disputes about such individual arrangements were the occasion of that part of the law which addressed civil or criminal disputes. Human progress required that we try to produce new things or arrangements with others. But we should agree on what we were doing, that it be fair, decent, and carried out according to our promises.

Distributive justice referred to the way goods of the polity were acquired from or returned to each member according to some principle of fairness. This form of justice did not deal with each member in exactly the same way but in proportion to his respective contribution to the common good or common burden. What exactly was "due" to each must be worked out by experience and reason. Justice could be violated if those who contributed more did not receive more, whether of monies, services, or even honors. Such things were "due" but, unlike the more exact sums of exchange, often could not be exactly mathematically calculated.

Aristotle also spoke of a natural justice, because he recognized that this virtue would exist even without a polity. Nor did the judgment of the polity by itself guarantee justice if there was not also an objective rightness in our actions. As we will see in Chapter 12, Aristotle devoted only one chapter to justice in the *Ethics,* but he devoted two chapters to friendship. This seemed to imply that justice has very severe limits by itself, however necessary it is for peace and fairness.

The intellectual virtue among the moral or cardinal virtues is called prudence, or moral wisdom, or sometimes practical (not theoretical) wisdom. This virtue is treated primarily in Book VI of the *Ethics.* Prudence is the chief moral virtue and is involved in all the other virtues. Why is this? Without prudence we could be neither just nor temperate nor brave. The object of prudence involves our practical intellects; that is, it involves our mind when it is considering what is to be done in this or that situation. If we are to be just or brave, we must not only do brave or just acts, but these actions must be ours. What makes this or that act to be an action of a given person is the intelligence he puts into the act or deed. All of the elements that go to make up any act—elements of time, circumstances, mode of doing, what the act is—are part of the prudential act of the practical intellect.

Prudence is the virtue whereby we habitually judge rightly of our actions, what they are and are not. Prudence remains within us as our virtue, but the action as it flows out of us and bears our stamp is seen for what it is intended to be only if we can see the intelligence that the author of the act put in it. Since every act that proceeds from a human being, to be his, must bear his personal stamp, this act will have to pass through his intelligence as he decides what is to be done, how, in what circumstances and conditions. Prudence, the intellectual virtue of the moral virtues, is the most important and necessary of the moral virtues.

10. *Control of Wealth, Anger, Speech, and Manners*

Aristotle, in Book IV of the *Ethics,* treated several other moral virtues that likewise had objects more or less subject to our guidance. The first of these was liberality, which referred to the way we stood to our own money or possessions. Our possessions were good. They too were to be used at the right time, in the right place, in the right circumstances. Possessions were not to rule us, but we were to rule them.

Also, one's character was revealed by how he stood to what was his but outside of himself, namely his possessions or wealth. Aristotle recognized, in a particularly sane understanding of human nature, that we normally needed a certain amount of material goods to be virtuous, although he also recognized that poor men could be liberal, could show mastery over themselves to use their meager goods for others, for proper purposes. For the rich, Aristotle had a special virtue called munificence or magnificence (1122a20–23b32). The magnificent rich man could use his goods for some worthy and noble purpose—to aid the polity, to foster beauty, to promote truth—in a way that revealed his soul and its understanding of the highest things.

Aristotle likewise saw that we all are given the capacity to be angry. Some things should anger us. Anger was a good and proper response to certain kinds of disorder or crime. No doubt, we could be too angry or too little angry. To rule our capacity for anger, we needed to judge and control ourselves. The rule of ourselves over ourselves included our control of our anger. Anger rightly ordered mirrored the order of virtue. Anger often displayed the peculiar character of the person by revealing what it was he thought to be good or evil.

Other areas of self-rule remained. We could rule our speech so that we told the truth. We needed to use humor and wit properly so that they did not injure others. But we ought not to be so sober that we failed to see the delight in something. Certain social graces were needed. Politeness and propriety in dealing with others are most fitting.

The whole scope of moral activity over which we had some control was the subject matter of the virtues. In separating the differing kinds of actions or passions over which we could have some control, we denominated the differing kinds of virtue and vice possible to human beings. The good man possessed the virtues in their proper proportions in relation to the nature of his own capacities. Each person had differing degrees of difficulty in each of these areas, so that some variety is found in what appeared as right order. But a right, objective order existed. To possess the virtues and to act according to them was to fulfill human potentiality, to be happy according to the possibilities given to a human being.

11. *The Magnanimous Man and Pleasure*

Aristotle called the person who possessed all the virtues, moral and intellectual, in proper proportion, the "magnanimous" man, one who was wise. The magnanimous man seems at first sight to be a rather proud man, for he was to acknowledge his own virtues. Some have seen this Greek ideal to be in conflict with later Christian notions of humility. Certainly there is some need for resolution here. The magnanimous man was in Aristotle's sense a thoroughly honest man. In acknowledging his virtues, he was not to boast or exalt himself. Rather, he possessed an objective awareness of what was the possession of a good person. The old Christian saying that "humility is truth" seems pertinent here if we would understand the good side of Aristotle's point about the magnanimous man.

The magnanimous man is perceived by Aristotle to have a sober loftiness by which he looks upon himself as objectively and accurately as possible. Aristotle's treatment of the magnanimous man does bring up the question of what is the highest form of life for man in this life. The possession of all the virtues, practical and theoretical, in the high and exalted form Aristotle provides for them, still can cause us to wonder whether this human fullness is enough for man. Perhaps at no other point in all of classical literature does the question of whether man is made for the virtues alone come up so poignantly as in Aristotle's treatment of the best, magnanimous man (1123a33–25a35).

After Aristotle had concluded his discussion of the virtues and of the reasons why we could err, he followed with two chapters on friendship. This will be the subject of Chapter 12, but it is well to stress that the whole discussion of moral life led to the discussion of the highest things and the possibility of perfection in human life. Again, the very conditions of moral living left imperfectly answered questions that arose within ordinary human and political life.

Aristotle saw that a further discussion of pleasure needed to be included properly to locate pleasure within the context of the whole of human life. Each activity possible to man had its own pleasure, which was not something independent of the activity itself. Pleasure varied according to the activity in which it existed. Pleasure was secondary to the activity, so that if the activity was good, the corresponding pleasure was good, whereas if the activity was bad, the pleasure was bad, not because of itself but because of the end for which it was employed.

Pleasure was something good in itself and needed no further apology. Yet it could be separated and looked on independently of the activity in which it existed. Anyone could make this separation and most did at many points in their lives, as Samuel Johnson pointed out in the reading at the beginning of this chapter. When pleasure as such became itself the end of our actions, then pleasure and not the end of the act in which pleasure occurs became the operative definition of happiness for the person. The distinction between pleasure and the activity in which it occurred made it possible to choose pleasure over the end of the action it accompanied. The discussion on pleasure defended its proper place, which was a noble one within practical life, without denying that pleasure could deflect man from his higher good.

12. *Two Kinds of Happiness*

Aristotle completed his discussion of the virtues by returning, in Book X of the *Ethics,* to his discussion of happiness. Aristotle held that two kinds of happiness could be distinguished. One was a practical happiness, the activities of all the practical virtues—the major and minor virtues—and the second was a speculative happiness, the activity of the intellect in knowing the truth of things. The practical or moral virtues enabled us to use our speculative powers for their own sakes. This use meant that the highest life was not that of the politician or the businessman but of the philosopher, whose task was to know the order of things, to know the truth insofar as it was given to human intelligence to know. The theoretic virtues, for their part, made it possible for the practical virtues to be properly guided. If we did not know what we were or what the world was, we could not act properly in it for our own highest end.

Though still most difficult, it was much easier to acquire the moral virtues than the speculative ones, but Aristotle admonished us not to listen to those who would have us look only to the political and moral virtues. Though the speculative virtues were more difficult to acquire and less certain when we tried to study them, nevertheless they were more worthy in themselves (1177b26–78a10). Human life needed to strive for something beyond itself because that was the very nature or purpose of the intellect.

At the end of the discussion on happiness in Book X, Aristotle began more formally to consider politics. He began his treatment not with the naturalness of politics, which he had touched on in Books I and VI of the *Ethics* and to which he would return in the *Politics,* but with the failure of the family to control or implant virtue in its youth. Aristotle had insisted that man is by nature a social and political animal. He could not be what he was by nature without establishing and living in an ordered polity wherein all his virtues, especially those related to justice, could be properly activated. Still politics began most obviously with a need of coercion or force to prevent worse evils from happening. Aristotle's *Politics* parallels his *Ethics.* Polities reflect the kinds of regimes formed by men with differing definitions of happiness and virtues. Some men choose wealth, power, honor, wisdom, or some other possible end for all their activities. The kinds of life were manifest in the regimes formed by those of similar purpose or definitions of happiness.

In ending his *Politics* with a discussion of leisure, moreover, Aristotle indicated that the purpose of the political life was not exclusively itself, however worthy it was. The end of political life was the contemplative life and the ordering of the practical life to its purposes. That leisure was the end of both ethics and politics meant that man's speculative powers were to be activated to know the truth of things, whereas his active or moral powers were to be used to enable him to live a human life in accordance with the truth of things. Civic beauty and the arts were designed to place in the city a reflection of the highest things known to reason.

Aristotle, though he realized not every regime could maintain this purpose, wanted a harmony between politics and philosophy that would enable both to exist together without the necessity of one destroying or hindering the other. His ethical and political analysis of the way men act for the most part recognized that few men or regimes ever attained the most exalted levels. Aristotle was content to achieve things gradually. He was aware of the difficulty in changing human habits and laws. He could recommend the second or third best regime, or even a better regime among those admittedly bad, because he knew human nature well enough to settle for a lesser good in place of a greater evil.

At the same time, Aristotle's philosophical analysis remained in place. The right order of thought and action was spelled out on the basis of the kind of nature given to men in the cosmos. Man was the highest of the beings containing matter but the lowest of the spiritual beings. It was good that man was what he was, the *microcosmos*, the being in whom every level of reality, from mineral to spirit, was contained. Aristotle reflectively took us through the steps by which we could understand our peculiar humanness and its limitations. Virtue was for itself, yet it seemed incomplete. The whole life of virtue was ordained to know the truth of reality, an achievement that even Aristotle thought was difficult and fleeting. In the tract on virtue, something remained unanswered precisely because the human conditions of virtue and vice were perceptively understood in what they actually were, curiously both complete and incomplete. This is why the tractates on virtue and vice needed to be seen in the light of the tractate on contemplation in Book X, the final and most extraordinary book of the *Ethics*.

PART IV

Political Philosophy and the Things of Uncommon Importance

TEN

Theology, Science, and Political Philosophy

*"You will, perhaps, wish to ask, what study I would recommend. I shall
not speak of theology, because it ought not to be considered as a question
whether you shall endeavour to know the will of God. I shall, therefore,
consider only such studies as we are at liberty to pursue or to neglect;
and of these I know not how you will make a better choice, than by
studying the civil law, as your father advises, and the ancient languages,
as you had determined for yourself; at least resolve, while you remain in
any settled residence, to spend a certain number of hours every day
amongst your books. The dissipation of thought of which you complain,
is nothing more than the vacillation of a mind suspended between different motives, and changing its direction as any motive gains or loses
strength."*
                    —SAMUEL JOHNSON TO JAMES BOSWELL, London,
                        December 8, 1763[1]

1. *The Background of Political Philosophy*

In Part IV of this book, I want to continue the approach of
Part III: not the "brilliant errors," but those intellectual and practical issues that leave us open to the higher things, leave us open
by being themselves. In this book, classical ethical and political
philosophy, particularly through Plato and Aristotle, Augustine
and Aquinas, have presented and deepened reflection on certain
perennial questions that arise in normal living, questions that

1. Samuel Johnson, *Rasselas, Poems, and Selected Prose*, ed. Bertrand H. Bronson (New York: Holt, Rinehart, and Winston, 1958), 6.

themselves are the signs of intellectual life, itself occasioned by human wonder and perplexity.

Part IV, then, begins with science, which in the modern world has seemed to present itself as the chief opponent of religion but which more and more can be seen as something that requires certain proper theological attitudes if it is to flourish and be intelligible to itself.[2] Both theology and what we now call science are, in their own ways, attempts to answer the questions about truth and the fullest meaning of human life in the cosmos.

In classical thought, man is by nature a political being. His nature is not of his own making. Rather this particular nature is discovered through experience and through the use of self-reflective intelligence, which is already operative within man himself. Man is a being who must choose to become what he ought to be. "Be thyself " is a function of "know thyself." The content or description of what man might be is what he can learn from self-reflection on the complexity of his own being.

Classical thought learns what man is from his nature. Once he learns this, man can attempt to rule himself according to this knowledge. Classical thought reveals itself to be a spirit of moderation.[3] Classical philosophy also recognized, in the myth of Prometheus (itself not unlike the account of the Fall in Genesis), that man could, if he chose, conceive his freedom to be directed against the gods, to claim powers that were not by nature his. Hubris or pride was the great sin, the claim of man to complete autonomy in each of his actions or words, a being subject to no intrinsic moderation. The spirit of moderation allowed man as a finite being to exist, to acknowledge a legitimate place and status for man in the universe. Immoderation or pride, on the other hand, meant that what man was in his given life was itself malformed, something that needed to be reconstructed according to man's, not nature's or God's, norms.

Man, in classical thought, is in a precarious position, since he can act contrary to his nature. His nature, though this is not its

2. See Stanley L. Jaki, *Chance or Reality* (Lanham, Md.: University Press of America, 1986); *The Absolute beneath the Relative* (Lanham, Md.: University Press of America, 1988).

3. Leo Strauss, "What Is Political Philosophy?" *What Is Political Philosophy and Other Studies* (Glencoe, Ill.: The Free Press, 1959), 9–55.

essence, is to have the capacity to act against his own nature. He can sin. He can act against what he ought to be. Praise and blame for his actions are possible only if man acknowledges simultaneously that it is possible, in each deed, to act freely and to act either for or contrary to what a person ought to do. Praise or blame validly arises only if there is a right thing to do, even if man does sin or act in a manner contrary to his nature.

The formulation of the best regime is the highest task of classical political philosophy. The description of the best regime enabled classical thought to classify those lives, and the polities formed by them, that were less than the best. This further classification of existing regimes as less than the best, which Plato did in the *Republic* and Aristotle refined in the *Politics*, was formulated according to the ends and purposes for which the regime was organized. In this sense it was possible to know ethical and political things.

Medieval and modern political philosophy built upon the classical heritage in various ways. Even when the bases of classical thought were rejected outright, as in the premises of modern theory, the nature of the rejection was unintelligible without an understanding of the foundations of classical and medieval theory. Medieval theory did not maintain that the classical tradition was wrong. It did insist that it needed to be completed by revelation, because classical thought was unable adequately to respond to questions that arose in political experience.[4]

Modern advocates of a return to the classical theories, those who do not see how revelation and reason can address each other, argue for the superiority of philosophy to revelation, not its valid "incompleteness" open to something beyond itself. The modern claim, on the other hand, is that essentially experimental "science" has replaced the classical and medieval premises of reason and revelation. This replacement is postulated in order to improve, if not perfect, man's lot. This claim, to be intelligible, requires some understanding of the classical notion of the best regime as well as

4. See Leo Strauss, "How to Begin to Study Medieval Political Philosophy," in *The Rebirth of Classical Political Rationalism*, ed. Thomas Pangle (Chicago: University of Chicago Press, 1989), 207–26; Ralph Lerner and Muhsin Mahdi, "Introduction," *Medieval Political Philosophy* (Ithaca: Cornell University Press, 1978), 1–21.

of the relation of modern regimes to those regimes, including democracy, described by the classical authors as less than good.

2. Reason and Revelation

Peculiar to the discourse of political philosophy as it arises in the classics and proceeds through medieval and modern theory is that classical political philosophy claims to be, and indeed proves itself to be, "universal." That is, we deal with a philosophy and a tradition that addresses itself to man as such, man of whatever time or place. It is a philosophy and philosophical argument locked in dialogue with any system or proposed alternative that might arise from whatever source—from theoreticians or from practice in existing states; from religion, economics, or psychology; or from politics.

In the realm of political philosophy, ancient, medieval, and modern theory all belong to the same discourse. No "theory" in other cultures is somehow independent of or superior to the consideration of political philosophy itself. All is part of and comprehensible within the same discourse. We can talk of different polities—Athens, Sparta, or Thebes—but not without comparing them by a single standard that has been tested by argument. We cannot claim that different political philosophies are each "true" unless their terms and concepts are tested by the same norms of political philosophy. Cultural relativism is self-contradictory.[5] Likewise, the political claims of the great religions, Eastern and Western, must be examined under the authentic light of political philosophy, at least to show that they are not contradictory to reason itself.

The difference between classical and medieval political philosophy has its origin in the distinction between revelation and reason. "The choice to live as a philosopher ceases to be simply an act of faith or of will," Thomas Pangle has written,

if and only if it is a choice to live as a philosopher preoccupied with the serious examination of the phenomena and the arguments of faith: if and only if, that is, the philosopher never completely ceases

5. See Hadley Arkes, *First Things* (Princeton: Princeton University Press, 1986), 134–58.

engaging in conversational scrutiny of those who articulate most authoritatively and compellingly the claims of the faithful, and if and only if through that perscrutation he repeatedly shows to his own satisfaction and to that of others that he has, not a definitive, but a fuller account of the moral experiences to which the pious point as their most significant experiences. The theme of such dialogues will always be in one way or another the human soul and the needs or longings of the soul which the pious claim allow us an intimation of the divine.[6]

Medieval political philosophy does not propose that philosophy can give a fuller account of human longings than faith. But it does argue that those longings are first intelligible in philosophy. Medieval thought continues, on reflection, to make philosophy to be more philosophy. The characteristic of medieval political philosophy is not reason or revelation, but reason and revelation.[7]

The test of whether a presumed revelation is "unbelievable" is not simply that it claims to have arisen from outside of human reason, but whether it specifically contradicts reason. If what is said to be revealed is irrational or contradictory, it cannot be believed, even according to revelation. The medieval controversy about the possibility of two contradictory "truths," one from reason and one from revelation, was precisely to address this question. Revelation as much as philosophy insists on the unity of the world, of the whole. The test of philosophy is, why can it not give a full account of the whole, although that is what it sets out to do? An even greater test is, why is it that properly formulated questions of philosophy have possible answers addressed to them by revelation?

Medieval theory, then, acknowledged that any revelation that contradicted reason could not be believed. Reason was more "reasonable" than it would have been without the revelation because it was forced by revelation to consider issues that it would not otherwise have had to engage. Medieval political philosophy, with its serious consideration of revelation, challenged the philosophers to complete the truths of philosophy already found in reason.

6. Thomas Pangle, "Introduction," in Leo Strauss, *Studies in Platonic Political Philosophy* (Chicago: University of Chicago Press, 1983), 22–23.
7. See Etienne Gilson, *History of Christian Philosophy in the Middle Ages* (New York: Random House, 1955).

Religion is looked upon in some classic writers (and in some modern thinkers following them) as primarily a myth used to control and rule those who cannot reason fully for themselves, as the philosophers supposedly can. But for the medievals, the philosopher needed revelation as much for his own profession, philosophy, as did anyone else in the normal course of human life, including the politician. If confronted with the problem of evil and punishment, the politician needed revelation to complete certain enigmas of politics. Likewise, the philosopher confronted by certain perplexities about truth and its origin needed revelation to clarify the whole, and the philosopher could not claim to be authentic to truth unless he so considered this revelational clarification.

In any given actual regime, a radical opposition may exist between reason and revelation, not because of thought itself or the supposed impossibility of considering revelation as a potential source of right order, but because every polity is based on some end, some chosen goal about which it constructs and legitimizes itself. This founding is the problem of civil religion or ideology. The potentiality for opposition between revelation and polities lies in the very structure of a human freedom that is capable of choosing an end contrary to the highest good. A polity may choose some particular "god" as its own, or it may exclude anything claiming revelation as a source. To exist in such a polity, revelation would have to be underground or private. The laws of this polity would allow no place either for revelation's transcendent claims to limit the political order or for revelation's influence on the actual souls of men.

3. The Permanent Discourse

For medieval thinkers, revelation defined better than politics what men ought to do and accounted for the grace that enabled them better to do what they ought. Revelation and grace both had origins outside of politics but not outside of reality. They reduced the disorders of any existing polity by enabling men to be better than what might be anticipated on the basis of realist expectations and experiences. This influence was why medieval political philosophy did not see revelation as completely independent of or indifferent to actual politics. The man to whom politics was addressed was the same man to whom revelation was directed.

For St. Augustine, who understood how grace and politics related to each other, social justice should receive its initial movement from the most final of causes, eternal beatitude, the just distribution of temporal goods making us proportionately like God, "the most just Disposer . . . of all the adjuncts of [temporal peace]—the visible light, the breathable air, the potable water, and all the other necessities of meat, drink, and clothing" (*City of God*, XIX, c. 13). This is the root of Christian social justice.[8] The doctrine about God led to the inspiration to do necessary things.

Man was the microcosmos, the being in whom all levels of being crossed. However difficult, it was inconceivable that these crossings were not ultimately harmonious and complete.

Faith and reason, though originating from the same transcendent source, are distinct yet not opposed. Beyond this view lies the more fundamental question of the unity of the universe and therefore the possibility of universal discourse, both over time and over space among all men, among all philosophers. This possibility would include the unity of man himself with the world, the fact that man is the in-between being who is legitimately and fully both matter and spirit.

Within himself, man joins the great spheres of being. This possibility of a single philosophy valid for all men was what Greek philosophy itself was about and why it was not simply "Greek" philosophy, but the irreducible foundation of philosophy as such. In the city of philosophy, Socrates and Plato are not merely ancient Athenians of a peculiar school of thought. They remain contemporary philosophers in any age, because the questions they raised belong in any polity.[9]

The great discussants in higher theoretical concerns, those who have formulated the issues that we must confront, often live before our time, often do not speak our particular language. The

8. Charles N. R. McCoy, *The Structure of Political Thought* (New York: McGraw-Hill, 1963), 114. See also, for a Protestant understanding of these issues in political philosophy, Glenn Tinder, *The Political Meaning of Christianity* (San Francisco: Harper, 1991).

9. See Henry Veatch, *Aristotle: A Contemporary Interpretation* (Bloomington: Indiana University Press, 1974).

great minds rarely exist when we exist, as Leo Strauss pointed out.[10] We encounter them initially in study, in books, though we are at liberty, as Samuel Johnson said, to neglect them. These books become alive to us only when we have actively made our own the point of their discourse, that is, when we realize that the questions the classical philosophers asked are our questions, questions addressed to man as man. At this level, the past is never really "past."

4. *Civil Order Not Its Own Judge*

Political philosophy obtains a certain priority over revelation and science. The polity, through a judicious use of force or opinion, can hinder or forbid from appearing in public the truths of revelation, prudence, or science. If the highest questions are to be welcome, the politician must be rendered benevolent to that which he does not himself fully know and over which he has no direct competence.

Moreover, the politician (though he himself should feel at least some of the pull of philosophy in his own being) is right in seeking to limit or confine the differences of the philosophers with one another to an arena that will not radically undermine the public order. If the philosophers cannot resolve with each other their struggles over the truth and order, the politician is right to encourage them to maintain a level of respectful or gentlemanly dispute. The religious person is right in maintaining that the particular and ultimate destiny of each person, his salvation, cannot wait until the time when the philosophers will have found the truth and agreed with one another that they have found it. For all its dignity, however, philosophy often appears to the ordinary man a mere confusion. Amid the conflicting claims of philosophers to the truth, the common man is not altogether wrong to be wary of the philosophers. St. Paul showed the same concern toward philosophers (1 Corinthians 1:20–22).

A given polity may insist that it be organized on a model that is not merely practical but theoretical. It may claim to be the

10. See Leo Strauss, *Liberalism: Ancient and Modern* (New York: Basic Books, 1968), chap. 1.

best regime. The order of the polity, even one that maintains it is the best, may in reality be based in opinions or in norms contrary to science and revelation. The regime always needs to be tested.

Science arose where it did and when it did, not through some arbitrary fortune or some injustice, but because science first required certain ideas from theology, reason, and moral habit without which it cannot exist.[11] In a case where scientific knowledge or another faith seems to threaten an existing political order, the actual well-being of the polity will be presumed to stand in opposition to the introduction or practice of science or another religion. Naturally, this fact of a closed polity precludes the discussion of the relative worth of the differing polities, which discussion might imply the need for a change in constitution. The distinction of polities according to the end or purpose for which they are organized suggests that not all existing regimes are the best. And if they are not the best, there will always be a desire to change them.

The real limits of political philosophy, thus, only arise when it is decided whether the Kingdom of God can or cannot be established in this world. If it cannot, which is the conclusion of revelation and the grounds of its own realism, then any effort to do so will be dangerous and destructive to actual human beings. The accurate description of the nature of existing regimes often requires an act of great intellectual and physical courage. The worst regimes want to appear to be the best.

This capacity of a polity to close off philosophical and religious discussion in order to preserve itself is why revelation cannot be totally indifferent to the forms of polity. Revelation claims to be addressed to all men in their particular lives. It also claims, if allowed to exist, to incite each polity nearer to the good that ought to be contained in its civil life, insofar as this is possible, remembering that a perfect regime is not politically possible. But if revelation admitted that a polity could legitimately exclude the presentation of its case about the ultimate meaning of human life at

11. See Stanley L. Jaki, *The Road of Science and the Ways to God* (Chicago: University of Chicago Press, 1978); William A. Wallace, *The Elements of Philosophy* (Staten Island, N.Y.: Alba House, 1977).

the level of religion, it would contradict its own claim to universality and its own response to questions that have arisen in actual polities. The constitutional effect of revelation is the limited state.

Present at the death of Socrates were not only the lawyer and the craftsman but also the poet. A poet sang the praises of what was before him, of this polity, of its arrangement, and of its end. This praise of a disordered particular polity, this fascination with republican and revolutionary songs, was why in Plato the poets were seen to be in opposition to truth.

If a polity is ordered not merely to itself but beyond itself to truth, it cannot be indifferent to what the poets sang and praised. Science and poetry were to be tested, not just by themselves, but by their relation to the order of civility. But was the order of civility to be judged by anything not itself? What judged the courts and parliaments when they rendered their final judgment?

The proposition that the civil order was its own judge and allowed no further discussion but what it decreed by itself has come to be known as "positivism," though this position has been present in one form or another from ancient times. Is there anything within the whole of reality that would permit the polity to be itself without implying or insisting that the polity is all there is? Are polities and cultures so "diverse" from each other that no comparison between them is possible because, as the historicist argues, everything is simply unique? Is the totalitarian regime, in other words, the best regime, as it claims to be?

5. *The Modern Solution*

Modern science joined modern political philosophy in believing that men could attain the best regime through the contributions of science and technology, quite apart from the conditions of virtue and goodness. "Modernity" proposed that the classical ideals of the best regime, which existed only in speech and therefore were impossible for actual men, be replaced by material norms. These norms prescinded from the question of virtue in the context of classical thought. Modern social and economic science proposed that the problem of virtue would be solved when the problem of well-being was solved. This solution was to be a technical achievement. A moderate amount of wealth would make virtue not only easier, as Aristotle held, but necessary, something Aristotle would never have held. Science would be achieved without relating itself to the problem of what in moral or ethical terms a regime was conceived to be.

Modern "democratic" regimes claimed to be silent about virtue and truth. The very proposition that virtue and truth existed and mattered to the actual polity came to be looked upon as "absolutist" or "totalitarian." The position that truth was possible, however, meant that the principle of ultimate doubt upon which, it was thought, modern polities alone could be built, was itself erroneous. The modern regime was threatened by classical philosophy and revelation that claimed to be true. To the relativist mind, the freedom of the polity depended on theoretic skepticism.

In classical political philosophy, though wide scope was given to the decisions of prudence and experience, philosophy was made possible by politics, which was devoted to character and the right order of virtue. Politics was not philosophy, but it was a necessary preparation that philosophy might happen in the contemplative life, in leisure. Politics provided the order in which the higher things could normally appear.

The modern solution to this problem was to embark on a long-range "education" to convert both philosophy and revelation to modernity. At first sight, this conversion seemed an impossible task. As it has turned out, the project was quite feasible, even well-conceived. In classical political philosophy the poets were seen picturing the gods as upholders of the city. In the poems themselves, the gods acted unjustly and approved of actions that militated against the well-being of the city. To save justice, it was necessary to rewrite the poems or forbid their being read.

The greatest philosopher of antiquity rewrote the poems, but as philosophy. This transformation was the purpose of the *Republic*. Plato knew that he had to convince and charm the nonphilosophers, especially the politicians. Aristotle understood this also.[12] But philosophy is universal and claims to be true. Classical philosophy thus cannot be open to political modernity, since modernity is based on the view that, for the good of the civil order,

12. See Carens Lord, *Education and Culture in the Political Thought of Aristotle* (Ithaca: Cornell University Press, 1982).

no truth is possible. The gods are only myths and the songs about them only songs. They can be listened to but not taken seriously.

6. Modern Science and Modern Politics

Did modern science claim to be "true"?[13] Did it recognize a human nature that it did not make? Or was existing human nature itself merely one potential form of rational being? Was the principled preservation of existing human nature through some natural law or right a threat to scientific liberty, which identified truth with the conformity of reality to the mind of the scientist (whatever it was that the scientist held)? Or were the universe and man in it constructed so specifically, so uniquely, that the discovery of what man was depended not on man's artistic and scientific mind but on his contemplative discovery of an order not made by him?

Aristotle taught that the highest of the practical sciences was politics. The practical sciences did not address themselves to the truths of the speculative sciences, but received them and were dependent on them. The practical sciences required some knowledge of the end of human action, a knowledge that was open to human reason. This knowledge was the purpose of Aristotle's discussions of happiness in Books I and X of the *Ethics*.

Human action in the concrete was the subject matter of a specific science, ethics-politics; freedom was its very substance. Right ought to be done, but men in their free agency frequently did not do what they knew they ought to do. One solution, that of Machiavelli, to this dilemma identified the ought and the is. What we did was what we ought to do if it got us what we wanted. This brilliant solution so lowered the moral level of man that he was no longer man in the classical sense. He had no agonizing choice of right and wrong, but only the possibility of success or failure.

The similar premise of Max Weber held that it was possible to tell us how to do something we wanted to do, whatever it was, but not at the same time tell us whether what we did was good or bad. We could be informed how to run a concentration camp or an art museum efficiently but not whether it was right to run either in

13. See Henry Veatch, *Human Rights: Fact or Fancy?* (Baton Rouge: Louisiana State University Press, 1985).

the first place. This power to decide right and wrong was not a function of reason or science but of will. Whatever was willed was identified with what was good.

At this point, the modern fields of science and technology joined with politics. Science was justified insofar as it provided the means for every man to get what he wanted. But we could not rationally debate about what we "wanted." That some men wanted what I had, or that science and technology came up with things that might destroy the very possibility of wanting, hinted at a "post-modern" world. Nietzsche apparently was right: we needed a morality "beyond" good and evil. But what was to be the source of this beyondness? It had to be the autonomous human intellect ruled by nothing but itself.

Modern philosophy had to distinguish itself from claims to order and truth that were said to lie outside of man's autonomous capacities. This meant, in practice, that classical ontology and ethics in their first principles had to be rejected, because they looked to an intelligible nature that was not ordered by human intellect to be what it was. The classical theories implied that the human intellect did not first know itself, but knew itself only in knowing what was not itself. That is to say, there was something to learn, something to be discovered. This position in turn suggested that man was not in fact autonomous.

7. *The Mediation of Political Philosophy*

Modernity argued that it was practical. Religion was said to diffuse man's attention by directing it to higher things, to the neglect of the "really" human things that prescinded from any higher concerns. Only if man could be weaned away from transcendence could he concentrate his attention on providing everything for needy man. Prosperity and fullness in this world denied the classical religious concerns but still absorbed them into the modern project itself as the solutions to what religion once claimed to achieve. Philosophy became, as Leo Strauss put it, "charitable and active."[14]

The cost of this charity and activity was, however, as C. S. Lewis

14. Leo Strauss, *The City and Man* (Chicago: University of Chicago Press, 1964), 3.

put it, quite heavy. "In lecturing to popular audiences," Lewis wrote, "I find it almost impossible to make them understand that I recommend Christianity because I thought its affirmations to be objectively true. They are simply not interested in the question of truth or falsehood. They only want to know if it will be comforting, or 'inspiring,' or socially useful."[15]

The encounter of science and revelation must first be mediated through a valid political philosophy that allows the questions of truth to be asked. Political philosophy is presupposed to both revelation and science. If the order of the polity, as upheld by its poets and laws, considers itself to be based on philosophic doubt or on ideological truth, only that revelation and that science which serve either will be allowed. And so we are left with problem found in Plato: the relation of the gentlemen to the philosopher, the willingness of those with power to allow themselves to be attracted to the higher things.

What seems new and ominous is that some elements within the revelational tradition are, sometimes knowingly, allowing that revelational tradition to see itself and to be seen through the ideologies of modernity. Those modern ideologies of course do not allow for transcendence.

The argument about the revival of classical philosophy is crucial to the question of the viability of revelation and science in the same world. Political philosophy is not absolutely central, but we encounter it first. For all but the very few, the polity is that body which, by its coercive or persuasive powers, permits or forbids the teaching of ultimate things.

The rendering of the polity open to what is beyond itself is the first requirement for a philosophy itself open to whatever might be addressed to it, even from revelation. It is a task of which we hear little in academia. As Voegelin suspected, the origin of the silence about the philosophical pertinence of revelation is the weak faith of clerics and philosophers.[16]

In the political sense, the recovery of an authentic revelation and philosophy is the first civic good. But the recovery is not, at

15. C. S. Lewis, "Modern Man and His Categories of Thought," in *Present Concerns: Ethical Essays* (London: Collins, 1986), 65.
16. Eric Voegelin, *Science, Religion, and Gnosticism* (Chicago: Regnery-Gateway, 1968), 108–10.

bottom, political. Socrates received his inspiration to think from outside the polity in which he lived. Modernity, insofar as it is reductionist and has place only for its own autonomous forms, cannot be called upon for this effort. A revelation that seeks to present itself in the categories of this same modernity will be seen for what it is, that is, modernity.

We will not go forward in an ultimate sense until we return to the philosophic questions about the highest things, and through them to the revelational answers addressed to such concerns. Science joins philosophy at the point where the specific order that science discovers is found in reality and does not reside merely in the mind of the scientist, with no reference to this same reality. But when the public order, in its constitutional form, reflects the mind of the ideologies—which through their historic constructions have now become the forms of public order—and when religion has accepted this same ideological construction as its own basis, then neither science nor philosophy nor revelation is possible.

The defense of science and revelation presupposes a political philosophy grounded in *what is,* not one grounded simply in the mind of the politician, scientist, philosopher, or theologian. A political philosophy based on *what is* must be legal; it must not ultimately be a violation of the laws of the polity to have the highest things considered. A polity open to truth is open to both revelation and science. A polity nevertheless has its own existence and proper actions. It seeks to put truth into its laws and ultimately into the things of uncommon importance that take place among human beings. Paradoxically, the truth of science in its classic understanding leads back to law and its own limits.

ELEVEN

Truth, Liberty, and Law

"It seems clear that the happiness of society depends on virtue. In Sparta, theft was allowed by general consent: theft, therefore, was there not a crime, but then there was no security; and what a life must they have had, when there was no security. Without truth there must be a dissolution of society. As it is, there is so little truth, that we are almost afraid to trust our ears; but how should we be, if falsehood were multiplied ten times? Society is held together by communication and information. . . ."

　　　　—SAMUEL JOHNSON, April 14, 1778[1]

"I (Boswell) asked him whether, as a moralist, he did not think that the practice of the law, in some degree, hurt the nice feeling of honesty." JOHNSON. *"Why no, Sir, if you act properly. You are not to deceive your clients with false representations of your opinion: you are not to tell lies to a judge."*

　　　　—SAMUEL JOHNSON, 1768[2]

1. Grounding Law

In 1778, Boswell recorded this first conversation with Samuel Johnson on the relation between truth, virtue, and society. In the second conversation, Johnson suggested that the lawyer could and should be honorable. It is in these relationships that the contrast between an autonomous modernity and a philosophic order based in a reality open to man but not made by him can be seen most clearly. The "web of communication," as Johnson called it, that

1. *Boswell's Life of Johnson* (London: Oxford, 1931), II, p. 222.
2. Ibid., I, p. 366.

holds society together is manifested in law, and its result should be a liberty based on virtue, truth, and honesty. The multiplication of falsehood must result in an insecure society, in one that literally cannot believe its own ears. The most destructive philosophy to be found in any society is that which does not believe, in principle, that truth is possible.

Law is rooted in something deeper than itself—in ethics and morals, indeed, in truth. Law does not arise from an abstract mind unaffected by any prior content or condition in that to which it addresses itself. Ethics and morals are in turn grounded in *what is*, in being, particularly in the kind of being to whom the law is consciously directed, that is, to someone who is capable of understanding and observing it. Because it establishes the order of the city, law is an appeal to intelligence that knows why there is a city with the differing sorts of rational beings who inhabit it.

The existence of the being who is to observe the law is itself not caused by the being in whom this law-directedness capacity exists. Politics and law not only do not create or cause man to exist in the first place; they also do not make man what it is to be a man either. For this reason, law is related to what is traditionally called the "higher law," which is manifested through reason and reflection on the reality of a limited finite being who can know.

Once laws are formulated on the basis of man's reason and freedom, they lead us to ask their end or purpose even when observed. It is at this point that law touches metaphysics and revelation.

St. Thomas Aquinas argued that positive, that is, civil, man-made law ought to be directed to that majority of people who are *not* perfect (I-II, 96, 2). Aquinas meant by this remark that lack of intelligence or virtue will be a fact in many circumstances and in most lives. If we insist on the strict observance of each positive law or make every virtue a law and every vice a crime, we will end up with something more dangerous than if we allowed for the fact that many people will not be able or willing perfectly to observe many laws in common usage.

Aquinas did not maintain that the effort to know the law or to observe and justify it was vain. Nonobservance of the law did not mean necessarily that the law as stated was wrong. It meant that for a variety of reasons, including in particular bad will, the law was not, in this or that specific case, observed.

Nonobservance might in fact mean that the law was right. The commandment holds even if its violation be widespread. The fact of error or of moral evil is not an argument against the truth or good that is contained in the law being violated. Crime and vice take their meaning from *what is* and from what ought to be done. The intelligibility of error, crime, evil, or disorder takes its primary content from that against which it stands or acts. The knowledge of evil or vice is not evil, but good and necessary.

2. *Law and Intelligibility*

Plato took great pains to insure that his potential philosophers would not be corrupted by the faults of the heroes whose deeds were praised by the poets and taught under the authority of the laws of the city. But he recognized that the fullness of moral education included an accurate knowledge of vice and evil. Knowledge of what is disordered should not come from evil deeds of the young themselves (though that is one possible, unwelcome origin of such knowledge), but from reading, observation of others, and instruction by the wisdom of the elders in speech and poetry.

It is possible to be virtuous in a world in which vice exists and even predominates. Any mature adult who did not know evil as an intelligible concept was quite dangerous. He did not have the full intellectual comprehension of any virtue or of the nature of the world in which he had to exist. Full knowledge included the knowledge of the vices opposed to the virtue.

Now knowledge included the reasons why the vices were vices in a rational being capable of virtue and vice. It included an intelligibility factor, a factor discovered, not made by the human intellect. Knowledge as such is good. It is only desire or will that can use it for good or evil. Or, as Chesterton quaintly put it, we should all commit crimes, even the most heinous ones, but we should do so in novels and stories we write, not in deed.

The integrity of the human condition requires that the law retain the intelligibility of principle even if the law is frequently violated. Modernity, which excuses or exempts man from his obligation to an objective order, produces a law with no higher content than itself. But doing what is right depends on more than what is stated in the law. There is a relation between the relative virtue of a people and the content of the law on its books.

Soulcraft is statecraft. The philosophic enterprise, the understanding of what is happening, remains operative even in the worst state. Whatever the nature of the regime may be, what is good or evil is not decided by willed law alone. Rather, by philosophic argument, the human intellect discovers the good, or truth. The discovery includes the deviations from the good—even those in one's own polity.

Philosophic doubt or theoretic relativism, in which all opinions are equal, makes truth and law as appeal to reason impossible, because it identifies truth with opinion. We should not forget that many things, particularly in politics, are at best matters of opinion. They lack the kind of certitude that is possible to the more philosophical or mathematical sciences.[3]

The integrity of the law requires that its violators have the possibility both of understanding why they are wrong in going counter to the law and of repenting the disorder they put in the world by this violation. Human wholeness requires the real possibility, based on introspective awareness of the causes and effects of our actions, of acknowledging one's errors and faults, even of a willingness to be punished for them. This requirement does not hold that everyone will so repent. But without this possibility of repentance, men will not recognize the disorder in their own actions. Even if one repents of his admittedly evil actions, it may still be prudent for the polity to proceed with civil sanctions. The area of the higher things, thus, is not co-terminus with that of the polity, even though the polity does live by and reflect such higher things as justice and mercy in its own realm.

The civil law has a vested interest in upholding the truth and integrity of the law in the light of its very nonobservance. The task of upholding the truth of the law belongs to the philosopher or even the prophet, both of whom are outside of the city but not outside of human nature. But the philosopher or prophet cannot

3. See Yves Simon, *A General Theory of Authority* (Notre Dame: University of Notre Dame Press, 1980).

forget that philosophers and prophets are themselves subject to corruption. There are false prophets and wild philosophers who reject truth.

3. Promulgation

When St. Thomas Aquinas placed "promulgation" as part of the very definition of law (I-II, 90, 1), he directed our attention to the relation between law, truth, and freedom. All codes of law provide for the terms of promulgation of new laws, of the time it might reasonably be expected to take for those citizens to whom the law is directed to learn of its existence. With this knowledge, they can gradually change their habits and conditions to be able to observe the law in a suitable fashion. Although this knowledge is largely common sense, we would miss something if we did not realize what Aquinas had in mind by his doctrine of promulgation.

Law is mind directed to mind. The city is to be ruled by argument, not by force. This communication between mind and mind is as much an aspect of natural as of civil law. At the beginning of *The Republic* of Plato, Polemarchus and his friends stop Socrates on the way back from the Piraeus to insist that he return to the home of Cephalus for an evening of discussion. In a playful manner, Socrates inquired about why he should so return. Polemarchus replied that he should look around and see that there were more of his men than of Socrates'. Socrates suggested that another way besides coercion to accomplish his end might be possible. Instead of threatening to force him to return by virtue of greater numbers, perhaps it would be possible to "persuade" him to return. This persuasion is what happened. The whole atmosphere of *The Republic* is bathed in the light of argument, not force.

In the beginning of *The Republic* (a book conspicuous for being based not directly on law but on the practical wisdom of the philosopher-king to account for the limits of law), we see the contrast of coercion and persuasion foreshadowed for the rest of political philosophy. Aquinas established the fact that law is not primarily coercion. He did this subtly by simply not listing coercion as one of the four essential elements in the definition of law.

Aquinas was not so naive as to think that coercion did not exist, nor did he deny that coercion is "reasonable." Its ultimate purpose is to re-establish reason, at least indirectly, in the life of the law-breaker.

Coercion is "reasonable," however, only when "persuasion" is inoperative or fails. Coercion has its own intelligibility once human nature and its dire conditions are accurately understood. The end of the law is not to coerce, even when it is reasonable to coerce, but to persuade. This "persuasion" in the understanding of the one who needed to be coerced may come only long after the actual coercion. But law addresses the intellect of the person who is being coerced with the claim of reason. Law does not reach its essence until it does persuade. Thus, an unjust law, since it is unreasonable, cannot really persuade.

The capacity of law to persuade is rooted in the reason common to the lawgivers and the law receivers. This is true both in existing cities and in cities in speech. The fact of revelation does not violate this principle. The law is the law of freedom when the law is understood to be a prudent or true expression of what is to be done based on *what is,* on the reality of what is given. When Aquinas asked whether everyone is subject to the law, he distinguished law as coercion from law as an intelligible proposition addressed to active intellects. The good and intelligent man who understands the proposition of the law as reasonable is not "coerced" by the law. He observes the law as the philosopher-king obeys the law, because it is reasonable to do so. This is the same idea we find in Plato's *Laws* with their famous "preambles."

The liberty of the law is never apart from the reasonableness of the law. Aquinas recognized, for example, that many of the precepts of the law were not obvious and might have been otherwise in their formulations. If this variability was the case, how can the law be said to be reasonable and obeyed? In a democratic society, the word "obedience" is often thought to be pejorative, but distrust of obedience to law arises when a democratic society defines itself on the proposition of theoretic relativism. If no truth is possible, obedience must be seen as an appeal to force, not as a mutual reason objectively shared by citizen and law-maker.

Obedience to the law is itself a rational proposition, whether it be in the family in which are found only two adults with fully

developed rational faculties or in a polity in which many free citizens decide. The argument for government not rooted exclusively in an Augustinian theory of the Fall (which has its own
intelligibility) recognizes that human action proposes many alternatives, not all of which are bad. Indeed, even within the range
of definitely bad actions, a wide variety of alternatives with varying degrees of disorder are discovered. Obedience is grounded
in the fact that many alternatives are possible, that not all of these
alternatives can be or need be put into effect. Therefore, one alternative must be chosen by a responsible authority if the community is to exist as community.

For anything to be accomplished, decisions must be made that
will not normally command complete agreement. This case can
be understood and the reasons to follow it can be also comprehended. Obedience is itself rooted in reason. To be obedient and
to be reasonable are not diametrically opposed positions. Without
obedience, we could not live in society. Even in a hypothetically
perfect society, we would still need obedience because alternatives
must still be selected to the exclusion of others. The more we
know, moreover, the freer we are and therefore the more alternatives we have to choose from. Obedience and freedom are not
opposed but aspects of the same reality.

4. Argument and Law

Behind the idea of promulgation lies an abiding respect for
argument and the nature of human thought. Argument is a product not merely of theoretical reason, but more especially of practical reason, of what is to be done as well as of what is true. What
Aquinas meant by promulgation of the law included both the
prior argument about what was to be done and the addressing of
the result of the argument to the mind of the one called upon to
obey it.

The law remains to be promulgated even to those who do not
observe it. Arguments persuasive of a good law remain to haunt,
to challenge the conscience of the doer who acts contrary to that
law. Obedience to the law might very well mean agreement, persuasion. Also, it might not. In this latter case, reasonable argu-

ment needs to follow the law when the reasons for the law are not agreed upon. Indeed, an argument needs to be made for enforcement of conformity when the good or existence of the community is at stake. All of this reflection had to be located within a system that allowed for the discussion to continue even while life went on, in terms of obedience to the law.

Tradition meant the accumulation of laws and customs, good and bad, passed down from those human beings who came before us. The thought of the past obliged us not because it was past but because it contained thought with which we had to reckon. We might be able to "prove" that old traditions or laws were wrong. But we had to try to prove it on some objective basis and not merely on the basis of the fact that it was old. The presumption, as a Burke would have it, is in their favor. In Chesterton's memorable phrase, if you see a fence across the road, the revolutionary shouts "Chop it down *because* it is there." The proper procedure is quite the opposite. If the fence is there, leave it there because it was put there for a rational purpose by some ancestor.

Once we discover *why* the fence was put there, however, we can take it down if need be, because then and only then can we argue with the man who put it up. That is, we can treat him as a reasonable being, even though he be dead. Constitutions and other fundamental documents fall within this background. The "self-evident" truths we hold remain self-evident even when philosophical passions deny there are such things. A thing that cannot be "held" in one age cannot be held in any other age. The intelligibility of law, even civil law, is addressed to all men. Law is intended to command the reasonable reflection of all, in whatever era or polity.

Aquinas argued that the law was to be promulgated because the law, to be law, had to recognize that those asked to observe it were themselves endowed with reason. Even if only a few or only the wise might understand the intricacies of a truth or practice, as was often the case with the more difficult principles of the law or of life, this difficulty did not lessen the need to preface the law with arguments that stated why this or that law in its particularities was justified. If a society was to survive, it could not be ruled mostly by coercion. It had to be ruled by law, that is, subjects had to will both the law and the truth of the law. St. Thomas justified civil disobedience when law was contrary to reason. He did not exempt anyone from the burdens of reason.

5. Reflection on Vice

Let me put in a good word here for vice, for what is the opposite of virtue. When it comes to our intellectual capacity, we are obliged to know both virtue and vice. Law needs to pay some attention to vice, especially as it harms others. When Aquinas argued that any civil society had to tolerate the existence of certain vices because their suppression might well entail greater vices, he had no intention of claiming that the tolerated vice or fault would not remain a vice. The tolerated vice would, subsequently, bring about its own dire effects, even if these effects might be less than others. The total composite of the human condition would include a multiplicity of various vices as well as various virtues. One could distinguish one society from another by the mixture and component proportions of its various vices. In some societies one had to worry about being robbed, in others about being lied to, in still others about being shot, in some all three.

In Judaeo-Christian theology, the doctrine of the Fall accounts for the fact and multiplicity of actual crimes and disorders that exist among men. If we read the classical authors, we will find that the same disorders described in Scripture were prevalent in societies without revelation. Human nature left to itself without law or custom was by no means a happy affair. Thucydides speaking of the plague and the revolution on Corcyra, or Aristotle speaking of the reasons we find vices recurring in all societies held that some root disorder was found among men. Paul Johnson echoed Aristotle's observation—that the greatest crimes are the result of bad philosophy—when he pointed out that the greatest crimes of the twentieth century were caused by intellectuals who gained political power in order to improve mankind.[4] Aristotle maintained that the cure for the greatest crimes is philosophy, that is, argument that establishes why crime is crime.

For Christianity, the correction of philosophy, and of crime too

---

4. Paul Johnson, *Modern Times* (New York: Harper Colophon, 1983), chap. 20.

for that matter, normally depended on something more than philosophy. As an example of the continuity of this tradition, the remarks of John Paul II, given January 27, 1990, in Guinea-Bissau in Africa, are worth citing: "[The Church] knows how much the Christian image of man, of his dignity and of his destiny, is projected, in a certain way, on to all sectors of life. Christ fully reveals man to himself. *It is the announcement of this revelation that leads humankind to rediscover the values of its humanity.*"[5] To be noted here is the relation of revelation to man's understanding of himself, of the values of his humanity.[6] Human understanding by itself can and does come to serious errors, "brilliant errors," as we have called them, about what man is.

Christianity's debate with both antiquity and modernity is on these issues. Crimes in their total intelligibility include something more than the disruption of the well-being of the polity. Statecraft might be dependent on soulcraft. But the soul is related directly to the divinity. For Christianity, the means to address the fact of sins or evils in their fullest extent does not lie totally within human reason, however much it is not against reason to seek to understand what such disorders are. Human reason, however, recognizes something wrong with its own powers to deal with its own aberrations. Grace does not oppose reason, but reason by itself is not simply grace. Even more fundamentally, grace heals nature by addressing nature's own aberrations and redirecting them.

In his argument for the need of revelation, Aquinas did not begin from revelation but from the unsolvable issues—"the inseparable imperfections" that perplex us at every turn, and the very nature of thought itself. Plato had realized that we could not rest content that there were crimes not punished in the polity and good acts not adequately rewarded. The philosophical discussion of immortality had political roots. We know without too much reflection that the greatest as well as the least crimes and wrongs originate in the human spirit, in the hidden area of our being impenetrable by normal civil law, even in the face of the sanction

5. John Paul II, Homily at Bissau National Stadium, January 27, 1990, in *L'Osservatore Romano*, English edition (February 12, 1990), 8 (italics added). See Harold J. Berman, *Law and Revolution: The Formation of the Western Legal Tradition* (Cambridge: Harvard University Press, 1983).
6. See John Paul II, *The Whole Truth about Man: John Paul II to University Faculties and Students*, ed. James V. Schall (Boston: St. Paul Editions, 1981).

of death. Aristotle had noticed that the tyrant wanted to make all thoughts of citizens public in order to control their actions (1313b10). The tyrannical effort to gain control of our thoughts, even our most vicious thoughts, was seen by the classical writers to be destructive to human nature.

Yet, acts of vice are manifested within and are destructive of any civil order. They corrupt the good of others as well as the good of their doers. At first sight, it would seem that civil society ought to reach into our thought-center in order that the common good be achieved. But Aquinas denied this alternative. Why? Because he saw that it is better that the state not perform the function of directly commanding our thoughts, even if it could. Aquinas did not deny that our desires needed control even for the highest ends of the polity.

It is one thing, however, to argue that the tolerant or liberal state ought not to control our thoughts, and another to maintain that these uncontrolled thoughts will have no dire effects on the civil order. But the control of the thoughts that might result in acts of vice or crime is properly a duty of the man himself who has the thoughts. If we are to leave mankind responsible for its acts, we must leave their thoughts, even their most horrendous ones, not to mention their most elevated ones, to themselves. Yet we should not deny the fact that the origins of vice lie not primarily in our habits or our urges or passions, but in our thoughts and hearts, in what we justify ourselves in believing about the world.

6. *Law and Thought*

Revelation, among its other functions, is directed to these very thoughts that do cause disorders in life and polity. The disorders resulting from our thoughts are perplexing to the human mind before any question of revelation arises. Aquinas was quite clear that, because He is our end and is what He is, it was a proper concern of God that we not only act correctly but think and desire correctly. God also had to address the free creature freely. No sound theology denies this. The admonitions of revelation not to covet and not to look greedily were capable of rejection. The law and the truth in the human creature remain subject to freedom, even in the case of dealing with the divinity.

What the civil law might prudently do, however, is not co-terminus with what we ought or ought not to do. The civil law can punish or reward only those actions over which it has some knowledge and control, and its punishments are themselves limited. In the view of St. Thomas Aquinas, it was only the divine law that could direct itself to our inner selves, wherein the ultimate disorders originate. But even here, we were addressed freely. "Thou shalt not" was not primarily a coercion but an appeal to reason and obedience. It was, like Socrates on the way back from the Piraeus, an effort to make divine persuasion the norm even of our inner lives, a norm that could be understood in terms of the reasonable experience we had with our own efforts to legislate.

In his Harvard Address, Alexander Solzhenitsyn was concerned that law itself could be used as a substitute for truth. Observance of the law substituted for the natural law or the City in Speech because law was seen merely as the abstract formulation of will—in other words, a typical artifact of modernity.

The limits of human rights and rightness are determined by a system of laws; such limits are very broad. . . . Every conflict is solved according to the letter of the law and this is considered to be the ultimate solution. If one is right from a legal point of view, nothing more is required, nobody may mention that one could still not be entirely right, and urge self-restraint or a renunciation of these rights, call for sacrifice and selfless risk: this would simply sound absurd. Voluntary self-restraint is almost unheard of: everybody strives toward further expansion to the extreme limit of the legal frames.[7]

Here we have the ultimate irony. The corruption of law is the observance of law. Yet, the point Solzhenitsyn made is valid. The civil law is not morality itself but a guide to or conclusion from morality that has its foundations elsewhere.

The lawless, it is often said, are the freest. Only those who observe the law are free is the counter-claim; only the truth will make one free. Aristotle had said that politics is the highest of the

---

7. *Solzhenitsyn at Harvard*, ed. Ronald Berman (Washington: Ethics and Public Policy Center, 1980), 7.

practical sciences, but not the highest of the sciences as such. Law, he said, is "reason without passion" (1287a32). Yet, all human beings have passion. The law in its purity seems to be more than human in the condition in which most human beings exist. Rousseau was the father of those modern thinkers who seek to move the cause of evil from inside the human heart (where St. Augustine had rightly located it) to outside the human heart. If the causes of evil lie outside of ourselves, the seriousness of our existence lies outside our wills, with those who form states and write constitutions. The multiplicity of laws will seem to contribute to the level of morality. Solzhenitsyn argued that the opposite is true: the multiplicity of laws more often is a sign of the abdication of law at a deeper level.

Aquinas asked whether the good man was subject to the law (I-II, 96, 5). Because his theory of law was directed to the intelligence of the observer of the law, Aquinas argued that the good man, the saint, did not observe the law. Aquinas meant that the good man did what the law required but that in seeing the reasonableness of any given law, the wise and good man observed the law willingly, not from coercion. He understood why it was promulgated in the manner in which it was formulated.

The good citizen, the good man, was free then because he observed the law not from fear of its punishments but because he saw the wisdom or necessity of a given law. Freedom and law were two aspects of the same principle. This conclusion still required the asking of whether the law was good. But in principle, this understanding of law as promulgated to or addressed to the reason of the one who obeys is the solution to Plato's philosopher-king problem or Aristotle's monarchy—that is, how do citizens participate in ruling in the best regime, even while they remain merely citizens or philosophers?

7. The Spirit of the Law

One function of the philosopher was to make a distinction between who is good and who is not. The letter of the law is not the law but a statement of its intelligibility. This intelligibility is the foundation that allows us to judge whether the law as stated needs to be corrected. Each case is different. Law by itself is inadequate.

It needs application to the particulars of each case. What substituted for the law was not the letter of the law. The law included the accurate knowledge of the circumstances in which the law was to exist in the light of a knowledge of the nature of man, his truth. Law had to be based in truth to be law. Freedom was not lawlessness but the complete observance of the law, including its intelligibility even in obedience.

Aquinas asked whether it was sometimes necessary to break the letter of the law to observe the law. He held that sometimes it was necessary, in order to keep the spirit of the law itself (I-II, 96, 6). The letter of the law was not the law. But the law of reason always held. Those who observed the law reasonably were able to understand the particulars in which each life must exist.

Christian revelation is not itself a code of laws. It argues that it is necessary to seek the end of the law in all cases of the observance of the law. The end of the law is the love of God and the sacrificial love of one's fellows, friendship with both God and man (I-II, 106–9). The New Law has no set doctrines or precepts, though it does not deny that these exist in reason and when reasonable ought to be formulated and followed.

But revelation is addressed to the ultimate good of each individual as seen in his every free act. The risk of the law is that nothing is unimportant. At any moment the possibility of choosing against the law is present. Freedom and law go hand in hand because freedom lies within our very acts. But this freedom can choose itself against law. Indeed, it can corrupt positive law itself. It can choose to make its own law in every act freely put into the world. Every act is, in its deciding, potentially its opposite.

The dignity of man is rooted not only in his nature but in the freedom active in and through this same nature. This dignity appears both in what man is and in what any person can do at any moment. Without his particular nature man could not act freely. But we do not know how he will choose until he acts. Even God is limited by this freedom. In this sense, damnation and salvation are very close to each other. Plato was not wrong to hint that the tyrant and the philosopher-king were quite possibly the same man. It was not a question of one man being more intelligent than the other, but of choosing different goods, different ends, something that was possible to anyone. The "limitations" of God derive from the condition of truth, liberty, and law. There can be no "answer" to the violation of law or truth that does not involve the freedom of the violator. Forgiveness, repentance, and purpose of amendment are the modes in which acts of crime or disorder confront the doer of evil acts.

Law is concerned with justice. Love is concerned with the fact that justice is not the highest virtue, with the fact that justice by itself easily leads to injustice. No response to injustice can deny the fact of injustice. The condition of forgiveness and repentance is to understand what injustice (or any other vice) is. We cannot rightly have sorrow for what is not wrong. The web of communication upon which society is based requires the upholding of truth, the recognition that virtue and vice are distinct and permanently what they are in an intelligible manner, that acts of vice have their own consequences even where they must be allowed for fear of greater damage.

When Aquinas insisted that promulgation was an essential element in the definition of law, he was aware that human society is composed of intelligent human beings locked in argument. Yet argument is not for its own sake, but for the sake of discovering what is true—not merely on the great issues but also on the acts and deeds of everyday life. Aquinas recognized that human beings do not themselves possess divine intelligences. They do possess intelligence, however, and their intelligence can be addressed by any intelligence, including that of the divinity. This possibility means that law is intended not merely for the ongoing affairs of society but also for the understanding of those beings who possess intelligence. Reason is not sufficient to rule the majority of mankind who do not easily follow it. But reason is the respect that each law and each violation of law owe to the acts we send forth into the world.

When Solzhenitsyn remarked that the observance of the law could be a sign of a greater evil carried out in the name of law, he recalled the tradition that understood that positive law must be set within the range of a higher law. The law is not merely what the lawgiver proposes, but what reason proposes (I-II, 94, 1–2). The communication of intelligence with intelligence is at the root of our relation to nature, to one another, and to God. The purpose of liberty and of law is to lead to truth. Truth as known can only be found in a being who possesses an intellect. The life of the being who is to know the truth, who is to know the consequences of his own acts, and to acknowledge the disorder that surround his faults and errors is not completed in society, or at least not in civil society. This is the truth that limits civil society to be what it is and only what it is. No other truth can make us so free.

Yet law, in St. Thomas's view, has one remarkable "end" or result that leads us to the final consideration about the incompleteness of political philosophy and how it, in some persistent manner, draws our attention to issues that philosophy itself leaves unsettling. Aquinas said that the end of the law is that we be friends (I-II, 105, 2. ad 1; see Plato, *Laws*, 862B-C). This purpose, of course, is rooted in Aristotle's discussion of friendship in the *Ethics*. What it means is that the highest end of law, society, and virtue, the web of communication in the highest things, leads political philosophy directly into the highest of realities and questions. The treatment of law in many obvious ways, as I have suggested from Aquinas, deals with disorder, with imperfect men. Yet law is also for the perfect, for the good man and the good philosopher. And it is precisely here, where we most want to be what we are that the proper questions formulated in political philosophy search for intelligible answers.

Friendship and Political Philosophy

"MRS. KNOWLES. 'I cannot agree with him [Soame Jenyns], that friendship is not a Christian virtue.' JOHNSON. 'Why, Madam, strictly speaking, he is right. All friendship is preferring the interest of a friend, to the neglect, or, perhaps, against the interest of others; so that an old Greek said, "He that has friends has no friend." Now Christianity recommends universal benevolence, to consider all men as our brethren, which is contrary to the virtue of friendship, as described by the ancient philosophers. Surely, Madam, your sect [Quakers] must approve of this; for, you call all men friends.' MRS. KNOWLES. 'We are commanded to do good to all men, "but especially to them who are of the household of Faith".' JOHNSON. 'Well, Madam. The household of Faith is wide enough.' MRS. KNOWLES. 'But, Doctor, our Saviour had twelve Apostles, yet there was one whom he loved. John was called "the disciple whom Jesus loved".' JOHNSON. (with eyes sparkling benignantly,) 'Very well, indeed, Madam. You have said very well.' BOSWELL. 'A fine application. Pray, Sir, had you ever thought of it?' JOHNSON. 'I had not, Sir'."

— SAMUEL JOHNSON, April 15, 1778[1]

1. Friendship in Human Discourse

Nothing is more surprising in the *Ethics* of Aristotle than the two books (Books VIII and IX; also, St. Thomas's *Commentary*) that the Philosopher devotes to friendship. Though we can speak of a "virtue" of friendship, friendship is not strictly speaking a specific virtue. Rather it presupposes the discourse on the virtues

---

1. *Boswell's Life of Johnson* (London: Oxford, 1931), II, p. 219.

that we have examined. Likewise, the discussion of friendship has to do with Aquinas's deliberations on law; friendship, he says surprisingly, is law's end or purpose. It is the condition of the flourishing of the virtues, the relationship in which they are most real. Friendship can be based on different kinds of communication, that is, on utility, or pleasure, or knowledge.

Friendship must also consider the relationship of the friends to each other. They might simply be good men or women, or husband and wife, brothers, sisters, companions, fellow citizens, or perhaps even strangers. Both the nature of the relationship and the basis of communication between friends enter into the worth and value of friendship. Friendships must be free and chosen, even when they arise in such relationships as that of brothers and sisters. At some level, friends must live in the same world, with the same or compatible understandings of truth and goodness.

We can paradoxically speak of "friendship" among thieves, though this friendship would be utilitarian and disordered. Plato remarked that we cannot do the maximum amount of injustice without some kind of agreed upon understanding of the "justice" existing among thieves or other sorts of unjust men (350C-52A). Scoundrels bound together in a kind of friendship are generally more dangerous than solitary evil men. The pseudo-"justice" existing among thieves could well indicate a kind of "friendship," however perverted in its ends. Like any of our capacities, which can be corrupted by the ends chosen by their possessors, friendship can be deflected from its highest purpose and used for devious ends.

Friendship, like justice, takes its highest meaning from right order in human relationships and from a right understanding of man's place in the world. Friendship takes its dignity from the truth and the good existing in reality and subsequently known and chosen by the friends as their own highest purpose. Friendship can exist only if something higher than friendship exists, something for which the friends themselves are seeking as the purpose of each life. Such was the lesson in Plato's *Symposium*. At this point, the discussion of happiness and friendship meet.

No one would call anyone "happy," Aristotle thought, who possessed everything else but lacked friends (1169b17–19). On reflection, this is one of the most profoundly true remarks in all of

classical thought; it still grounds the final meaning of political philosophy. Nothing can substitute for the reality of friends. Since
friendship is the most profound point to which classical political
philosophy brings us, it can serve also as the final consideration
of those questions and answers that fall within the surprising incompleteness of political philosophy. We deal here still with "brilliant errors," yet somehow this question of friendship intimates
for political philosophy rather some few "brilliant answers" to the
perplexing and insufficiently comprehended questions of political philosophy.

Aristotle recognized that a complete account of our moral activities included a description not only of the vices opposed to the
virtues but also of the kinds of friendship that were based on deviant purpose as well. Oligarchs who chose wealth as the specific
end of their proper activities and lives could be friends in a pleasurable or utilitarian mode because of shared ends. The worthiness of a friendship depended upon the nature and dignity of the
relationship it created and of the end on which it was based.
Friendship as a moral exchange itself depended on the distinction
in reality of good and evil, of truth and falsity. Friendship rests
on an acknowledgement of *what is*.

2. *Friendship in Political Philosophy*

The discussion on friendship leads directly from political philosophy to further questions that remain perplexing even to
philosophy. A central task of political philosophy, as I have suggested often, is to spell out the paradoxical nature of these questions, of how they lead into issues of the highest order, to questions
that are the subject matter of the communications among good
friends, where alone some topics can be thoroughly discussed.

Of all the topics of philosophy, friendship was among the most
profound and fascinating, even the most urgent. No topic, except
perhaps death (Chapter VI), was capable of raising more enigmatic questions than friendship. The treatise on friendship, however seldomly treated in a thorough manner, is fundamental in
political philosophy. Likewise, it is fundamental in understanding
that incompleteness of political philosophy that requires us to lis-

ten to, search for answers for our questions because the treatise on friendship clarifies what is at stake.

Friendship arises directly from the conditions of human living together. No human life will avoid—nor should it—the deepest perplexities caused by the reality of friendship. But questions that friendship implies require considerations that do not seem capable of being solved by political living or by philosophy alone. And even in revelation, we are left in hope, not vision.[2] Friendship both as a reality and as a topic of reflection seems to leave the philosopher in a condition of anxious waiting, of anticipating answers to questions he suspects are impossible of resolution.

Yet, if he be honest, the philosopher remains unsatisfied that this seeming "impossibility" is necessarily the case. Like virtue, which appeared incomplete precisely when it seemed most completely elaborated, the examination of friendship yields perplexities that seem odd, that seem to involve considerations that flow beyond the boundaries of the initial subject itself, and yet are rooted in fundamental issues and questions that do arise in ethical, political, and intellectual life.

In Book X of Aristotle's *Ethics*, he advised us not to listen to those who told us to limit ourselves to the merely human considerations. Similarly, E. F. Schumacher wrote, in discussing the limits of modern science:

At the level of man, there is no discernible limit or ceiling. Self-awareness, which constitutes the difference between animal and man, is a power of unlimited potential, a power which not only makes man human but gives him the possibility, even the need, to become superhuman. As the Scholastics used to say: "*Homo non est proprie humanus sed superhumanus est*"—which means that to be properly human, you must go beyond the merely human.[3]

This openness to something higher than man was not a sort of Nietzschean appeal to a superman. Nor was it a doubt about the metaphysical goodness of man itself. It was a recognition that

---

2. See Josef Pieper, *Hope and History* (New York: Herder and Herder, 1969).

3. E. F. Schumacher, *A Guide for the Perplexed* (New York: Harper, 1977), 38. See James V. Schall, "The Law of Superabundance," *Gregorianum* 72, no. 3 (1991): 515–42.

man's natural being yearned for something that nature itself could not fulfill.[4]

The life of actual virtue does not appear sufficient to itself, though the activities of the virtues are fulfilling and seem to accord with the purposes of the differing capacities we have been given in our natural being. Without denying the good or the strength of reason, we do seem to need more than ourselves even to be naturally virtuous. Yet, such was Aristotle's way of emphasizing the point, no one would choose a life of all the virtues or with all the wealth if it meant being without friends.

The practical or moral virtues are valuable and valid in themselves, but they lead beyond themselves. Particularly when they are best do the virtues hint at their own openness to something more than themselves. The brave man is most brave when he dies. The good man seems most incomplete when he is good, as if to say that goodness portends a good "in itself," a source of the real good that we discover through virtuous activities.

3. *Unique Limitations of Friendship*

The virtues enable thought and love to take place. Even if we are lovable or good, we still may not be loved. This situation implies a kind of ultimate loneliness. Thought, the pursuit of the knowledge of the whole and the place of particular things within the whole, in its turn leads to wonder about the whole and its origins.

Love, for its part, leads us to the understanding of the objects we love: What are they? What is their permanence? What is their reality? As love of its essence demands free reciprocity, we can only love other persons capable of responding to us. Something that seems passing and destined for death, namely our particular life, takes on a kind of permanence when seen in the light of friendship.

The virtues also seem to lead to considerations of friendship as the highest form of human living. The virtues call forth a kind of inner composure or rule. But in almost every case, the practice of the virtues requires others for whom these activities are like-

4. See C. S. Lewis, "Preface to the Third Edition," *The Pilgrim's Regress* (Grand Rapids, Mich.: Eerdmans, 1986), 5–14.

wise good and formative. However, neither justice nor courage nor temperance nor liberality requires friends to be practiced. We must often be brave or temperate or just or liberal to those we do not know or do not like. There can be a kind of stoic grimness to the virtues without the tract on friendship.

The possession of good habits, however, makes us good and therefore more lovable to others. Friendship is always possible, even though we should not forget that we can refuse to love the good somehow. This possibility reminds us that friendship will be free even in the good. Even without the prospect of friends, moreover, we ought to acquire virtue to rule ourselves and thereby to become capable of dealing properly with others.

But if we limit ourselves to these formal relationships demanded by the virtues, we lack something that seems proper to human well-being and completion. The activities of the virtues, however formal in themselves, are best elicited in friendship. Aristotle devoted much time to the fact that we also "need" friends, even for practical or pleasurable purposes. But friendship is always a free choice, not a "need." Friendship cannot be coerced. No one can demand it.

Nevertheless, friendship seems dependent on strict limitations. Aristotle did not think that we could have more than a few good friends, perhaps not more than one or two, in the course of a complete lifetime. At the head of this chapter, Samuel Johnson cited the ancient Greek saying, "He who has *friends* has no *friend*." Aristotle was not being merely a realist or a pessimist. He observed that we could not be friends with everybody in any deep sense. If we tried to do so, we would end, as Johnson said, with no friends.

Ironically, the very claim to be friends with everyone indicated that no real friendship existed. The proposition that everyone should have some good friends did not mean that we would ourselves have many friends or be friends with many. Rather it meant that a healthy society or human condition manifested itself when many individuals within it had one or two or a few good friends. The level of communion of friendship was not to be lowered so that everyone could have the same friends but on a superficial basis of communication. The existence of friendship, of its very nature, demanded a certain strict exclusivity.

Modern theories of civil communication and brotherhood often make the mistake of implying that by following their program everyone could be "friends" or "comrades." In practice, they "lower our sights" so that we base our relationships with others on the lowest, not the highest, possible basis. Brotherhood or fraternity can become antiphilosophical in the name of political philosophy when it promises a friendship it cannot guarantee.

In Aristotle's analysis of tyranny, both philosophy and friendship came to be seen to be inimical to the state (1314a16–18). However, in good polities, communication of friends should be possible. At least some persons should be friends at the highest level. The well-being of mankind required at least some true friendships existing within society, some relationships that were devoted to the highest things. The notion that a few good or holy persons could save society was not totally ill-founded.

The reason for this limitation in the number of friends is important to understand. The limitation implied that most men, even of the same polity, would remain fundamentally unknown to each other at the deepest levels. Could we be content with this truth of few friends in theory? Does not this violate the scriptural admonition to love one another? Ought we not seek to overcome this limitation to found a polity in which everyone would be friends in the deepest sense?

For Aristotle, all tyrants consider friendships of good men to be dangerous to their deviant rule, which rule is defined by the tyrants' freedom to direct all things to themselves. It was in the interest of the tyrannical state to prevent friendships of the highest order. Friendship implied a level of commitment to real persons and a devotion to truth that the tyrant could not control or even fathom. The tyrant's own evil activities would not be seen with approval by good friends who could, because of their friendships, generate the confidence to overthrow him.

All men in the tyrant's view should be merely "friendly" but in a superficial way. All their activities should be public. No excellence, no depth of the human spirit, could be allowed in such a polity. In a democracy, in Aristotle's view, the same sort of thing happened in a different way. For in a democracy, which had no settled concept of truth, there was no subject of communication between friends. The fool and the philosopher, it appeared, spoke the same effective nonsense.

Vague, general comradeship was to be a safer political environment for a tyrant than one in which there were many true friendships. Yet, this comradeship was an aberration of the most fundamental sort. The tyrant as a kind of perverted philosopher-king had to corrupt the most exalted of human relationships in order to secure his own safety and to prevent his rule from being questioned by those devoted to something other than his own success or interests.

4. Friendship and Justice

What was the nature of a regime in which true friendships were encouraged? Aristotle was quite sure that civil societies depended for their peace more on friendships than on justice (1155a25–28). Justice, unlike friendship, looks not to the particular person in his uniqueness toward whom one is just. Rather justice looks to the relationship itself and to one's own part in it, to what is "due."

Justice is a harsh virtue. Blind to the persons involved in its exchange, its symbol is a blindfolded maiden with sword and scales in her hands. She is blind to the individual peculiarities of the persons involved in a controversy of justice.

To be just to one another, we do not need to know each other. Indeed, it may be a detriment to know one another because it could corrupt the objectivity justice demands. Contemporary juries are not composed of those who "know" either the defendant, the prosecution, or the case. The virtue of justice allows us to exchange and deal with persons whom we do not know and whom we have no desire or need of knowing except around some transient exchange or disorder that needs rectification.

The nature of justice at its best, then, would hint that something beyond it is needed for human completion. The highest things, on this basis, are not conceived in justice, or at least not in justice alone. Aquinas even argued that the universe itself was established in mercy, not justice (I, 21.4). Since the existence of the universe, creation, was not "owed" or "due" to anyone, something more than justice seemed to regulate its ultimate order. This view of St. Thomas is one of the deepest insights in all for political philosophy to consider.

Friendship requires a certain sort of justice. We cannot cheat our friends for long and expect them to remain friends. Justice and friendship are not intrinsically opposed. In each of the kinds of justice relationship we can have—those based on utility, those based on pleasure, and those based on wisdom—there is a corresponding kind of friendship. All three kinds of friendship can exist towards the same person.

The relationship of justice is softened and deepened by friendship, even when the primary exchange remains one of justice. Friendships based on utility lighten and humanize what goes on between persons. Commerce at its best, though it usually requires detailed contracts and potential civil enforcement of breaches, is based not merely on the exchange of just and fair price but on a friendship that would unite seller and buyer or worker and owner in a bond of more than simple justice. Utilitarian friendship added to a commercial transaction based on justice mitigates the abstractness and harshness of the exchange.

Indeed, some kind of friendship is what ought to happen. Commerce, manufacture, and work are based in justice but strive for something more than justice even to achieve justice. All justice seeks equity or mercy, seeks the mitigation and understanding of friendship. Aristotle, in his discussion of justice in Book V of the *Ethics,* treated equity as an aspect of the insufficiency of pure justice. In a perfectly just world, we would be intrinsically lonely. We would deal only with relationships, not persons. Friendship exists that we might not, ultimately, be lonely.

Exchanges based solely on pleasure are themselves disordered only insofar as they separate the action in which the pleasure exists from the pleasure itself. Friendships of pleasure, like those of utility, recognize not just the pleasure but the source of the pleasure. This source is the whole being of its origin. As something given and something received, pleasure originates in a particular human being.

Pleasure paradoxically is, or at least can be, the beginning of that deepening spiritual process that looks beyond the pleasure to its source. Through pleasure we can come to look at the activity and its object in the person experiencing the pleasure.

Both friendships of utility and friendships of pleasure are capable of leading to friendships of the highest sort, though normally they do not and need not. In themselves they indicate the normal relation we have to a good number of people who are related to us not merely by the more harsh relationship of justice. Friendships of the highest sort will include aspects of utility and pleasure as part of the wholeness of the persons involved in them. A world full of friendships of utility and pleasure is not a disordered world but a world that recognizes the kinds of relationships we can and ought to have with many people whom we cannot know well enough to be friends in the deepest sense.

In principle, nothing is wrong with exchanges of usefulness or pleasure in their proper context. Most of our actual relationships with others will be of this sort. If we attend to the good, we attend to the pleasure that the good produces. If our relationships are modified or deepened by a kind of friendship, this makes the whole society, including ourselves, better. Thus Aristotle argued that cities are safest and most bound together because of their friendships, even utilitarian and political ones. Justice, however necessary, was not adequate.

5. *Virtue and Friendship*

The restriction on the number of friends one might have implied some sort of unfinished agenda in the universe, an agenda with which we seem to be involved: that the highest purpose of this life could be completed without our being friends with everyone who ever existed. We could not be friends with everyone because human life at its best lasted four score and ten years. During this time, human life passed through the stages of birth, childhood, youth, adulthood, middle age, old age, and death. Friendship required a certain maturity. Friendships of the young, which were so unstable, were mostly based on passing pleasure and changed frequently. Friendships of old age were rather more based on utility, on the increasing needs the old had for help, comfort, and assistance. (Even here, the revelational tradition has suspected that the friendship of the old needs to be supplemented with a kind of sacrificial charity really to meet the needs of the old.) While these were natural conditions of youth and old age, they did not deal with the highest sort of friendship, that of good persons through friendship engaged in the exchange of the highest things for their own sake.

Time itself was one of the main reasons we could not have many friends. To do friendship "justice" required experience, the opportunity to live together and to learn character, to choose and to hold the highest truths in common and yet also to experience the ordinary things of life (1156b25–32). Friends recognized that they were engaged in a similar pursuit of truth and a true understanding of the good life that included questions of the deepest philosophic and religious import. Plato insisted in his *Symposium* that love required that friends be honorable. Their honor included objective truth and wisdom that were not subject merely to the wills of the friends.

Since much of a lifetime was required to know someone else sufficiently well to be friends, and since friendship required a certain common life in which the exchanges proper to friendship could happen, the natural order of things intimated that we each, if we were fortunate, would have but few friends. It is at this point also that the Christian doctrine of marriage meets in a most surprising manner the Aristotelian doctrine of friendship.

In a healthy society, no doubt, many mutual friendships would exist. These depended for their dignity on the common pursuit of being, truth, beauty, and ultimate order. This pursuit was implied by the very nature of our minds whose object was *all that is*. While the natural order of this world explained why we could have few friends, it also indicated in what these friendships consisted.

Friendship was proper to the end of the polity, to leisure. Friendship supported that condition in which what needs to be done morally and materially for a full life is in fact done. If the polity is the product of the highest of the practical sciences, the citizens of the polity still will not have activated those virtues of intellect and speculation that would satisfy all there is to being human.

Josef Pieper remarked, "All practical activity, from practice of the ethical virtues to gaining the means of livelihood, serves something other than itself." He continued:

And this other thing is not practical activity. It is having what is sought after, while we rest content in the results of our active efforts. Precisely that is the meaning of the old adage that the *vita activa* is fulfilled in the *vita contemplativa*. To be sure, the active life contains a felicity of its own; it lies, says Thomas, principally in the practice of prudence, in the perfect art of the conduct of life. But ultimate repose cannot be found in this kind of felicity. *Vita activa est dispositio ad contemplativam*; the ultimate meaning of the active life is to make possible the happiness of contemplation.[5]

The highest forms of friendship penetrate to this life of contemplation, which itself is ordained to the objects of contemplation, to the order of being.

Polity and family exist for virtue, but virtue exists for friendship, for the activities of the virtues. The highest things exist in the one place where they can exist, in the conversations and exchanges of friends. Aristotle discussed the intellectual virtues in particular—wisdom, science, first principles—in Book VI of the *Ethics*. These virtues make possible that peculiar unity of the mind's own search for truth and the exchange of this search in the friendship of those who also understand and know. The search for truth or the meditation on beauty, however solitary, seeks an overflow in friendships.

6. *Human Completeness*

Two other questions about friendship needed philosophical attention for Aristotle. The first was the question of whether we wanted the best possible condition for our friends (1158b25–36). Would we want the best for our friends, that they become kings or gods, for instance? What lay behind this consideration of whether we would want our friends to be something else was whether it was all right to be a human being. Would it not be better to insist that human beings were poorly "made" so that they would be better to be "gods" or more perfect beings?

The effort to create a "new man" has been a persistent one,

5. *Josef Pieper—an Anthology* (San Francisco: Ignatius Press, 1989), 121.

usually a destructive one, in political history. Aristotle took it for granted that we could not be a friend of God. Too much distance separated the realm of human life and divine life (1159a3–5). Friendship required a certain equality of nature or condition. Human friendships demanded that friends be human beings, otherwise any understanding of friendship would be ambiguous.

The problem can perhaps be illustrated in another passage found in Boswell. In a conversation with Samuel Johnson that took place in 1772, Boswell remarked:

Finding him [Johnson] in a very good humour, I ventured to lead him to the subject of our situation in a future state, having much curiosity to know his notions on that point. JOHNSON. "Why, Sir, the happiness of an unembodied spirit will consist in a consciousness of the favour of God, in the contemplation of truth, and in the possession of felicitating ideas." BOSWELL. "But, Sir, is there any harm in our forming to ourselves conjectures as to the particulars of our happiness, though the scripture has said but very little on the subject? 'We know not what we shall be.'"

JOHNSON. "Sir, there is no harm. What philosophy suggests to us on this topick is probable: what scripture tells us is certain. . . ." BOSWELL. "One of the most pleasing thoughts is, that we shall see our friends again." JOHNSON. "Yes, Sir; but you must consider, that when we are become purely rational, many of our friendships will be cut off. Many friendships are formed by a community of sensual pleasures: all of these will be cut off. We form many friendships with bad men, because they have agreeable qualities, and they can be useful to us; but, after death, they can no longer be of use to us. We form many friendships by mistake, imagining people to be different from what they really are. After death, we shall see everyone in a true light. . . ."[6]

These remarks of Johnson underscore the problem of friendship as it existed in Aristotle: namely, what is the relation of the whole person, body and soul, to a friendship with another that includes the whole person? We want to recognize our friend as a complete human being, not as a god or pure soul.

Johnson followed the Greek idea of the immortality of the soul as that question was used by Christian theologians to explain the

6. *Boswell's Life of Johnson* (London: Oxford University Press, 1931), I, p. 446.

continuity of individual being after death. Nothing unorthodox is found in Johnson's response either in the Greek sense or in the Christian sense. Our wish for the good of a friend does not want him to be someone other than himself. We do not wish the good of someone by wishing that he were someone else. Friendship must include a desire that the whole person be involved in friendship, even after death, if the logic of the argument is to be maintained.

This position hinted that something is incomplete about the response of Johnson, as he would admit. For it did not include a discussion of the resurrection of the body, a doctrine that is directly related to the discussion in friendship as it existed in the philosophical considerations of the Greeks. We want to remain ourselves throughout our relationships with others, including God. For the same reason, we want God to be God. Particularly we want our friendships to remain. The philosophic exchanges of disembodied spirits, which are all the natural philosopher can be expected to justify and to which Johnson referred, are not the whole of what is implied in friendship, however much these exchanges of pure soul solve the problem of human continuity after death (see *The Apology*, 41).

This same conclusion comes even more to the fore in considering the question of whether we can be friends with God. Aristotle, in his discussion of this topic, approached it not from the side of human friendship but from the side of God. Recognizing that friendship was a perfection in men of the highest order, it seemed to indicate a lack in God if He could have no friends. Even though Aristotle's God or First Mover was understood to be the kind being that moved others by love and knowledge, this inner life evidently implied no direct relationship with what was not God.

Unlike the Christian doctrine of the Trinity, which identified otherness of persons in God, Aristotle's First Mover seemed to be merely solitary. Besides, what was not God would not be adequate to His friendship, even though there are theories that postulated that for this very reason of loneliness, God was necessitated to create something besides Himself to love. This lack of any apparent possibility of friendship in God seemed to suggest that

God was incomplete, or that what was not God, that is, the rest of the cosmos, was designed to make up for this lack in God. But a God who lacked would not seem to be a God at all.

Friendship implied not merely otherness, but an otherness with an independence and an inner life free enough to will or choose what was not itself. This choosing in turn presupposed a genuine knowledge that was properly possessed by a being as its own. Aristotle did not see any possibility of a friendship between man and God, and he seems at first sight and in reason to be correct in this position. Still his theory of knowledge and choice did leave open some link or relationship that would not merely be inert. Johnson, with distinct overtones from Plato and Aristotle, described what an immortal soul separated from its body might know. His description would have been perfectly intelligible to Plato and Aristotle. The separated soul, for Johnson, had "a consciousness of the favour of God, in the contemplation of the truth, and in the possession of felicitating ideas." Likewise this was in part a description of the activity of the philosopher in this life. This question was what was behind the position that the highest kind of life was that of the philosopher, the contemplative or divine life.

Political living naturally raised the question of the purpose of the virtues, while the virtues enabled the philosopher, at least, to ask questions concerning the highest things. Among the highest things were considerations of friendship. Was friendship not the context of the reality of the highest things, the proper mode of their existence? The question of friendship with God implied that the highest relationships with the deity would include a friendship between God and rational beings. That such a relationship did not seem, on philosophical grounds, to be possible did not prevent the question from being asked with some force and logic.

7. Friendship in the Highest Things

The argument about the existence of God, of a First Mover, was the most important question the philosopher in his leisure confronted (1072a18–76a4; I, 2–11). If the cosmos indicated a specific ordering of its parts, this meant that the property of the highest things included mind or spirit, since mind could arise from no other source but mind itself. Order came neither from nothing, nor from chaos, but from mind.

Aristotle did not idly wonder then whether God was not lonely because His kind of being implied, as far as Aristotle could tell, no friends. Aristotle allowed this question to stand as he found it, namely, unsolvable, but perplexing none the less. Aristotle seemed correct in maintaining that too much distance in the level of their respective being existed between them for such two diverse beings ever to be friends in any proper sense.

Once we have these two questions or perplexities clearly in mind—namely, the apparent loneliness of God and the presumed impossibility of friendship between God and men—we can understand their force as philosophical propositions apparently incapable of solution. Did they indicate some disorder in the universe? Or were there solutions that philosophy, though it could naturally formulate the question, could not comprehend by its own powers? These questions arose out of the classical ethical and political books. It is on this issue that reason and revelation confront one another, not apart from but within questions that must be legitimately felt and formulated by the experience of politics and philosophy.

Revelation presented itself in two essential propositions. The first is that an ordered inner life exists in the Godhead. This life manifests a diversity of persons. This diversity of persons, usually discussed under the heading of Trinity, addressed the philosophical question of whether God was intrinsically lonely.

If God was not in fact lonely, then what was not God existed not because it was "needed" by God to complete Himself. The philosophical perplexity about divine incompleteness, a perplexity caused by the suspicion that God lacked what was the highest relationship among other rational beings, was resolved in revelation, which described God as Three Persons in a complete life. God, in other words, was not lonely. Friendship was possible within the Godhead. What was not God, but contained reason, bore this image.

This resolution did not mean that the teaching of revelation about the inner life of God suddenly became something the philosopher could reach by his own methods. The teaching that God is not lonely because of the Trinity of persons remains closed to proper philosophical argument. But philosophy cannot demonstrate that such an understanding of the Godhead is impossible, nor can it pretend not to understand its implications.

Philosophy, if it is to be honest and open to *all that is*, must recognize that this teaching does address itself to what are apparently insoluble but genuine philosophical problems. The net effect of the comparison of revelational and philosophical teachings is that an incompleteness in the universe, suspected by the philosopher, may not be a full description of reality. The unity of the whole remains an intellectual possibility even for the philosopher on this basis.

8. *The Incompleteness of Philosophy*

The second teaching of revelation is that one of the members of the Trinity, the Second Person, became man and dwelt among men for a given time in a given place. Though many people will know that this is the teaching of revelation, it will not take on full meaning until the philosophical question of friendship in all its power is posed, intellectually posed. This teaching of revelation about the fact that God became man was addressed to the second major perplexity arising from the treatise on friendship. The distance between God and man was too great to expect any communication between them in terms meaningful to human beings, as seemed to be the case to the philosopher. The impossibility could, however, be overcome if God became man.

It is therefore striking in the Gospel of John, in particular at the Last Supper, that the relationship between Christ and His disciples is presented as a form of proper friendship. The disciples are called not servants but friends, because the highest things are communicated to them. Both the notions of friends and communication of the highest things are grounded in the classic treatment of friendship.

That Christ was man-God cannot be "proved" in terms of philosophic demonstration. What can be shown is that such an eventuality is not absolutely contradictory. What does seem striking from this discussion of friendship is that the philosophical reasons for denying the possibility of friendship with the Godhead are set aside if in fact, in the Incarnation, God possessed also a human nature while remaining God. For it was this lack of the possibility of friendship with God that made some plausible argument in philosophic terms that there was a fundamental disorder in the universe.

The philosophical perplexities about friendship with God and the loneliness of God confront implicitly the two central difficulties that arise from the treatise on friendship: namely, (1) the limitation of friends to merely a few and (2) our remaining ourselves in receiving the highest things with the best of friends. The unsatisfactoriness of the "philosophic" solution to our not knowing many others as true friends, that is, our lack of time or virtue, is a condition of the wholeness of the friendships we do have as mortals. If we would not want to cease to be ourselves in our friendships, and if the human being in his natural state includes his body and soul, then again the teachings of revelation on eternal life and resurrection exactly respond to these difficulties.

That we could only have a few friends in this lifetime seemed both necessary and good in the order of mortality as experienced by men in the polity. But our intelligence was in its nature *capax omnium*, capable of knowing all things, including all other finite beings and perhaps in some fashion the divinity itself, as Johnson intimated. The possibility of a proper friendship with everyone could not be automatically excluded. The doctrine of the resurrection of the body answers to a perplexity in the treatise on friendship as it arose in political philosophy but was never able to be resolved. It is also a response to the problem of the actual unity of all men in the highest things, both those we know, those in our time, and those in any time. The doctrines of eternal life and of its relation to time, finally, relate to the problem of the shortness of time in which we, the mortals, can know *all that is,* all who are.

9. *The Response of Friendship*

One final lesson can be drawn from the treatise on friendship. Man was happy not by the possession but by the activities of the virtues. Ideas and truths did not exist unless they were actually being thought. Friendship implied that the highest things existed in the communications of friends with all the depth of goodness, truth, and passion that such an activity implied and the nature of their being allowed.

While human affairs, including those of politics, were worthy endeavors and closest to us in terms of understanding and familiarity, still we were warned, even by Aristotle in Book X of the *Ethics*, not to listen to those who told us to look only to human affairs. Rather, we should devote our attention to the highest things, which would often seem tenuous and difficult but would be worth all our efforts. And Plato had said in the *Laws*, that God alone is serious, that human affairs in comparison are lightsome. The only really serious thing in the universe was God; we were but God's playthings, as Plato taught in *The Laws*, where "playthings" meant objects of delight, independence, and autonomy. Our response to God, Plato thought, was to be that of singing, sacrificing, and dancing (803). That is, we stood to the Godhead as receivers of the highest things. What we could do was respond in delight to what was given to us not of our own making.

This response did not mean that we should not perform proper human activities, even political activities, to respond to this reality, to *what is*. But it did mean that what was happening in the world fell more into the category of praise and affirmation than into an object constructed by purely human powers. This difference between making and praise indicates the ultimate answer to modernity's obsession with self-constructed worlds and knowledges. The highest things are given to, not made by, man.

By themselves, the many ironies and perplexities of the treatise on friendship provide intellectual stimuli of the highest import and provocativeness. By neglecting the transcendent import of friendship, political philosophy has avoided its most fascinating enterprise and dignity. The loneliness of God, the fewness of our friends, the communications on which friendship is based, the relation to those who cannot be our friends in this life, friendship with God, the relation of our practical activities in this life to contemplation, these questions arise naturally and insistently. We are not fully human until we feel their urgency and, perhaps more profoundly, charm in our own souls.

That revelational responses are posed to these very questions arising naturally, inevitably in political philosophy can, finally, be looked upon either as an accident, or as an uncanny coincidence, or with the suspicion that some wholeness exists even beyond philosophy. Political philosophy in its true sense exists that these deeper questions may properly be formulated in every city and be proposed there to every human person, in friendship, beyond politics. No earthly city is the City of God. The understanding of our evil and finiteness moderates any claim that such a city can be built by our own power in time.

The question of the location of the City of God, of the ultimate reaches of friendship with God and with one another, nonetheless, is formulated by political philosophy in its history and proper reflection on itself. Loyalty to *what is* requires that we notice all the answers posed to these enigmas of the tractates on friendship. Some answers, at least, will seem surprisingly to be addressed to the questions as asked, to the questions arising in our experience of the highest things, which live in friendship with one another.

This very fact—that, based on the experience of *what is*, the treatise on friendship in political philosophy poses the exact questions human beings need to ask of themselves and of the world itself—constitutes the true dignity of political philosophy. Aquinas understood the brilliance and daring of Aristotle because he understood that the answers of revelation needed questions of philosophy. The wholeness of man, God, and universe is guaranteed by proper intelligence, that is, by a polity in which philosophy can pose the true questions and in which all answers are considered, not just for their own sakes, but for the sake of the questions as posed. These are things of uncommon importance. It is right that we should consider them.

Conclusion
"To Those That Study Politicks"

> "The direction of Aristotle to those that study politicks, is, first to ex-
> amine and understand what has been written by the ancients upon gov-
> ernment; then to cast their eyes round upon the world, and consider by
> what causes the prosperity of communities is visibly influenced, and why
> some are worse, and others better administered.
>
> "The same method must be pursued by him who hopes to become
> eminent in any other part of knowledge. The first task is to search books,
> the next to contemplate nature. He must first possess himself of the in-
> tellectual treasures which the diligence of former ages has accumulated,
> and then endeavour to encrease them by his own collections."
> —SAMUEL JOHNSON, *The Rambler*, September 7, 1751[1]

This book is a discourse in political philosophy. It is addressed,
in Johnson's words, "to those that study politicks." The uniqueness of this discourse at the limits of political philosophy, its specific emphasis, is found in the particular way that certain basic
questions in political philosophy, questions uncommonly important in themselves, lead to answers that are not specifically political. Strong souls recognize that such questions do exist even in
ourselves. This higher side of political philosophy, both in academic courses and in the literature in the field, is frequently neglected or treated with a certain cautious embarrassment, if not
methodological hostility.

---

1. Samuel Johnson, *Rasselas, Poems and Selected Prose*, ed. Bertrand H. Bronson
(New York: Holt, Rinehart, and Winston, 1958), 106–7 (italics added).

Yet such neglect of the higher philosophic reaches of political things deprives and lessens us. It dispossesses of their rightful heritage those young potential philosophers to whom the highest things ought to be most attractive. It also frustrates those mature and even aging thinkers who still ponder these ultimate things, mindful both of their dangers and of their fascination. The argument presented in this book has treated these ultimate issues as proper and legitimate concerns of political philosophy.

The deepest disorders in human life arise initially in disagreements in the minds of the philosophers about the nature of *what is*. These disagreements seem like so many "brilliant errors" because they do strive to explain, however oddly, things that exist in ordinary human experience. Because they sense the danger in these errors without being able exactly to explain why they are dangerous, many honest citizens and politicians hesitate to consider political philosophy's ultimate reach. Small errors, they know with Aristotle, do lead to great ones.

Modern political philosophy is grounded in a curious intellectual toleration that attempts to tame or even to coerce those philosophers and citizens who would take the ideas about the limits of the discipline and of the politician most seriously. Such profound and radical differences among philosophers and believers, it was feared in modern political philosophy, would erupt in the public order in the form of wars or strife or civic hostility. This eruption has no doubt happened. But in its reaction to the dangers of pursuing the highest things, modernity proposes a kind of weak-souled man, whose highest ethical norm is self-preservation or gratification, a man who has somehow inured himself against the lure of the highest things themselves. The result has produced a kind of "bravery" against truth, against the argument that something in fact might be true and might be knowable by the human mind even amidst the multitude of "brilliant errors."

Yet, the relativist principles on which this toleration in modernity was argued left unfaced the annoying fact that certain issues had to be thought out, beginning with the issue of whether relativism itself was true. The disturbing logical paradox that if relativism is true, it cannot, by that very fact, be true, goes unnoticed. In the pursuit of the truth, intellectual courage was required to affirm that the weak-souled solution of modern relativism was seriously flawed. A second, more ominous, alternative philosophy turned these unresolved questions about human meaning and intellectual relativism over to antirational or antireligious forces such as fascism, positivism, Marxism, some forms of liberalism, or deconstructionism. Such forces presented themselves, however, as philosophically valid, as right ways to act and exist once granted that no truth existed. If truth did not exist, man evidently was free and obliged to will some order into being from his own resources if only for practical reasons.

Political philosophy, in being true to its own questions, had a "defensive" purpose: to protect openness to the truth of the higher things from dangers to it arising from within the polity itself. At the same time, it rejected the skeptical notions that nothing could be true or that any sort of enthusiasm would fill the heats of men. Aristotle put it very simply when he remarked in the Sixth Book of *The Ethics* that "the work of both the intellectual parts [theoretical and practical], then, is truth" (1139b12).[2] The truth is what is of the most uncommon importance to us in political philosophy itself. This truth is not fanatical, not outside our possibilities, not apart from our very lives. The heart of political philosophy is not betrayed when we acknowledge that the truth is what we are seeking in political philosophy.

Political philosophy, because of its knowledge of imperfect regimes, was interested in finding a polity, or at least an academy, in which it was legitimate to take the highest concerns with great soberness and philosophic attention.[3] The philosopher had both to enflame the souls of the youth so that contemplation could begin and to moderate the passions of the politician enough to let the philosopher exist. The politician, for his part, recognized that philosophy could drive some of its practitioners mad, that not all philosophers were wise or honest, that philosophy did itself require some political judgment.

This book is a guide through classical topics and readings that

2. For a discussion of truth and reason in *The Rhetoric*, see Larry Arnhart, *Aristotle on Political Reasoning* (DeKalb, Ill.: Northern Illinois University Press, 1981).
3. See Ellis Sandoz, *A Government of Laws* (Baton Rouge: Louisiana State University Press, 1990).

initially establish what are these issues that mankind cannot avoid thinking about because of its experience in civil life. Students are told that there are alternatives or substitutes to the classical works in which these issues are presented most directly. Without denying that good thinkers and books exist in many places and times, some students remain foolish enough to believe this subtle doctrine of cultural relativism, that the classical authors do not retain an unequalled authority among us. The soul deprived of the best intellectual food remains a dangerous thing.

No doubt, a certain faith is needed even to be reasonable, even to recognize that philosophers exist who have thought their way through the deepest of issues. A student from whatever background will not have read well until he has read and pondered the classical and revelational sources within which political philosophy arose in the first place.[4] We can, to be sure, have answers before we have problems. But in the intellectual life, no answers are secure until we really know the questions to which they are designed to respond and clarify. The purpose of teaching political philosophy as such is to take the student through the classic texts that establish the questions in our souls, without neglecting (for that would be dishonest) the answers that various political philosophers and even believers give to these same questions.

Political philosophy is likewise of great service to religion and theology. The religion and theology that most potential philosophers meet today are themselves often filled with ideology, doubt, and confusion in their understanding of themselves. Religion during the last hundred years has itself been surprisingly susceptible to ideology. I have argued here that revelation, properly understood, directs itself to certain clearly articulated questions in political philosophy. Political philosophy from its own resources raises issues for which specific theological teachings—those of the Trinity and the Incarnation, for example—provide accurate answers. Without political philosophy, theology is ungrounded. Without revelation, political philosophy appears frustrating, because it leads to a continued series of brilliant errors in efforts to answer its own questions.

Political philosophy is important for its capacity to keep the

---

4. See Christopher Dawson, *The Crisis of Western Education* (Garden City, N.Y.: Doubleday Image, 1965).

right questions in the forefront of thought. Those theological answers or interpretations that do not maintain the essential revelational content turn out, in fact, on examination, not to be answers to the questions argued and presented in political philosophy. In this sense, political philosophy is itself a service to revelation, a service that keeps reason and revelation in some fundamental contact, keeps them in the same world, in the same minds.

To recall the introductory passage from Frederick Wilhelmsen, this book is the text of a professor. Sometimes, no doubt, we ought to laugh at professors, sometimes we ought to ignore them, sometimes we ought to be frightened by them. But professors ought to tell us what they hold to be true, without neglecting to tell us why they have come to conclude to this truth. What is presented here is not conceived to be just one more academic opinion among a thousand others equally valuable, equally obscure, and equally indefensible. Unless we are vain, stubborn, scatter-brained, or illogical, our discourse should conclude to the truth about a thing and state it as true when known. Aristotle said that even the little truth we know about the highest things is worth all else that we know and that we should not doubt this. The argument, successfully or not, addresses itself to the truth of the issues arising properly in political philosophy.

The subject matter of this book, then, is political philosophy as it becomes more fully itself, that is, as it touches the whole in which all being is articulated and discretely contained. Political philosophy begins not with minerals or with plants, not with the stars or the gods, though it is aware of them all. Rather it begins with a certain reality, the human reality, insofar as human reality does what is specific to itself. We are surprised to discover, however, that political philosophy, by being itself, is also a means to something higher. Political philosophy provides the grounding for the higher things in this world. It provides a place where the highest things can take root in real human questions, validly formulated, and freely comprehended.

We might initially have wondered what death, friendship, virtue, salvation, law, hell, or eternal life had to do with politics. First we found, with Samuel Johnson, that those who were wisest in this field saw fit to address themselves to these issues. Secondly, we discovered that the questions did arise for our consideration, either dramatically in the trials of Socrates and Christ, or more prosaically in the discussions of Aristotle, or more passionately in the writings of St. Augustine, or more immediately from our own experience.

A certain caution, a certain realism, even pessimism, inheres in these reflections. Politics, for all its dignity, must deal with the messes we make of human lives. The very subtitle of this book speaks of "brilliant errors," as if we should know that there are errors, that they are in fact sometimes "brilliant," and that they compose a good part of the history of political philosophy. When Samuel Johnson spoke about the "inseparable imperfections of all human government," he implied that wisdom in human affairs is not on the side of those who would tell us how to be perfect by our own endeavors.

Political philosophy leads us to the paradoxical conclusion that the most dangerous people among us are, most often, those who look to government to perfect us (but government *does* have a role in helping us to be virtuous). The recent, presumed death of socialism, one ill-starred form of this position, has not discredited the perfectionist thesis. Recall Aristotle's statement, the epigram that begins this book: we should not listen to those who tell us that politics is the most important affair. His admonition directs us to the most dangerous philosophical fact about us, namely, our capacity to choose with apparent reason against right order, beginning with the right order of our own souls.

We can, therefore, choose philosophic rebellion as our response to existence. This rebellion can manifest itself in a withdrawal from this world or, contrariwise, it can seek to establish a perfect city in this world over against all actual ones. It can also express itself in a kind of Epicurean moderation that fears any philosophic endeavor. Philosophers have chosen one or another of these routes. But the inseparable imperfections remain. They continue to incite us to ask about the meaning of this human condition, of these very imperfections. We have seen that, in defending the imperfections, we have also been defending the possibility of there being such a being as man in the first place. It is a worthy defense.

Some powerful thinkers such as Machiavelli have argued that

these imperfections should themselves be the norm of our conduct. The believing realists like St. Augustine or Burke have rather argued that we should not lower our standards, even though we will not be completely good in this life. Aristotle and his followers like St. Thomas have maintained that there is such a thing as a human enterprise, something to do in this world that is valid, worthy, and significant, something not to be neglected. The political life leads to what Aristotle called leisure, a status in which further reflection is to take place about what we are, about what is true, and about what makes us happy. Both the imperfections and the works of leisure lead to a "surprising incompleteness" in political philosophy. I do not mean to suggest that political philosophy is missing something, but rather that it leads by its very nature to something it itself is not.

Socrates spoke to his friends about the immortality of the soul on his last day, while Aristotle doubted that we could be friends with God. The trials of Socrates and Christ elaborated what is at stake, both in the polities of this world and in the transcendent meaning of man. The questions asked at both trials must still be asked. This is why we read the accounts of these trials again and again, why, if we do not, we miss the real heart of political and human things. But the answers that are found in both trials remain fundamental—that it is never right to do evil, in the case of Socrates, that we are made for friendship with God, in the case of Christ.

Modern philosophy has sought to reclaim the notion of possible human perfection either through technology or through ideology. Charles Taylor's account of the politics of recognition, authenticity, and dignity remind us of nothing so much as theological reflections on the nature of being and the category of relation in the Trinity, only now relocated in this world as if man were the highest being.[5] The ancients and the medievals were accused of deflecting man from his true earthly task by talk of philosophy and the gods. This accusation Aristotle already warned us not to listen to if we chose to be what we are, a choice we had to make if we wanted to remain ourselves. The revelational tradition did not abandon the notion of perfection—"Be ye perfect

---

5. Charles Taylor, "The Politics of Recognition," in *Multiculturalism and "The Politics of Recognition"* (Princeton: Princeton University Press, 1992), 25–74.

as your heavenly Father is perfect" (Matthew 5:48)—but it did not locate it as the product of man's own powers or as completely possible in this world.

This conclusion, that the ultimate terms of our perfection were not in our hands, had the advantage of allowing imperfect men to acknowledge their imperfections without at the same time claiming the power of making what is evil to be good. It allowed them, in other words, to acknowledge evil as evil, good as good. It allowed them to live according to reality. This acknowledgment was the purpose of the intellect with which each person was endowed as a part of his very human being. The intellect, in other words, had its own integrity, its own purpose in reality.

At the beginnings of the Royal Societies in seventeenth century Europe, Samuel Johnson wrote to this point words that remain substantially true:

When Philosophers of the last Age were first congregated into the Royal Society, great expectations were raised of the sudden progress of useful Art; the time was supposed to be near when Engines should turn by a perpetual motion, and Health be secured by the universal Medicine; when Learning should be facilitated by a real Character, and Commerce extended by ships which could reach their Ports in defiance of the Tempest.

But improvement is naturally slow. The Society met and parted without any visible diminution of the miseries of life. The Gout and Stone were still painful, the Ground that was not plowed brought no Harvest, and neither Oranges nor Grapes would grown upon the Hawthorne. At last those who were disappointed began to be angry; those likewise who hated innovation were glad to gain an opportunity of ridiculing men who had deprecated, perhaps with too much arrogance, the Knowledge of Antiquity. And it appears from some of their earliest Apologies, that the Philosophers felt with great sensibility the unwelcome importunities of those who were daily asking, "What have ye done?"[6]

Let me emphasize this extraordinarily insightful remark of Johnson: "*Those [philosophers] who were disappointed began to be angry. . . .*" This anger of the philosophers takes us to the heart of modern philosophy, of modernity, to the desire of men to be responsible for the content of a seemingly intractable world. It takes us to the

6. Samuel Johnson, *The Idler*, December 22, 1759, in *Rasselas*, 191–92.

refusal to accept the "inevitable imperfections" not only of "all human government" but of human life itself. The "modernity" that we confront in political philosophy reminds us of nothing so much as that knowledge that was dangerously promised in Genesis. Eating the fruit gave man, it was claimed, the divine power to form what was good to be good and what was evil to be evil. Satan even told Eve in this famous account that if she should eat of this fruit, she would not die (Genesis 3:4).

Yet, both classical philosophy and revelation addressed themselves to man's imperfections and to his immortality. When oranges and grapes subsequently became available by international commerce, when gout was cured by a pill through universal medicine, and when ships found their ports in any sort of tempest, the world still found itself by its own testimony to be miserable. Abundance, however noble it might be, and it is an achievement, did not calm the human soul. More and more, philosophy denied that there was a soul to disquiet. The philosophers and scientists ever more frequently came to be asked by a worried mankind, "What have ye done?" And they were not sure.

It is not the argument here that no development in arts and sciences and even in morals is possible. Rather, such development occurs, but it must not be confused with the ultimate destiny of each particular human being. Some significant light can be shed on our personal destiny as it relates to improvements, changes, or even declines in arts and morals. The meaning of man as a responsible agent in the world is that he should do something about the world itself in the process of doing something about himself, about his moral and transcendent purpose.

The discourse on human virtue is a necessary discourse even for the world. Knowledge of the structure of the physical world and of the human world does not leave men themselves unaffected. But men do not determine why the world or they themselves are as they are, nor does scientific knowledge of the world substitute for investigations about the highest good. Philosophers may be angry that their solutions neither work nor are the best for which men might hope. But we wonder if what is the best we might hope for can possibly exist? We think it unlikely on our own terms. What does seem strange, however, is that, when properly formulated, the essential outlines of what it is we want are described as achievable. But this description exists in its fullness only in revelation, and there it is offered in ways we ourselves would never have conceived or chosen.

Political philosophy does not argue that revelation is philosophically "necessary." What it does suggest, however, from its own point of view is that what philosophy would want if it could have it is found in the terms in which revelation pictures human life at its completion. We will not understand revelation if we do not understand political philosophy, if we do not understand ourselves. Revelation does not substitute for philosophy. Strictly speaking, the two do not stand in opposition to each other. Revelation is not unreasonable. Indeed, revelation seeks reason in its own terms. The position that religion is but a substitute in the masses for what the philosopher knows in his dialectics does not confront the real claim of revelation. But revelation must be itself. Theology has itself spoken with very confused words in modern times, usually in imitation of modern theories, so that its real content is obscured or effectively denied.

Revelation true to itself, faithfully handed down, however, does not make any theoretical sense until the questions to which it responds are first asked in the souls of those "that study politicks." When these questions are finally formulated, over a reading of Plato perhaps, or over a lifetime of suffering, or over living in an unjust regime, or even over a moment of intense joy, reason can see that revelational answers are likely and are in fact directed to these questions. These answers from revelation, on the basis of what is asked in political philosophy, do make curious sense. They make sense in terms of the questions found in human life as elaborated in the books of the philosophers and in the experience of the actual politicians: questions of death and friendship, of love and evil. Revelation is not a conclusion of human reason. If it were, we would already be gods. Revelation is not contradictory to reason, for if it were we could in no way believe it. Belief itself must be consistent with what is at least possible and thinkable. That proposition itself, that faith cannot contradict reason, is a tenet of faith as well as grounded in a first or self-evident principle of reason.

Discourse in political philosophy is successful if we realize that such questions, which have been asked by the great thinkers, are also our questions. In some sense, revelation implies that the distance between the philosopher and the ordinary man is not as great as it appears in philosophy alone. Such questions unavoidably arise in our souls because of what we are. Only at this point can we seriously ask what sorts of answers have been given to such questions. If we are free, we will be ready to consider those answers that are in fact responses to these questions as they are asked by the philosophers, by the politicians, and by ourselves.

Indeed, it is right, in conclusion, to consider political philosophy as a "doctrine that claims to be true." When we so consider it, we will see that the "brilliant errors" that constitute the history of political philosophy are themselves efforts to answer the same questions that we find also treated in revelation. Political philosophy is no mean enterprise when it endeavors to grasp intellectually that perhaps there are not two worlds but one, and in that one world answers are given in revelation to questions properly formulated in political philosophy at its best.

When we finally take our stand here, we can see that political philosophy itself has led us, by its own inner energy and logic, to look beyond its limits. We too have wondered about the confines and contours of our full lives. We have been concerned about those actual experiences that awakened in our souls questions about the highest things. We realize in political philosophy that we are not beings who question for the sake of questioning but beings who want and who expect to find answers that are true. We do not think we are beings created "in vain," beings with no meaning.

The thesis of this book is that a coherent relationship between what we are and what we would have if we thought about it does exist. Such is our very nature, that we can refuse even to think about this curious correlation, even when it is plausible. The dignity of political philosophy is to be measured primarily in the service it can give to these, the higher and most surprising of endeavors, to which the being who is "naturally political" can be led by his encounters with *what is*. In the end, we need not be "disappointed philosophers" who become intellectually "angry" because we could not explain the world in our own terms. Above all else, political philosophy, rightly, openly considered, I think, is not a sign of disappointment but a hint of glory.

BIBLIOGRAPHY

This bibliography does not include standard classical texts in political philosophy that are easily available in a number of editions or translations. Aristotle, Plato, Cicero, Plutarch, Marcus Aurelius, Thucydides, the Scriptures, St. Augustine, St. Thomas Aquinas, Machiavelli, Hobbes, Rousseau, Kant, Hegel, Marx, Nietzsche, and Heidegger, among others, should, of course, be basic texts.

Alvis, John, and Thomas G. West. *Shakespeare as a Political Thinker.* Durham, N.C.: Carolina Academic Press, 1981.
Arendt, Hannah. *Between Past and Future: Eight Exercises in Political Thought.* New York: Viking, 1968.
———. *The Human Condition.* Garden City, N.Y.: Doubleday Anchor, 1959.
———. *The Origins of Totalitarianism.* New York: Meridian, 1958.
Arkes, Hadley. *Beyond the Constitution.* Princeton: Princeton University Press, 1990.
———. *First Things: An Inquiry into the First Principles of Morals and Justice.* Princeton: Princeton University Press, 1986.
———. *The Philosopher in the City: The Moral Dimensions of Urban Politics.* Princeton: Princeton University Press, 1981.
Arnhart, Larry. *Aristotle on Political Reasoning: A Commentary on The Rhetoric.* DeKalb: Northern Illinois University Press, 1981.
Babbitt, Irving. *Representative Writings.* Edited with an introduction by George A. Panichas. Lincoln: University of Nebraska Press, 1981.
Balthasar, Hans Urs von. *Convergences: To the Source of Christian Mystery.* Translated by E. A. Nelson. San Francisco: Ignatius Press, 1983.
———. *The God Question and Modern Man.* Translated by Hilda Graef. New York: Seabury, 1968.
———. *A Theology of History.* New York: Sheed & Ward, 1963.
Barker, Ernest. *Greek Political Theory: Plato and His Predecessors.* London: Methuen, 1960.

————. *The Political Thought of Plato and Aristotle*. New York: Dover, 1959.

Bartlett, Robert C. "Aristotle's Science of the Best Regime." *American Political Science Review* 88 (March 1994): 143–55.

Bate, Walter Jackson. *Samuel Johnson*. London: Hogarth Press, 1975.

Beisner, E. Calvin. *God in Three Persons*. Wheaton, Ill.: Tyndale House, 1984.

Belloc, Hilaire. *The Path to Rome*. Garden City, N.Y.: Doubleday Image, 1956.

Berman, Harold J. *Law and Revolution: The Formation of the Western Legal Tradition*. Cambridge: Harvard University Press, 1983.

Bishirjian, Richard. *The Development of Political Theory: A Critical Analysis*. Dallas: The Society for the Study of Traditional Culture, 1978.

Bloom, Allan. *The Closing of the American Mind*. New York: Simon & Schuster, 1987.

————, with Henry V. Jaffa. *Shakespeare's Politics*. Chicago: University of Chicago Press, 1964.

Bochenski, Joseph M. *Philosophy—an Introduction*. New York: Harper, 1972.

Boswell, James. *Boswell's Life of Johnson*. 2 vols. London: Oxford University Press, 1931.

Brezik, Victor B., ed. *One Hundred Years of Thomism: Aeterni Patris and Afterwards: a Symposium*. Houston: University of St. Thomas Press, 1981.

Brown, Peter. *Augustine of Hippo: A Biography*. Berkeley: University of California Press, 1967.

Bruell, Christopher. "On Plato's Political Philosophy." *Review of Politics* 56 (Spring 1994): 261–82.

Budziszewski, Jay. *The Resurrection of Nature: Political Theory and the Human Character*. Ithaca, N.Y.: Cornell University Press, 1986.

————. *True Tolerance*. New Brunswick, N.J.: Transaction, 1992.

Burke, Vernon J. *Will in Western Thought*. New York: Sheed & Ward, 1964.

Burns, J. H., ed. *Cambridge History of Medieval Political Thought c. 350–c. 1450*. Cambridge: Cambridge University Press, 1988.

Butterfield, Herbert. *Christianity and History*. London: Fontana, 1964.

Camus, Albert. *Lyrical and Critical Essays*. Translated by E. C. Kennedy. New York: Vintage, 1970.

————. *The Rebel: An Essay on Man in Revolt*. A revised and complete translation by Anthony Bower. New York: Vintage, 1956.

Carey, George W., ed. *Order, Freedom, and the Polity: Critical Essays on the Open Society*. Lanham, Md.: University Press of America, 1986.

Carey, George W., and James V. Schall, S.J., eds. *Essays on Christianity and Political Philosophy*. Lanham, Md.: University Press of America, 1984.

Cassirer, Ernest. *An Essay on Man*. Garden City, N.Y.: Doubleday Anchor, 1944.

————. *The Myth of the State*. New Haven: Yale University Press, 1944.

———. *The Philosophy of the Enlightenment.* Translated by Fritz C. A. Koelln and James P. Pettegrove. Boston: Beacon Press, 1955.

Catechism of the Catholic Church. Vatican City: Libreria Editrice Vaticana, 1994.

Chenu, M.-D. *The Scope of the Summa.* Translated by R. E. Brennan and A. M. Landry. Washington, D.C.: Thomist Press, 1958.

Chesterton, G. K. *The Autobiography.* San Francisco: Ignatius Press, 1988. *Collected Works,* vol. 16.

———. *Orthodoxy.* San Francisco: Ignatius Press, 1986. *Collected Works,* vol. 1.

———. *St. Thomas Aquinas.* San Francisco: Ignatius Press, 1986. *Collected Works,* vol. 2.

———. *What's Wrong with the World.* San Francisco: Ignatius Press, 1987. *Collected Works,* vol. 4.

Choron, Jacques. *Death and Western Thought.* New York: Collier, 1963.

Christenson, Reo M. *Heresies, Right and Left: Some Political Assumptions Reexamined.* New York: Harper, 1973.

Cochrane, Charles Norris. *Christianity and Classical Culture: A Study of Thought and Action from Augustus to Augustine.* London: Oxford, 1977.

Collins, James. *God in Modern Philosophy.* Chicago: Regnery, 1959.

Cooper, John M. *Reason and Human Good in Aristotle.* Indianapolis: Hackett, 1986.

Copleston, Frederick C. *Medieval Philosophy.* New York: Harper Torchbooks, 1961.

Cropsey, Joseph. *Political Philosophy and the Issues of Politics.* Chicago: University of Chicago Press, 1980.

Cullmann, Oscar. *The State in the New Testament.* New York: Scribner's, 1956.

Dawson, Christopher. *Beyond Politics.* New York: Sheed & Ward, 1939.

———. *Christianity and the New Age.* Manchester, N.H.: Sophia Institute Press, 1985.

———. *Crisis of Western Education.* Garden City, N.Y.: Doubleday Image, 1965.

———. *The Historic Reality of Christian Culture: A Way to the Renewal of Human Life.* New York: Harper Torchbooks, 1960.

———. *The Judgment of the Nations.* New York: Sheed & Ward, 1942.

———. *Medieval Essays.* Garden City, N.Y.: Doubleday Image, 1954.

———. *The Movement of World History.* New York: Sheed & Ward, 1959.

———. *Religion and the Rise of Western Culture.* Garden City, N.Y.: Doubleday Image, 1958.

Deane, Herbert A. *The Political and Social Ideas of St. Augustine.* New York: Columbia University Press, 1966.

de Grazia, Sebastian. *Machiavelli in Hell.* Princeton: Princeton University Press, 1989.

Dennehy, Raymond. "The Intellectual Disarray of Freedom." *New Scholasticism* 54 (Summer 1980): 326–41.

————. "The Ontological Basis of Human Rights." *The Thomist* 42 (July 1978): 434–63.

————. *Reason and Dignity.* Washington, D.C.: University Press of America, 1981.

————. "Unreal Realism." *The Thomist* 55 (October 1991): 631–55.

Derrick, Christopher. *Escape from Scepticism: Liberal Education as if the Truth Mattered.* La Salle, Ill.: Sherwood Sugden, 1977.

————. *The Rule of Peace: St. Benedict and the European Future.* Still River, Mass.: St. Bede's Publications, 1980.

Deutsch, Kenneth L., and Walter, Nicgorski, eds. *Leo Strauss: Political Philosopher and Thinker.* Lanham, Md.: Rowman and Littlefield, 1994.

Dobbs, Darrell. "Piety and Thought in Plato's *Republic.*" *American Political Science Review* 88 (Spring 1994): 668–83.

Dougherty, Jude P. "Appropriating Tradition." *Proceedings, Eighth International Conference on the Unity of Science.* The International Cultural Foundation, 1980.

Durrwell, F. X. *The Resurrection, a Biblical Study.* Translated by Rosemary Sheed. London: Sheed & Ward, 1964.

East, John P. *The American Conservative Movement: The Philosophical Founders.* Chicago: Regnery, 1986.

Eliot, T. S. *Christianity and Culture: The Idea of a Christian Society and Notes Towards the Definition of Culture.* New York: Harvest, 1968.

Emberley, Peter, and Barry Cooper, eds. *Faith and Political Philosophy: The Correspondence between Leo Strauss and Eric Voegelin, 1934–1964.* University Park, Pa.: The Pennsylvania State University Press, 1993.

Fairlie, Henry. *The Seven Deadly Sins Today.* Notre Dame: University of Notre Dame Press, 1979.

Finnis, John. *Natural Law and Natural Rights.* New York: Oxford, 1980.

Fortin, Ernest L. *Political Idealism and Christianity in the Thought of St. Augustine.* Villanova, Pa.: Augustinian Institute, Villanova University, 1972.

Fukuyama, Francis. *The End of History and the Last Man.* New York: Free Press, 1992.

————. "Against the New Pessimism." *Commentary* 97 (February 1994): 25–29.

Germino, Dante. *Political Philosophy and the Open Society.* Baton Rouge: Louisiana State University Press, 1982.

Gilby, Thomas. *Principality and Polity: Aquinas and the Rise of State Theory in the West.* London: Longmans, Green, and Company, 1958.

Gilder, George. *Microcosm: The Quantum Revolution in Economics and Technology.* New York: Simon & Schuster, 1989.

————. *Wealth and Poverty.* New York: Basic Books, 1981.

Gilson, Etienne. *Being and Some Philosophers.* Toronto: Pontifical Institute of Mediaeval Studies, 1949.

————. *A Gilson Reader.* Edited with an introduction by Anton C. Pegis. Garden City, N.Y.: Doubleday Image, 1957.

————. *God and Philosophy.* New Haven: Yale University Press, 1941.

———. *A History of Christian Philosophy in the Middle Ages.* New York: Random House, 1955.

———. *Methodical Realism.* Translated by Philip Trower. Front Royal, Va.: Christendom Press, 1990.

———. *Reason and Revelation in the Middle Ages.* New York: Scribner's, 1938.

———. *The Spirit of Thomism.* New York: P. J. Kenedy. 1964.

———. *Thomist Realism and the Critique of Knowledge.* San Francisco: Ignatius Press, 1986.

———. *The Unity of Philosophical Experience.* New York: Scribner's, 1937.

Graham, George J., and George W. Carey, eds. *The Post-Behavioral Era: Perspectives on Political Science.* New York: David McKay, 1972.

Grisez, Germain. "The 'Four Meanings' of Christian Philosophy." *Journal of Religion* 42 (April 1962): 103–18.

Guardini, Romano. *The Conversion of St. Augustine.* Chicago: Regnery, 1960.

———. *The Trial of Socrates.* New York: Sheed & Ward, 1948.

Gunnell, John G. *Political Theory: Tradition and Interpretation.* Cambridge, Mass.: Winthrop, 1979.

Hallowell, John H. *Main Currents in Modern Political Thought.* New York: Henry Holt, 1950.

Havard, William C. *The Recovery of Political Theory: Limits and Possibilities.* Baton Rouge: Louisiana State University Press, 1984.

Hayes, Carlton J. H. *Christianity and Western Civilization.* Stanford: Stanford University Press, 1954.

Himmelfarb, Gertrude. *The New History and the Old: Critical Essays and Reappraisals.* Cambridge: Harvard University Press, 1987.

———. "Of Heroes, Villains, and Valets." *Commentary* 91 (June 1991): 20–26.

Hittinger, Russell. *A Critique of the New Natural Law Theory.* Notre Dame: University of Notre Dame Press, 1987.

Hodgson, P. E. "The Significance of the Work of Stanley L. Jaki." *Downside Review* 105 (October 1987): 260–76.

Howard, John A., ed. *Belief, Faith, and Reason.* Belfast: Christian Journals Limited, 1981.

Howard, Thomas. *Chance or the Dance? A Critique of Modern Secularism.* San Francisco: Ignatius Press, 1989.

Hütter, Horst. *Politics as Friendship: The Origins of Classical Notions of Politics in the Theory and Practice of Friendship.* Waterloo, Ont.: Wilfrid Laurier University Press, 1978.

Jackson, Michael P. "Leo Strauss' Teaching." Ph.D. dissertation, Georgetown University, 1985.

Jaffa, Henry V. *The Conditions of Freedom: Essays in Political Philosophy.* Baltimore: The Johns Hopkins University Press, 1975.

Jaki, Stanley L. *The Absolute beneath the Relative.* Lanham, Md.: University Press of America, 1988.

——. *Chance or Reality?* Lanham, Md.: University Press of America, 1986.

——. *The Road of Science and the Ways to God.* Chicago: University of Chicago Press, 1978.

Jarrett, Bede. *Social Theories of the Middle Ages.* New York: Frederick Ungar, 1966.

The New Jerome Biblical Commentary. Edited by Raymond E. Brown, Joseph A. Fitzmyer, and Roland E. Murphy. Englewood Cliffs, N.J.: Prentice-Hall, 1990.

John Paul II. *See* Wojtyla, Karol.

Johnson, Paul. *Intellectuals.* New York: Harper & Row, 1988.

——. "Is Totalitarianism Dead?" *Crisis* 7 (February 1989): 7–16.

——. *Modern Times.* New York: Harper Colophon, 1983.

Johnson, Samuel. *Rasselas, Poems, and Selected Prose.* Edited by Bertrand H. Bronson. New York: Holt, Rinehart, and Winston, 1958.

Jones, E. M. *Degenerate Moderns: Modernity as Rationalized Sexual Behavior.* San Francisco: Ignatius Press, 1993.

Kasper, Walter. *Faith and the Future.* New York: Crossroad, 1982.

——. *Jesus the Christ.* New York: Paulist, 1976.

Kass, Leon R. *Toward a More Natural Science: Biology and Human Affairs.* New York: Free Press, 1985.

Ker, Ian. *John Henry Newman: A Biography.* Oxford: Oxford University Press, 1988.

Kirk, Russell. *Reclaiming a Patrimony: A Collection of Lectures.* Washington, D.C.: Heritage Foundation, 1982.

——. *The Roots of American Order.* La Salle, Ill.: Open Court, 1974.

Kolakowski, Lezek. "Le diable, peut-il être sauvé?" *Contrepoint* (Paris), no. 20 (1976), 130–38.

Kramnick, Isaac, ed. *Essays in the History of Political Thought.* Englewood Cliffs, N.J.: Prentice-Hall, 1969.

Kreeft, Peter. *Back to Virtue: Traditional Moral Wisdom for Modern Moral Confusion.* San Francisco: Ignatius Press, 1992.

——. *A Summa of the Summa: The Essential Philosophical Passages of St. Thomas Aquinas' Summa Theologica.* San Francisco: Ignatius Press, 1990.

Lerner, Ralph, and Muhsin Mahdi, eds. *Medieval Political Philosophy.* Ithaca: Cornell University Press, 1961.

Lewis, C. S. *The Abolition of Man.* New York: Macmillan, 1947.

——. *The Four Loves.* New York: Harcourt, 1960.

——. *God in the Dock: Essays on Theology and Ethics.* Edited by Walter Hooper. Grand Rapids, Mich.: Eerdmans, 1970.

——. *Mere Christianity.* London: Fontana Collins, 1961.

——. *Miracles: A Preliminary Study.* New York: Macmillan, 1960.

——. *The Pilgrim's Regress: An Allegorical Apology for Christianity, Reason, and Romanticism.* Grand Rapids, Mich.: Eerdmans, 1986.

——. *Present Concerns: Ethical Essays.* London: Collins, 1986.

——. *The Problem of Pain.* New York: Macmillan, 1962.

————. *Till We Have Faces: A Myth Retold.* Grand Rapids, Mich.: Eerdmans, 1956.

————. *The Weight of Glory, and Other Addresses.* New York: Macmillan, 1980.

Lindsay, Thomas K. "Politics and Religion in Aristotle's *Politics.*" *Review of Politics* 53 (Summer 1991): 488–509.

Lobkowicz, Nicholas. "Christianity and Culture." *Review of Politics* 53 (Spring 1991): 373–89.

Lord, Carnes. *Education and Culture in the Thought of Aristotle.* Ithaca: Cornell University Press, 1982.

Lubac, Henri de. *Catholicism: Christ and the Common Destiny of Man.* Translated by Lancelot Sheppard and Elizabeth Englund. San Francisco: Ignatius Press, 1989.

————. *The Christian Faith.* Translated by Richard Arnandez. San Francisco: Ignatius Press, 1986.

————. *A Brief Catechism on Nature and Grace.* Translated by Richard Arnandez. San Francisco: Ignatius Press, 1984.

McCoy, Charles N. R. *On the Intelligibility of Political Philosophy.* Edited by James V. Schall and John J. Schrems. Washington, D.C.: The Catholic University of America Press, 1989.

————. *The Structure of Political Thought.* New York: McGraw-Hill, 1963.

Machiavelli, Niccolo. *Florentine Histories.* Translated by Laura Banfield and Harvey Mansfield. Princeton: Princeton University Press, 1988.

McIlwain, Charles H. *The Growth of Political Thought in the West, from the Greeks to the End of the Middle Ages.* New York: Macmillan, 1932.

McInerny, Ralph. *St. Thomas Aquinas.* Notre Dame: University of Notre Dame Press, 1982.

————. *Thomism in an Age of Renewal.* Notre Dame: University of Notre Dame Press, 1982.

MacIntyre, Alasdair. *After Virtue: A Study in Moral Theory.* Notre Dame: University of Notre Dame Press, 1981.

Madariaga, Salvador de. "The Europe of the Four Karls." *The Tablet* (London) (June 23, 1973), 580–81.

Marcel, Gabriel. *The Mystery of Being.* 2 vols. Chicago: Gateway, 1960.

Maritain, Jacques. *Art and Scholasticism.* Translated by Joseph W. Evans. Notre Dame: University of Notre Dame Press, 1962.

————. *Christianity and Democracy and The Rights of Man and the Natural Law.* San Francisco: Ignatius Press, 1986.

————. *The Education of Man.* Edited with an introduction by Donald and Idella Gallagher. Garden City, N.Y.: Doubleday, 1962.

————. *Integral Humanism: Temporal and Spiritual Problems of a New Christendom.* Translated by Joseph W. Evans. Notre Dame: University of Notre Dame Press, 1973.

————. *Man and the State.* Chicago: University of Chicago Press, 1951.

————. *Notebooks.* Translated by Joseph W. Evans. Albany, N.Y.: Magi Books, 1984.

————. *The Peasant of the Garonne: An Old Layman Questions Himself about the Present Time.* New York: Holt, Rinehart, and Winston, 1968.

————. *The Range of Reason.* New York: Scribner's, 1952.

————. *Scholasticism and Politics.* Garden City, N.Y.: Doubleday Image, 1960.

————. *The Social and Political Philosophy of Jacques Maritain.* Edited by Joseph W. Evans and Leo R. Ward. Notre Dame: University of Notre Dame Press, 1976.

Maritain, Raïssa. *Raïssa's Journal.* Presented by Jacques Maritain. Albany, N.Y.: Magi Books, 1974.

Mascall, Eric L. *The Christian Universe.* London: Darton, Longman, and Todd, 1966.

————. *Theology and the Future.* New York: Morehouse-Barlow, 1968.

Meilaender, Gilbert C. *Friendship: A Study in Theological Ethics.* Notre Dame: University of Notre Dame Press, 1981.

————. *The Taste for the Other: The Social and Ethical Thought of C. S. Lewis.* Grand Rapids, Mich.: Eerdmans, 1978.

Midgley, E. B. F. "Authority, Alienation, and Revolt." *Aberdeen University Review* 44 (Autumn 1976): 372–83.

————. "Concerning the Modernist Subversion of Political Philosophy." *New Scholasticism* 53 (Spring 1979): 163–90.

————. *The Ideology of Max Weber: A Thomist Critique.* Aldershot, Hants.: Gower, 1983.

————. *The Natural Law Tradition and the Theory of International Relations.* London: Elek, 1975.

————. "On 'Substitute Intelligences' in the Formation of Atheist Ideology." *Laval théologique et philosophique* 34 (October 1980): 239–53.

Mitchell, Joshua. *Not by Reason Alone: Religion, History, and Identity in Early Modern Political Philosophy.* Chicago: University of Chicago Press, 1993.

Molnar, Thomas. *The Church: Pilgrim of Centuries.* Grand Rapids, Mich.: Eerdmans, 1990.

————. *Politics and the State.* Chicago: Franciscan Herald Press, 1980

————. *Twin Towers: Politics and the Sacred.* Grand Rapids, Mich.: Eerdmans, 1988.

Montgomery, Marion. *Men I Have Chosen for Fathers: Literary and Philosophical Passages.* Columbia: University of Missouri Press, 1990.

————. *The Prophetic Poet and the Spirit of the Age.* 3 vols. La Salle, Ill.: Sherwood Sugden, 1982–84.

————. *Virtue and Modern Shadows of Turning: Preliminary Agitations.* Lanham, Md.: University Press of America, 1990.

Moore, Barrington. *Reflections on the Causes of Human Misery and Upon Certain Proposals to Eliminate Them.* Boston: Beacon Press, 1969.

Morrall, John B. *Aristotle.* London: George Allen & Unwin, 1977.

————. *Political Thought in Medieval Times.* New York: Harper Torchbooks, 1958.

Muggeridge, Malcolm. *The Chronicles of Wasted Time.* 2 vols. New York: William Morrow, 1974.

_____. *The End of Christendom.* Grand Rapids, Mich.: Eerdmans, 1980.
Mulgan, R. G. *Aristotle's Political Theory.* Oxford: Clarendon Press, 1977.
Navone, John. *Self-Giving and Sharing: The Trinity and Human Fulfillment.* Collegeville, Minn.: Liturgical Press, 1989.
_____. *A Theology of Failure.* New York: Paulist Press, 1974.
Neuhaus, Richard John, ed. *Augustine Today.* Grand Rapids, Mich.: Eerdmans, 1993.
Newman, John Henry. *The Idea of a University.* Garden City, N.Y.: Doubleday Image, 1959.
_____. *Parochial and Plain Sermons.* San Francisco: Ignatius Press, 1981.
Novak, Michael. *The Spirit of Democratic Capitalism.* New York: Simon & Schuster, 1982.
O'Connor, Flannery. *Collected Works.* Edited by Sally Fitzgerald. New York: The Library of America, 1988.
_____. *The Habit of Being. Letters.* New York: Vintage, 1979.
Orr, Susan. *Reason and Revelation in the Works of Leo Strauss.* Lanham, Md.: Rowman and Littlefield, 1995.
Passerin D'Entreves, Alessandro. *Natural Law: A Historical Survey.* New York: Harper Torchbooks, 1965.
Pegis, Anton C. *At the Origins of the Thomistic Notion of Man.* New York: Macmillan, 1963.
Percy, Walker. *Lost in the Cosmos: The Last Self Help Book.* New York: Farrar, Straus, & Giroux, 1983.
_____. *The Thanatos Syndrome.* New York: Farrar, Straus, and Giroux, 1987.
Pieper, Josef. *The End of Time: A Meditation on the Philosophy of History.* Translated by Michael Bullock. New York: Pantheon, 1954.
_____. *Enthusiasm and Divine Madness: On the Platonic Dialogue "Phaedrus."* Translated by Richard and Clara Winston. New York: Harcourt, Brace, and World, 1962.
_____. *The Four Cardinal Virtues: Prudence, Justice, Fortitude, Temperance.* Translated by Richard and Clara Winston et alia. Notre Dame: University of Notre Dame Press, 1966.
_____. *Guide to Thomas Aquinas.* Translated by Richard and Clara Winston. San Francisco: Ignatius, 1991.
_____. *Happiness and Contemplation.* Translated by Richard and Clara Winston. New York: Pantheon, 1958.
_____. *Hope and History.* Translated by Richard and Clara Winston. New York: Herder and Herder, 1969.
_____. *In Defense of Philosophy: Classical Wisdom Stands up to Modern Challenges.* Translated by Lothar Krauth. San Francisco: Ignatius Press, 1992.
_____. *In Tune with the World: A Theory of Festivity.* Translated by Richard and Clara Winston. Chicago: Franciscan Herald Press, 1973.
_____. *Josef Pieper—An Anthology.* San Francisco: Ignatius Press, 1989.
_____. *Leisure, the Basis of Culture.* New York: Mentor-Omega, 1963.
_____. *Living the Truth: The Truth of All Things and Reality and the Good.* San Francisco: Ignatius Press, 1989.

———. *Problems of Modern Faith: Essays and Addresses.* Translated by Jan van Heurck. Chicago: Franciscan Herald Press, 1985.

———. *Scholasticism: Personalities and Problems of Medieval Philosophy.* New York: McGraw-Hill, 1964.

———. *The Silence of St. Thomas.* Translated by John Murray and Daniel O'Connor. Chicago: Regnery-Gateway, 1957.

Pirenne, Henri. *Economic and Social History of Medieval Europe.* Translated by I. E. Clegg. New York: Harvest, 1937.

Plamenatz, John. *Man and Society, A Critical Examination of Some Important Social and Political Theories from Machiavelli to Marx.* 2 vols. New York: McGraw-Hill, 1963.

Ratzinger, Josef. "Focus: Some Perspectives." *30 Days* (February 1990): 49.

———. *"In the Beginning . . ."* Translated by B. Ramsey. Huntington, Ind.: Our Sunday Visitor Press, 1990.

Rahner, Karl, ed. *Encyclopedia of Theology: The Concise 'Sacramentum Mundi.'* New York: Seabury, 1975.

Reinhardt, Kurt F. *A Realistic Philosophy: The Perennial Principles of Thought and Action in a Changing World.* New York: Frederick Ungar, 1962.

Rommen, Heinrich A. *The Natural Law: A Study in Legal and Social History and Philosophy.* St. Louis: B. Herder, 1947.

———. *The State in Catholic Thought.* St. Louis: B. Herder, 1945.

Rougemont, Denis de. *Love in the Western World.* Translated by Montgomery Belgion. New York: Schocken, 1983.

Royal, Robert. *1492 and All That: Political Manipulations of History.* Washington, D.C.: Ethics and Public Policy Center, 1992.

Rutler, George W. *Beyond Modernity: Reflections of a Post-Modern Catholic.* San Francisco: Ignatius Press, 1987.

Ryn, Claes G. *Democracy and the Ethical Life: A Philosophy of Politics and Community.* Washington, D.C.: The Catholic University of America Press, 1990.

———. "Universality and History: The Concrete as Normative." *Humanitas* 6 (Fall 1992/Winter 1993): 10–39.

Sabine, George H. *A History of Political Theory.* New York: Holt, Rinehart, and Winston, 1956.

Sacks, Robert. "The Lion and the Ass: A Commentary on Books I-X of *Genesis* (Strauss)." *Interpretation* 8 (May 1980): 29–101.

Salkever, Stephen G. *Finding the Mean: Theory and Practice in Aristotelian Political Philosophy.* Princeton: Princeton University Press, 1990.

Sandoz, Ellis. *A Government of Laws: Political Theory, Religion, and the American Founding.* Baton Rouge: Louisiana State University Press, 1990.

———. *The Voegelinian Revolution: A Biographical Introduction.* Baton Rouge: Louisiana State University Press, 1981.

Sayers, Dorothy L. *The Whimsical Christian: 18 Essays.* New York: Macmillan, 1978.

Schall, James V. *Another Sort of Learning.* San Francisco: Ignatius Press, 1988.

———. "Aristotle on Friendship." *Classical Bulletin* 65, nos. 3 & 4 (1989): 83–88.

———. *Christianity and Politics.* Boston: St. Paul Editions, 1981.

———. *Does Catholicism Still Exist?* Staten Island, N.Y.: Alba House, 1994.

———. *Far Too Easily Pleased: A Theology of Play, Contemplation, and Festivity.* Los Angeles: Benziger-Macmillan, 1976.

———. *Human Dignity and Human Numbers.* Staten Island, N.Y.: Alba House, 1971.

———. "Human Rights as an Ideological Project." *American Journal of Jurisprudence* 32 (1987): 47–61.

———. "The Law of Superabundance." *Gregorianum* 72, no. 3 (1991): 515–42.

———. *Liberation Theology in Latin America.* San Francisco: Ignatius Press, 1982.

———. "The Mystery of the 'Mystery of Israel'." In *Jacques Maritain and the Jews.* Edited by Robert Royal. Notre Dame, Ind.: University of Notre Dame Press/American Maritain Association, 1994.

———. "On Being Dissatisfied with Compromises: Natural Law and Human Rights." *Loyola Law Review* 38, no. 2 (1992): 289–309.

———. "On the Teaching of Political Philosophy." *Perspectives on Political Science* 20 (Winter 1991): 5–10.

———. "On the Uniqueness of Socrates." *Gregorianum* 72, no. 2 (1995): 343–62.

———. "Political Philosophy: Remarks on Its Relation to Metaphysics and Theology." *Angelicum* 70 (1993): 487–503.

———. *The Politics of Heaven and Hell: Christian Themes from Classical, Medieval, and Modern Political Philosophy.* Lanham, Md.: University Press of America, 1984.

———. "Post-Aristotelian Philosophy and Political Theory." *Cithara* 3 (November 1963): 56–79.

———. "Post-Aristotelian Political Philosophy and Modernity." *Aufstieg und Niedergang der Römischen Welt.* Edited by Wolfgang Haase and Hildegard Temporini. Part 2, vol. 36, 4902–36. Berlin: Walter de Gruyter, 1994.

———. *Reason, Revelation, and the Foundations of Political Philosophy.* Baton Rouge: Louisiana State University Press, 1987.

———. *Redeeming the Time.* New York: Sheed & Ward, 1968.

———. *Religion, Wealth, and Poverty.* Vancouver, B.C.: Fraser Institute, 1990.

———. "Transcendence and Political Philosophy." *Review of Politics* 55 (Summer 1993): 247–65.

———. "Transcendent Man in the Limited City: The Political Philosophy of Charles N. R. McCoy." *The Thomist* 57 (January 1993): 63–95.

———. *What Is God Like?* Collegeville, Minn.: Liturgical Press, 1992.

Schlier, Heinrich. *The Relevance of the New Testament.* New York: Herder and Herder, 1968.

Schnackenburg, Rudolf. *The Moral Teaching of the New Testament.* Translated by J. Holland-Smith and W. J. O'Hara. London: Burns and Oates, 1962.

Schrems, John J. *Principles of Politics: An Introduction*. Englewood Cliffs, N.J.: Prentice-Hall, 1986.

Schumacher, E. F. *A Guide for the Perplexed*. New York: Harper, 1977.

Scott, Norman A. *The Broken Center: Studies in the Theological Horizon of Modern Literature*. New Haven: Yale University Press, 1966.

Senior, John. *The Restoration of Christian Culture*. San Francisco: Ignatius Press, 1983.

Sertillanges, A. G. *The Intellectual Life: Its Spirit, Conditions, Methods*. Washington, D.C.: The Catholic University of America Press, 1988.

Shafarevich, Igor. *The Socialist Phenomenon*. Translated by William Tjalsma. New York: Harper and Row, 1980.

Sibley, Mulford Q. *Political Ideas and Ideologies: A History of Political Thought*. New York: Harper and Row, 1970.

Simon, Julian L. *The Ultimate Resource*. Princeton: Princeton University Press, 1981.

Simon, Yves. *Freedom of Choice*. New York: Fordham University Press, 1987.

———. *A General Theory of Authority*. Notre Dame: University of Notre Dame Press, 1980.

———. *The Philosophy of Democratic Government*. Chicago: University of Chicago Press, 1951.

———. *The Tradition of Natural Law: A Philosopher's Reflections*. New York: Fordham University Press, 1965.

Skinner, Quentin. *The Foundations of Modern Political Thought*. 2 vols. London: Cambridge University Press, 1978.

Sloyan, Gerard S. *Jesus on Trial: The Development of the Passion Narratives and Their Historical and Ecumenical Implications*. Philadelphia: Fortress Press, 1973.

Smith, Janet. Humanae Vitae: *A Generation Later*. Washington, D.C.: The Catholic University of America Press, 1991.

Sobran, Joseph. *Single Issues: Essays on the Crucial Social Issues*. New York: Human Life Press, 1983.

Sokolowski, Robert. *The God of Faith and Reason: Foundations of Christian Theology*. Notre Dame: University of Notre Dame Press, 1982; reprinted 1995 by The Catholic University of America Press.

Solzhenitsyn at Harvard: The Address, Twelve Early Responses and Six Later Reflections. Edited by Ronald Berman. Washington, D.C.: Ethics and Public Policy Center, 1980.

Strauss, Leo. *The City and Man*. Chicago: University of Chicago Press, 1964.

———. *Liberalism: Ancient and Modern*. New York: Basic Books, 1968.

———. *Natural Right and History*. Chicago: University of Chicago Press, 1953.

———. *Persecution and the Art of Writing*. Westport, Conn.: Greenwood Press, 1973.

———. *The Political Philosophy of Hobbes: Its Basis and Its Genesis.* Chicago: University of Chicago Press, 1963.

———. *Political Philosophy: Six Essays.* Edited by Hilail Gildin. Indianapolis: Bobbs-Merrill, 1975.

———. *The Rebirth of Classical Political Rationalism: An Introduction to the Thought of Leo Strauss.* Selected and introduced by Thomas L. Pangle. Chicago: University of Chicago Press, 1989.

———. *Studies in Platonic Political Philosophy.* With an introduction by Thomas L. Pangle. Chicago: University of Chicago Press, 1983.

———. *Thoughts on Machiavelli.* Glencoe, Ill.: Free Press, 1958.

———. *What Is Political Philosophy? and Other Studies.* Glencoe, Ill.: Free Press, 1959.

———, and Joseph Cropsey. *History of Political Philosophy.* Third edition. Chicago: University of Chicago Press, 1987.

Talmon, J. L. *The Origins of Totalitarian Democracy.* New York: Praeger, 1960.

Taylor, Charles. "The Politics of Recognition." *Multiculturalism and "The Politics of Recognition."* Princeton: Princeton University Press, 1992.

Tinder, Glenn. *The Political Meaning of Christianity: The Prophetic Stance: An Interpretation.* San Francisco: Harper, 1991.

———. *Political Thinking: The Perennial Questions.* Boston: Little, Brown, and Company, 1974.

Veatch, Henry. *Aristotle: A Contemporary Appreciation.* Bloomington: Indiana University Press, 1974.

———. *Human Rights: Fact or Fancy?* Baton Rouge: Louisiana State University Press, 1985.

———. "The Idea of Christian Science and Scholarship." *Faith and Philosophy* 1 (January 1984): 89–110.

———. *Rational Man: A Modern Interpretation of Aristotelian Ethics.* Bloomington: Indiana University Press, 1966.

———. *Swimming Against the Current in Contemporary Philosophy: Occasional Essays and Papers.* Washington, D.C.: The Catholic University of America Press, 1990.

Voegelin, Eric. *Anamnesis.* Translated and edited by Gerhart Niemeyer. Columbia: University of Missouri Press, 1989.

———. *Conversations with Eric Voegelin.* Edited by R. Eric O'Connor. Montreal: Thomas More Institute Papers, 1980.

———. *The New Science of Politics: An Introduction.* Chicago: University of Chicago Press, 1952.

———. *Plato.* Baton Rouge: Louisiana State University Press, 1985.

———. *Science, Politics, and Gnosticism.* Chicago: Regnery-Gateway, 1968.

Wallace, William A. *The Elements of Philosophy: A Compendium for Philosophers and Theologians.* Staten Island, N.Y.: Alba House, 1977.

Walsh, David. *After Ideology: Recovering the Spiritual Foundations of Freedom.* San Francisco: Harper, 1990; reprinted by The Catholic University of America Press, 1995.

Walzer, Michael. *The Revolution of the Saints: A Study in the Origins of Radical Politics.* New York: Atheneum, 1968.

Weaver, Richard M. *The Southern Essays of Richard M. Weaver.* Edited by G. Curtis and J. Thompson. Indianapolis: Liberty Press, 1987.

Webb, Eugene. "The Epochal Particularism of Modernity." *Gallatin Review* 12 (Winter 1992–93): 87–96.

Weisheipl, James A. *Friar Thomas d'Aquino: His Life, Thought, and Works.* Washington, D.C.: The Catholic University of America Press, 1983.

Wilhelmsen, Frederick D. *Christianity and Political Philosophy.* Athens: University of Georgia Press, 1978.

———. "Great Books: Enemies of Freedom." *Modern Age* 31 (Summer/Fall 1987): 323–31.

———. *Man's Knowledge of Himself: An Introduction to Thomistic Epistemology.* Englewood Cliffs, N.J.: Prentice-Hall, 1956.

Williams, Charles. *The Figure of Beatrice: A Study in Dante.* New York: Farrar, Straus, and Cudahy, 1961.

Wilson, William R. *The Execution of Jesus.* New York: Scribner's, 1970.

Wippel, John F. *Metaphysical Themes in Thomas Aquinas.* Washington, D.C.: The Catholic University of America Press, 1984.

Wiser, James L. *Political Theory: A Thematic Inquiry.* Chicago: Nelson-Hall, 1986.

Wojtyla, Karol. *The Acting Person.* Translated by Andrzej Potocki. Boston: D. Reidel, 1979.

———. *Crossing the Threshold of Hope.* New York: Knopf, 1994.

———. *Towards a Philosophy of Praxis.* New York: Crossroads, 1981.

——— (John Paul II). *Veritatis Splendor.* 1993.

Wolin, Sheldon. *Politics and Vision: Continuity and Innovation in Western Political Theory.* Boston: Little, Brown, and Company, 1960.

Woznicki, Andrew N. *Karol Wojtyla's Existentialist Personalism.* New Britain, Conn.: Mariel, 1980.

Wright, John H. "The Eternal Plan of Divine Providence." *Theological Studies* 27 (March 1966): 27–57.

Wulf, Maurice de. *Philosophy and Civilization in the Middle Ages.* New York: Dover, 1953.

Zaehner, R. C. *The City within the Heart.* London: Unwin, 1980.

INDEX OF NAMES

INDEX OF SUBJECTS

268